THE BEAUTY OF
SEPHARDIC LIFE

Scholarly, Humorous and

Personal Reflections

Sam Bension Maimon

Edited by

Albert S. Maimon

Eugene Normand

MAIMON IDEaS Publications

Seattle, WA

Copyright © 1993

MAIMON IDEaS Publications

ALL RIGHTS RESERVED

No part of this book may be reproduced in any form, including
photocopying and retrieval systems, without written permission from
the copyright holder, except by a reviewer who wishes to quote brief
passages.

Drawing of Maimonides reprinted by permission from *The Jewish
People, Book Two*, by Deborah Pessin, © 1952 by United Synagogue
of Conservative Judaism.

ISBN 0-9636764-0-7

Library of Congress Catalog Card Number 93-92700

Frontis. Sam Bension Maimon at home, 1980.
(Courtesy of Rochelle Casserd)

© Cover design & photography by Jacques Frances New York 1993.

About the cover: The theme of the book is illustrated by the photo detail
of a *chevre*, an 18th century embroidered heirloom, from the Romaniote
family of Jacques Frances (gold thread on royal blue velvet)

MAIMON IDEaS Publications
5241 S. Holly
Seattle, WA 98118

Printed in the United States of America by
Malloy Lithographing, Inc, Ann Arbor, Michigan

In loving memory of our parents,

Sam Bension Maimon, z"l
(1907 - 1992)

author of this book, and his *Eshet Hayil*, his devoted wife,

Lucy, z"l
(1915 - 1985)

Sam Bension Maimon

About the Author

Sam Maimon was the product of another era, the Jewish world of the waning Turkish Empire, transplanted to the shores of Puget Sound in the American Pacific Northwest. Although he arrived at the age of sixteen and was lacking an advanced formal education, he was able to thrive and excel culturally and intellectually in all endeavors that were important to him: family life, synagogue life, Jewish law, Sephardic traditions, secular literature and teaching the Jewish/Sephardic heritage at all levels.

For almost forty years he earned his living as a grocer in the Central Area of Seattle, Washington. Before he retired in 1969 he used his spare time to expand his knowledge of his people, the Turkish Sephardim, through every available means: reading, talking to elders, listening to and singing Sephardic liturgy and *romansas* to develop his own *hazanut* (cantorial) style and even joking to pick up Ladino expressions. But as much as he picked up, he gave back even more. He taught and entertained his customers in the store, his congregants in the synagogue and his students in the many and varied classes that he conducted. In addition, he inspired his fellow congregants as a *hazan*, a *na'im zemirot Yisrael* (pleasing singer of Israel) and the special way he carried out his cantorial duties.

Once the store was closed and he had more time available, his role as a teacher greatly expanded. He taught young boys Hebrew and prepared them for becoming Bar Mitzvah, he taught grown men the Jewish law and traditions they did not learn in their youth, and he taught his entire synagogue community through the columns he wrote in the *La Boz* (The Voice), newsletter of the Sephardic Bikur Holim Congregation, from 1971 until 1982.

Sam Bension Maimon, known affectionately as "B'sion" and later as "Uncle Sam," was born in the Turkish city of Brusa in 1907. His father, Rabbi Abraham Maimon, and his mother, Victoria (Vida) Maimon nee Franco, were from families that had lived in Brusa for many generations. His father, known as Haribi Avram, decided to become a rabbi, a *haham* in Sephardic terminology, when Sam and his two older sisters were very young. Once certified as a *haham*, Haribi Avram served in two smaller Turkish towns before 1911 when he was offered the position of *haham* in the city of Tekirdag, about seventy miles southwest of Istanbul in the European part of Turkey.

It was in Tekirdag that Sam received much of his formal education, and it was his father who had a great influence on how he would lead his life. The Jewish educational system in Tekirdag was centered around the Alliance Israelite Universelle school (secular classes plus some Jewish topics), supplemented by after-school Judaic classes in the *meldar* (old-style Talmud Torah). A great deal was also learned in the synagogue. Secular classes were in French, they spoke Ladino amongst themselves, synagogue services were in Hebrew and they picked up Turkish to be able to converse with their non-Jewish neighbors (Turks, Armenians and Greeks).

As Sam and his younger brothers, Jack, Isaac, Morris and Solomon, got older, Haribi Avram became concerned for the future of his sons. Mustapha Kemal had taken control of Turkey by 1922, and among the many reforms he instituted was the obligation of all Turkish citizens to serve in the army. Haribi Avram was not going to let his sons be conscripted because he had seen first-hand how young Jewish men could be changed by their stint in the army. He was open to a rabbinical position abroad. Thus, in 1924 when he was contacted by members of Sephardic Bikur Holim (SBH) synagogue in Seattle, Washington to serve as their rabbi, he readily accepted. Agreement was reached for Haribi Avram to serve as their spiritual leader, and so the family, Rabbi and Mrs. Maimon, Sam and his five younger siblings (four brothers and sister Rachel), was transplanted to the Pacific Northwest. His older sisters, Fanny and Louise, joined the family a few years later.

In Seattle, Sam first learned English and then attended Garfield High School for two years. Sam needed to go to work to help his parents support the large Maimon family. (Because he was lacking one or two credits he never officially graduated, but that was remedied some fifty years later when he was given an actual Seattle Public School diploma at an SBH testimonial dinner in his honor.) Nevertheless, there were many opportunities for him to read and learn outside of school, and he availed himself of them. His brother Isaac recalls how Sam would be up reading books late at night, hovered over the single light in the bedroom, while his four younger brothers were falling asleep on the mattresses stretched out across the floor.

As the 1930s opened, the Maimon family was devastated by the untimely death of their patriarch, Haribi Avram, in January of 1931. The family pulled together, as the older brothers took on the financial responsibilities of the family. Sam formed a partnership with a friend of his, Jack Funes, and the two opened up a grocery store, the 24th Avenue Market, located at 24th Avenue and Yesler Way. Sam operated that store for almost forty years, and it quickly became one of the gathering places for the Sephardim in Seattle. In 1941 Jack Funes left the store for other business ventures, and Sam's brother, Isaac, who had already been working there, became his partner. That partnership lasted until they sold the store in 1969.

Sam got to know all the Sephardim in Seattle, not only those from his own synagogue, but also those from Ezra Bessaroth (whose members came from the island of Rhodes), and Ahavath Ahim (whose members came from the island of Marmara). Sam developed and perfected his humor, his story-telling techniques, his informative style and his Ladino expertise in that store. The many men who had worked as delivery boys over the years, including his brother, Rabbi Solomon Maimon, his son Albert and many nephews, fondly remember their years in the store and the wisdom and humor of one of the men who made it so memorable.

Down the block from the 24th Avenue Market lived Reverend Morris Scharhon and his large family. Reverend Scharhon had been a student and friend to Haribi Avram, but Sam took special notice of the oldest daughter, Lucy, who chauffeured her father around. They were engaged in 1933 at the wedding of Sam's brother Jack; Lucy and Sam were wed on August 12, 1934. The following year their first child, Victoria (Vicki) was born.

Sam and his father-in-law had become good friends. They shared similar interests. Both were *hazanim* (cantors) in their synagogues. Sam had an exceptionally rich voice, but with his father gone, he had to turn elsewhere to learn the wide variety of Sephardic tunes and *makamot* (musical modes) appropriate for the various prayers and poems to be chanted on the many special days of the Jewish calendar. He learned much from Nessim (Sam) Azose whose father had been a *haham*, and with whom he shared *hazanut* duties in SBH from the mid-1930s to mid-1940s.

There was also a great deal of Jewish law to be learned, beyond what he had acquired in his youth. He enriched his learning in many ways. He studied with a number of rabbis in the Jewish community at large, but probably the person who taught Sam the most in the study of *Gemara* (Talmud) was an Ashkenazic man, Shabbsi Lewis, who often learned and prayed at Sephardic Bikur Holim. Sam also studied a great deal on his own. One of the methods he used was to pick a Biblical commentator for an entire year. Each week he would read the explanations offered by that rabbi on that particular week's *perashah* (Torah portion). The next year he would choose a different commentator, and he continued the cycle for quite a few years. In addition, Sam and his brother Jack would teach classes at the synagogue on such topics as *Ein Yaakov* (non-legal aspects of Talmud) and *Me'Am Lo'Ez* (a unique encyclopedia-like Biblical commentary written in Ladino, which is fully described in one of his articles in this book). Sam also enjoyed reading secular books of all kinds, and Mark Twain was his favorite American author.

The 1940s brought significant changes. Albert was born in 1941, the same year Sam and Lucy moved into a spacious house on 24th and Spruce, (two blocks from his grocery store), and Esther was born in 1946. Sam, Jack and Isaac had helped send their youngest brother, Solomon, to Yeshiva University. Solomon returned in 1944 with his rabbinical ordination and took on the position of rabbi of Sephardic Bikur Holim Congregation. Haribi Avram's sons had filled the large gap that their father's death had left; Solomon as rabbi, Sam as assistant *hazan* (cantor), with Jack and Isaac also taking on cantorial and other duties.

The 1950s were years of exercising his role as father and father-figure. He taught Albert his Bar Mitzvah *perashah* and as much Jewish law and Sephardic lore as an American teenager was willing to absorb. The arrival of Rev. Samuel Benaroya to serve as the official *hazan* of SBH reduced only slightly Sam's active role as assistant *hazan*. He continued teaching congregants, nephews, and all those who were interested about the vast richness of the Sephardic *hahamim* (sages). When his nephew, Isaac Azose, became *hazan* of the sister Seattle Sephardic congregation, Ezra Bessaroth, Sam spent a great deal of time teaching him the fine points of *hazanut* and the details of how the prayers are to be chanted. He was equally important as "Uncle Sam" to his many other nephews, for his jokes, his wisdom and his inspiration regarding the value of Jewish learning.

During the 1960s Sam took on a new role, that of *papu* (grandfather) to nine grandchildren. His children all chose Ashkenazic spouses: Vicki married Sid Schain in 1956, Albert married Jean Yablok in 1964 and Esther married Eugene Normand in 1967. Each couple gave Sam and Lucy three grandchildren. *Papu*-hood came easily to Sam because it allowed him to do so many things he loved to do, tell stories and jokes, sing and laugh, all to a new captivated audience. Sam not only taught all six of his grandsons their Bar Mitzvah *parashiot* (Torah portions), but also studied Bible and Talmud with those grandsons who attended Hebrew day school and yeshiva high school.

Sam expanded his knowledge of Sephardic *halacha* (Jewish law), customs, history and culture through reading, but the sources he had access to in Seattle were limited. This improved when his son-in-law, Eugene Normand, then a graduate student at the University of Washington (UW) began bringing him books and journals from the large UW library. Later, his access to new sources of Sephardic-related reading material expanded as he combined visits to his children with opportunities to read more. This occurred first in Israel in 1970 when Sam and Lucy joined Albert, Jean and family for an extended stay in Haifa where Albert was living. One or two mornings a week Sam would board the bus in Haifa that would take him to Jerusalem, change buses and end up at the Ben Zvi Institute where he would spend hours reading the books and manuscripts that the Institute had collected. The same procedure was followed in Chicago where Esther and Eugene lived during the 1970s. Sam would travel from Esther's West Rogers Park neighborhood by bus and train to the Spertus College library in downtown Chicago which had an extensive Judaica collection. He would spend hours reading those books of special interest to him before returning at the end of the day for dinner with the family.

By 1969 several factors had combined to prompt Sam and Isaac to sell the 24th Avenue Market. Like all other Sephardim, they and their synagogue had moved to another part of the city, so the store was no longer close by. Sam had already turned sixty and was interested in concentrating on other activities. The social disturbances that erupted in the late 1960s hastened their decision. Sam now had the time to pursue full-time the role he had always loved, that of teacher. He was a substitute teacher at the Seattle Hebrew Academy, the school his children had graduated from and which his grandchildren were attending, and a full-time teacher at the after-school Sephardic Religious School sponsored by SBH. He also became a private tutor, preparing boys for becoming Bar Mitzvah, and teaching adult men the Jewish law and traditions that they had bypassed in their youth.

Because so many people were continually asking him about Ladino and Sephardic customs, he began organizing in his own mind the best way to explain an entire tradition to a large audience. He had to formalize his approach in 1975 because, through the efforts of his friends David and Esther Raphael, he was asked to teach a course, "Ladino: Language and Literature" at the University of Washington. Later, he taught similar classes at the Jewish Community Center. These classes led him to compile Ladino words which, after several years, culminated in his first-of-its-kind English dictionary of non-Spanish Ladino words, "Ladino-English Dictionary" that was published in 1980 in *Studies in Sephardic Culture, The David N. Barocas Memorial Volume*, Marc Angel, Editor.

Sam's audience multiplied even further with the advent of his column in the SBH monthly newsletter, *La Boz*. The first article appeared in the October, 1971 issue of *La Boz* and it continued uninterrupted until September, 1982 when he suffered a heart attack. These articles rekindled in the Sephardic old-timers, as well as their children and grandchildren, the spark of customs, sayings and events that most had heard about and practiced, but had since forgotten. He taught through his writings in a folk-scholar style that everyone found appealing.

His knowledge of Sephardic customs and language was vast, and his reputation for this knowledge spread far beyond Seattle. He was consulted as a major source by Rabbi Herbert Dobrinsky for his book *A Treasury of Sephardic Laws and Customs*, and Joseph Papo for his book *Sephardim in Twentieth Century America*. Students at all levels sought out his advice. One to whom he devoted considerable effort was Nancy Kobrin, a graduate student at the University of Iowa, for her transliteration of the Ladino ethical tract *Tokpho Shel Yoseph* (The Strength of Joseph). Students sought out their Sephardic identity through questions directed to him, and he always responded favorably. One such venue was the class he taught in Sephardic History and Customs at the after-school High School of Jewish Studies in Seattle. But he was just as likely to get a phone call asking a specific question, or to be button-holed in synagogue for an explanation.

Unfortunately this came to a halt in September, 1982. His younger brother, Morris, had died and several days later, during the *Shachrith* (morning) service of Rosh Hashanah, Sam suffered a heart attack in synagogue. He recovered, but was never able to completely return to the person he had been, intellectually or physically. *La Boz* reprinted some of his previous articles for a year or two; he never wrote any more. Afterwards, his brother Isaac took over with his own column, "News from Isaac," which has a different focus. Isaac has also continued the tradition of teaching Ladino classes, using the same course material that Sam had developed.

Sam and Lucy celebrated their fiftieth anniversary in August, 1984 at a dinner party given by their children. In June of the following year, Lucy suffered a heart attack and died suddenly. Sam was not able to continue living in the home that he had shared with Lucy. He was slowed, but still showed flashes of his earlier brilliance and keen sense of humor. He was able to teach his two youngest grandsons their Bar

Mitzvah *parashiot*, although he did it mainly from memory, listening and correcting them while his eyes were firmly closed.

For the next six and a half years he lived primarily in the homes of his children Albert and Esther. As he had done several times a year, in December 1991 he took a train to spend some time with his daughter Vicki in Salem, Oregon. While there he suffered a gall bladder attack, requiring an operation. He never recovered and died on January 18, 1992. His body was returned to Seattle to be buried alongside his wife. On his tombstone are the following Hebrew passages which epitomize the man who was Sam Bension Maimon:

Ish makir tov v'ohaiv shalom lomaid um'lamaid
Ashrei mi sheba l'caan v'talmudo b'yado
Odeh Hashem m'od bphi, uv'toch rabim ahal'lenu

A man who appreciated the good in all, loved peace, studied and taught (A. Maimon)
Happy is he who comes here (Heaven) with his teachings in his hand (Babylonian Talmud, *Ketubot*, 77B)
I will thank G-d exceedingly with my mouth, and amid the multitude I will praise him (Psalms, 109,30)

About the Book

Sam Maimon was a man who had the insight to recognize that his people, the Levantine Sephardim, were at a crossroads in their history. He also had the talent and interest to help them successfully cross from the Old World to the New. As he wrote in many of his articles, his main goal was to stimulate the younger generation to learn about, appreciate and embrace the beauty of Sephardic life, so as to integrate the richness of the past into an emerging future. While he gladly shared his extensive knowledge about Sephardic culture, his real interest was to challenge and encourage people to translate that knowledge into living the Sephardic life.

He fully understood that the world of his youth in Turkey was foreign to his younger readers. He also recognized that very few people anywhere had the interest or resources to research the rich history of Sephardic life going back a thousand years or more. He had the first hand experience of both the Old and the New Worlds and personal contacts with many very knowledgeable people. G-d had given him the motivation and talent to study and understand the rich primary and secondary sources written in Hebrew, French and Ladino that linked his two worlds to the roots of early Jewish history. His sources included classical writers, available and well-known to the general Jewish scholarly world, such as Benjamin of Tudela and Cecil Roth. However, more importantly, they also included the books of less well-known, more recent writers, such as Rosanes, Molho, Almaleh, Galante and Gaon as well as numerous journals, magazines and newspapers in Hebrew, Spanish or Ladino.

His humor and folk style of writing enabled him to reach and relate to a wide general public with his message, in a manner reminiscent of the effective blending achieved in the original *Me'Am Lo'Ez*. Using this style, he covered many topics, including places, people, practices, language and social and religious institutions to convey the "feel" of Sephardic life most effectively to his audience.

At one level, this book is simply a compilation of Sam Maimon's articles written over an eleven year period of time (1971-1982) for *La Boz*, the monthly newsletter of Sephardic Bikur Holim Congregation in Seattle, Washington. Taken as such, each article can be read and enjoyed for its own content. The reader will gain knowledge on a wide variety of topics, relating to Sephardic life (primarily Levantine Sephardim), history, language, customs and social practices.

Taken as a whole, however, the book takes on a much broader purpose, and provides the reader with a unique opportunity to catch a glimpse of a part of Jewish history which has been essentially closed to the English-speaking public. The overall effect is like seeing a panoramic view of personal and communal experiences, primarily in the Ottoman Empire among the Ladino-speaking, Levantine Sephardic Jews, painted in brightly colored, broad brush strokes.

To capture his readers' interest, he had to bridge many gaps between his subject and his readers' frame of reference. For example, we do not learn much about the Ottoman Empire in our schools. What we do learn is taught from a Western orientation, and does not promote understanding of the culture or the people. Thus he first had to provide some basic information. Before he could introduce the Alliance movement and its unsettling effect on the community, he had to first explain the traditional methods of education. He had to introduce the basics of the background of Ladino and certain social realities, before the richness of some expressions and phrases could be appreciated. He had to remind the reader of social practices or the limited availability of certain technology in order to set the stage for understanding the meaning and value of customs and events.

In editing these articles for publication, we endeavored to change as little as possible, and only changed when we believed it would enhance clarity or understanding and/or benefit from having the articles presented together. We edited lightly to preserve his personal, informal style, so the reader will find some "not-so-perfect" grammar, some apparent redundancy and some modest inconsistency.

Similarly, rather than use academically "correct" translation and transliteration conventions (with "x"s and special characters, hard for the uninitiated to decipher), we chose an informal convention (much like he used in his original articles, essentially phonetic, but not entirely consistent). We used the Sephardic pronunciation and terminology except where we felt it would inhibit understanding among a more general readership. In such cases, we used the Sephardic term initially to give a "flavor" of the word or expression, but then switched to the more common term. For example, the Sephardic usage for rabbi is either "haham" or "haribi," so the reader will find those terms used with we felt the usage would be clear; but in most places we used "rabbi."

We used italics to indicate words not commonly recognized or used by the English-speaking Jewish community (e.g., Ladino or

Hebrew words and phrases). He translated many of the Ladino passages in his original articles, and we have provided additional English translations where there were none originally.

To promote clarity and understanding of the articles taken as a whole, we have grouped them into chapters, each chapter based on a common theme. Within each chapter we have chosen a specific order appropriate to that chapter; chronologically for most chapters, but by geographical proximity or some other measure of importance for others.

We have also inserted explanatory editors' notes where appropriate, as well as two types of cross references to assist the reader in finding many of the inter-related subjects. First, in the text we have added parenthetical references, i.e., "(see p. #)," and secondly, a major subject cross reference index is provided in Appendix IV.

Since he wrote extensively on the positions of *Haham Bashi* (chief rabbi of the Ottoman Empire) and *Rishon LeZion* (chief rabbi of Jerusalem and Israel), and also on many of the rabbis who held those positions, we have also included a list of the rabbis who have held those positions, in Appendices I and II, respectively.

Since he sometimes refers to events contemporary to the time of his writing a particular article, we have left the original date of the article along with the title to give the reader historical perspective. Furthermore, Appendix III provides a chronological listing of the articles.

The task of bringing this book to print would have been much more difficult, if not impossible, were it not for the assistance and contribution of many people. We thank them all, but can not mention all of them here by name. Those whom we must acknowledge here are:

Rabbi Solomon Maimon who provided us advice and counsel and, especially, encouragement to carry out the project, even when we got so stalled that we couldn't seem to get things moving.

Professor David Romey who provided an invaluable editorial review of much of the material, and made many suggestions for improvement.

Dr. and Mrs. David Raphael who, as they have so often done in the past, shared generously of their experience and ideas to help us in this project, regarding both our general approach and some very specific suggestions for improvement.

Mr. Isaac Maimon (Uncle Ike) who graciously and expertly took on the tasks of review much of the book, as well as translating virtually all of the previously untranslated Ladino material.

David Hyman who provided his technical and professional assistance on many aspects of the "esthetics" of the book as well as its title.

· Ruth Hyman who started her involvement with this project as the typist (word processing person), a function that she performed most efficiently and professionally. But she got so "hooked" on the content that soon it became "her baby" so, in the end, she in effect became our partner in the editing process.

Our sister and brother-in-law Vicki and Sidney Schain who participated in all major decision-making leading to our joint commitment to publish this book, and who offered support in many ways.

Finally, our wives, Jean and Esther, who have given their time, talent and energy to the project. They graciously and supportively gave their permission for us to work on and complete this book, even at the expense of much-needed time together, and putting off many other high priority tasks. Our "job jar" is full, and now, *si quiere el Dio*, we'll get to them soon. (They're probably saying to themselves -- "*a la otra venida . . .*" loosely translated as "and if you believe that . . .")

*   *   *

Sam Bension Maimon, z"l, our father and father-in-law, possessed a rare blend of wisdom and humor, and a gift for taking a simple phrase, even in English, and investing it with special meaning to people and events that personalized it for them. He touched every one he knew in a particular way that became important to each one of them. We would like to convey to the reader the uniqueness of the Sam Maimon approach to life, and give a sense of his remarkable trait of capturing special meaning with a single phrase. To do this we will share with you some of his best remembered phrases, and indicate their connection to the publication of this book.

"It can not be helped"
Editing this book has been a labor of love, the fruition of a longtime ambition, a much talked-about but never-realized goal during the author's lifetime. It therefore leaves us with a sense of bittersweet accomplishment. Completing the book provided us great joy and satisfaction, but also sadness in that neither parent was able to enjoy the experience of seeing it published. There always were other priorities, other family matters to be attended to, and the editing

process was a major task, so, in Dad's words, "It can not be helped" that it took so long. We also hope that our efforts might have brought comfort to his *neshama* since working with his writings has somehow kept us closer to him so that, in our consciousness, he is very much still alive.

"Take a chance!"

In bringing this work to print, we have been driven by a strong sense of *kibud av va'em* (honoring our father and mother). This has led us to some dilemmas in the editing of this book. For example, in the interest of adhering to the accepted writing conventions, we have used the familiar third person or, in many places, his first name, instead of "Dad" or "Father." As editors, our task was to objectively ensure the accuracy and integrity of the reprinted articles as best reflecting the author's message, despite the personal nature of some of these messages to us. The final product is ours. We are responsible for any errors of omission or commission in the book, and hope that if there are any, they will not diminish the impact of the author's ideas and experiences. We ask, in the words of the author, that you the reader, "Take a chance!", read and hopefully feel, the vibrancy of the lifestyle of the Turkish Sephardim as he expressed it.

"If that's the case, *L'chaim!*"

In summary, we hope and pray that this book promotes the overriding purpose of the author when he wrote these articles, i.e., to capture and pass on the best of what true Sephardic life in the Ottoman Empire and the United States has to offer. As Dad would have done, we toast you the reader with "If that's the case, *L'chaim!*" and hope that you enjoy and are enlightened by his writings. If his message is passed on, it will truly bring honor to the memory of the lives of Sam and Lucy Maimon *TNZB"H* (May their souls be bound up in the bonds of life, amen.)

A. S. Maimon/E. Normand
Nisan 5753/April, 1993
Seattle, Washington

Introduction

by Rabbi Marc D. Angel

The Torah teaches that we are obligated to keep G-d's commandments and "to walk in His ways" (Devarim 28:9). Rabbi Hayyim Palachi, a leading sage of Izmir during the last century, commented that the requirement "to walk in His ways" is an active one, not merely a passive one. One should not simply sit home and wait for the opportunity to fulfill mitzvot. Rather, one should be actively searching for possibilities to do acts of kindness and righteousness. A truly good and pious person is characterized by his willingness "to walk," to go out, to involve himself in the lives of others.

The Sephardic community of Seattle was blessed for many years with the dynamic presence of Mr. Sam (Bension) Maimon. During the course of his long life in Seattle, he was not just another person -- he was a presence, a force in the cultural and spiritual life of the community. He knew what it meant "to walk in His ways."

Everyone who had the privilege of knowing him will remember him with positive and happy memories. We will remember his beautiful voice, his singing in the synagogue, his phenomenal sense of humor. We will remember that every family celebration was made happier by his presence. We will remember attending *selihoth* services where he would look at the Hebrew text and sing the translation in Ladino. We will remember how he brought a spirit of liveliness and joyousness through his witticisms.

Sam Maimon can fairly be described as one of the folk heros of the Sephardic community of Seattle. His knowledge of Judaism was extensive. He was deeply imbued with the traditions of the Sephardim of Turkey. He loved books, he loved ideas, he loved the culture of which he was part. He was not an external student of Sephardic history and culture; he was himself a living representative of the Sephardic way of life. He was one of the best and one of the last genuine examples of a folk scholar raised in the Judeo-Spanish tradition of Turkish Jews.

Sam Maimon was always available and eager to help members of the younger generation learn more about the Sephardic tradition. In my own research over the years, I turned to him often -- and he was always enthusiastic and generous in his assistance. He taught me to decipher the Sephardic cursive writing in some old manuscripts from the Island of Rhodes; he read with me a number of Ladino newspapers which were in his collection, which shed light on a period of Sephardic history which I was then studying. He provided translations of Ladino words, explanations of Ladino phrases. In 1980, Sephardic House published a volume which included a Ladino-English dictionary which he had prepared. Many students have found this work to be helpful in their own studies.

Sam Maimon's family is to be commended for preparing this volume of his writings and teachings. They are the reflections of an optimistic, fun-loving folk scholar, who also understood the seriousness of his task. Through his teachings, writings and classes, he wanted to convey the traditions of the Turkish Sephardic Jews to coming generations. This is a book which will bring smiles and tears to the sensitive reader. I am sure it would have been Sam Maimon's hope that the ideas and information presented in this book will deepen our own understanding and appreciation of Sephardic tradition, thereby deepening our connection to Judaism and the Jewish people.

Preface

by Dr. David Raphael,
author of *The Alhambra Decree*

Bension Maimon was a *Sephardi tahor*, a pure Sephardi who lived and breathed the Ladino tradition. As a cantor with a hauntingly beautiful voice, he moved us at prayer. As a self-taught scholar immersed in Ladino lore and literature, he was sought out by Spanish and Jewish academicians alike. In his delightful manner, he taught us as we walked to synagogue, *caminando y hablando*. He gave of himself in many ways to friends, family and community. Now he has left us something very precious: a collection of his writings as lively, thoughtful and thoroughly Sephardic as the man himself.

Table of Contents

THE BEAUTY OF
SEPHARDIC LIFE

Scholarly, Humorous and

Personal Reflections

Chapter One

Sephardic Communities Far and Wide

March 1978   1 Adar/2 Adar 5738

Spain

A few weeks ago, the Sephardic chief rabbi of Israel, Rabbi
Ovadia Yoseph, made a historic trip to Spain. The *Rishon LeZion* was
invited to attend the opening of a Center of Young Leadership Institute
in Madrid. While there, Rabbi Yoseph also attended the opening of
the first Jewish school to be established in Spain since our forefathers,
the Sephardim, were expelled in 1492. Authorities agree that the
Spanish Expulsion edict, which was in effect for almost 400 years, was
effectively lifted when Spain became a republic in 1858. General Prim
said then that Jews were permitted to tread once again upon Spanish
soil.

For a while, though, Jews were not permitted to have any public
building where they could hold religious services. In 1917 some
refugees from World War I established a little synagogue. Among
these refugees was the famous Max Nordau. The Spanish government
helped many Jews from Salonika and other places to emigrate to Spain
during Hitler's Holocaust. A spirit of good will towards Jews moved
the bishop of Huelva recently to issue a remarkable statement, saying,
"We regret and deplore that we once banished the Jews from Spain."
And a professor from Madrid University said, "We realize the great
injustice, and we now want to rectify it." This proves that the Spanish
people want us to renew our contact with the country where our
Sephardic ancestors had a glorious past.

That is all very well. But, what about our attitude, our side of the
story? Can we forget and forgive what painful heartaches our
forefathers endured? We were led to believe that there was a *herem* (a

rigorous rabbinic ban) against anyone going back to Spain to live! We were told this *herem* was decreed by the expelled rabbis and scholars in their newly formed communities and that it carried the strict penalty of a very stiff curse on anyone who ever dared to go back and live in Spain. This was a very solemn restriction, and fearful of the terrifying penalty, no decent Sephardi would ever step on Spanish soil again.

Now come the three crucial questions. First, was such a *herem* ever proclaimed? Second, if so, has anyone ever seen it? And, third, the fact that so many people believe it prompts one to ask, if this *herem* actually existed, has it ever been recorded any place, or has it been recorded in the form of an official document? We do possess hundreds of books written by great rabbis and scholars of that period, in which they describe, in minute detail, the conditions that existed before, during and after the Expulsion of our ancestors from Spain, and how they settled in the Turkish Empire and other Mediterranean cities.

In order to answer these puzzling questions and in order to resolve, once and for all, whether such a *herem* ever existed, the late eminent historian and author Mr. Cecil Roth launched an inquiry into this riddle. He read all the relevant historical literature but found no reference to the unseen and awesome *herem*. He also decided to ask around to several Sephardic experts, among whom was the former chief rabbi of Israel Rabbi Yitzhak Nissim, who referred him to inquire from Mr. Meir Benayahu (Rabbi Nissim's son) who is very proficient in Sephardic history and literature. (See p. 210)

Mr. Benayahu, in his reply to Mr. Roth, explained that he also studied this puzzling subject and that in all of his studies had never come across any book that mentioned, specifically, the existence of such a *herem*, adding that all he saw written about the matter was a quotation in one of the books containing the following: "It's our fervent hope that none of our dear brothers will ever return to the land of Spain." Of course, this phrase advocating "hope" cannot be construed as an official, authoritative *herem* by any stretch of the imagination. So the conclusion that scholars came to finally is that it is very possible that a *herem* may have existed and, perhaps, in the course of these many long years it might have gotten lost.

Obviously, Rabbi Ovadia Yoseph is of the opinion that no official *herem* ever existed or, if it ever did, it's not in effect any longer. Otherwise, the chief rabbi would never have made this historic visit to Spain.

February 1974 Shevat/Adar 5734

Early Sephardim in Spain

The question is often asked: How far back in history can we trace the beginnings of a Jewish community in Spain? The answer, of course, is very complex. Historical authorities differ, some suggest there were Jews in Spain right after the Roman conquest of *Eretz Yisrael*.

For now, we shall deal with the Golden Age of Spanish Jewry, which comprises the immortal works on literature, *halacha*, philosophy and poetry produced by our great Sephardic sages.

One of the persons to whom we can assign the honor of being "The First Mover of the Epoch of the Golden Age" was Hasdai Ibn Shaprut. He was born in Jaen, Spain in 915 and moved later to Cordova.

Along with his various other studies, he studied medicine and became a top physician to the Mohammedan ruler of the time who respected his judgment so much that he made Hasdai his foreign minister, entrusting him with very important missions. Those of our readers who are interested should read up further on this remarkable man and his important role with the *Kazars*, a people in the Crimea that adopted the Jewish religion.

At this period in history, the center of Jewish learning was still in Babylonia. However, these Jewish centers were beginning to disintegrate, so it was necessary for the academy in Sura to send out emissaries to the different communities in the Diaspora to collect funds to maintain the academies.

The story is that in the year 960, four great *hahamim* from Sura set out on a similar mission to collect funds, but they were all captured by pirates, who sold them to different communities around the Mediterranean. One of these captives was a *haham* by the name of Rabbi Moshe Ben Hanoh, who had his son with him, and somehow later he found his way to the town of Cordova in Spain.

The story continues that one day Rabbi Moshe, unknown to anyone, appeared at the *yeshiva* in Cordova and he listened to the director Rabbi Nathan delivering a Talmudic discourse on the very complicated tractate of *Yoma*.

Rabbi Nathan noticed a stranger wearing torn and ragged clothes sitting in the back row. However, by the tone and depth of the questions that Rabbi Moshe asked, Rabbi Nathan realized that this was no ordinary stranger but someone who possessed a high degree of knowledge. Rabbi Nathan introduced Rabbi Moshe to Hasdai who was so impressed with Rabbi Moshe that he opened a *yeshiva* for him where Hasdai himself enrolled as one of the students. Hasdai hired scribes to copy all new books for this *yeshiva*. Rabbi Moshe's greatest gift was his ability to explain the most difficult passages of the Talmud in such a way that they became clear to every student.

When Rabbi Moshe died there was a competition as to who should succeed him as head of the academy. Among other qualified candidates for this post was the renowned scholar Rabbi Joseph Ibn Abitur. Hasdai Ibn Shaprut, however, decided in favor of Hanoh, the son of Rabbi Moshe. Hanoh was educated under his father and was well qualified for this high position and so Rabbi Hanoh was installed as the head of the academy.

Our readers should certainly recall that Cordova produced a number of scholars, and it was later to become the birthplace of the greatest scholar and philosopher of the Golden Age, the Rambam (Rabbi Moshe Ben Maimon, or Maimonides).

January 1981   Teveth/Shevat 5741

Butchering in the Jewish Community of Zaragoza

(La Carniceria de la Aljama Zaragozana)

Sometime ago, my son-in-law, Eugene Normand, brought me a magazine named *Sefarad* from the University of Washington library. In it I found a very fascinating article entitled "*La Carniceria de la Aljama Zaragozana*" (*Butchering in the Jewish Community of Zaragoza*).

Sefarad is published in the Spanish language by a society called *Arias Montano* of Madrid. The scholars and professors who write these articles have been discovering a wealth of interesting material such as historical documents in the ancient archives of Spain.

This ancient document from Zaragoza deals with strict rules and regulations by the *Aljama* (Jewish community) of the city of Zaragoza on the sale of kosher meat. Written in our ancient cursive (Hebrew script), in the Spanish-Ladino language (with a few Hebrew words mixed in), it consists of sixteen sheets of paper and is dated 1488. One of the main sources of income that the Jewish communities of Spain had was to impose on the membership a tax on certain commodities, such as meat, wine, etc. In our own time, in Turkey, this tax was called *gabella*, but in this 1488 document, our Sephardic ancestors called it *sisa*.

To make it convenient for the *Aljama*, the leaders devised a plan whereby one individual was selected every year to assume the responsibility of paying to the community a fixed sum, arrived at by the estimated number of heads of families and the average amount of meat they would consume. This man was called *el arrendador* or the leasor of kosher butcher shops who was given the right to collect or levy "*cinco dineros por libra de carne vendida*" (five coins per pound of sold meat). In order to be fair to this *arrendador*, the leaders of the Aljama would guarantee him certain privileges, such as, no one was allowed to slaughter, on his own, for kosher consumption. All meat had to be bought from one of the kosher butcher shops in town, and no member was allowed to import any kosher meat from out of town. The religious authorities, this document says, were able to enforce all these rules with government backing and authority. We see a few sample pages of the original document in this Zaragoza *Aljama*. It's divided into numbered chapters, each chapter regulating the different rules, such as the cuts of meat, even as to how much they were to charge the customers, also covering the rules of *shehita* (ritual slaughtering) and qualification of the *shohet* (ritual slaughterer), including *carne de carnero, de ternero, de oveja, de vaca*, etc. (different kinds of meat). It also regulated the price on the *minudos* such as *los rinones, corazon, pulmones, cabeza, patas, higado, lengua, mollejas, utera de vaca, las tripas*, etc. (kidneys, heart, lung, head, legs, liver, tongue, sweetbreads, beef udder, intestines, etc.)

Among the names of the charitable institutions maintained by the *Aljama de Zaragoza* was *La Societa Bikur Holim*. No doubt this has the same origin as the name of our *kahal*, Sephardic Bikur Holim in Seattle. This document contains a tremendous amount of rules. The name of the *arrendador* for 1488 was Benveniste who leased out six kosher butcher shops. The owner of one of the butcher shops was Yaakov Franco, and one of the co-signers was Rabbi Moshe Bivas. The *arrendador* was even instructed that in case he sold some meat to charitable institutions, it was exempt from paying the *sisa*, the *arrendador* having the right to deduct the amount from his next payment. *Pesah* time, the butcher shops were instructed to distribute meat to a number of poor people of the community, this amount being paid by the treasurer of the *Aljama*.

On reading this Zaragoza document dated 1488, one can only conclude that the Spanish Jews of the time didn't have the slightest hint or the fear of being expelled in 1492 -- just four short years away.

These newly discovered Spanish documents are certainly an excellent source of information to future history writers, especially depicting how well-organized these Sephardic communities were.

April 1974   Nissan 5734

Who Was There? (The Romaniotes)

On that horrible summer of 1492, when our forefathers were inhumanly expelled from Spain, thousands were about to locate themselves in North Africa, some settled in Italy, but the bulk of them found refuge in what was then the lands of the Ottoman Empire.

The Ottoman Turks had conquered Asiatic Turkey over a hundred years earlier before they were finally able to capture Constantinople in 1453. When the Spanish Jews came in 1492, the Sultan had accorded them a very warm welcome through the *Haham Bashi* (chief rabbi), Rabbi Moshe Capsali, who lived then in Constantinople.

Who were these Jews that received these refugees? A small Jewish community of Greek-speaking Jews that had lived around those areas for hundreds of years and who called themselves *Romaniotes*, (meaning, Greek-speaking Jews).

Even in our own day those Greeks that still lived in European Turkey called their language Romeka. If someone asked you the question: *Ekseris Romeka?* It meant: Do you know how to speak Greek? The Turkish name for the Greeks was *Ouroum* and the Turkish name for European Turkey was and still is *Rou Eli*, which included cities like Edirne, Tekirdag, Gallipoli, and even Sofia and Salonica.

As we mentioned, these Jews used to speak Greek in their home, until some years passed after the enormous Sephardic population settled into these areas. These *Romaniote* Jews had to yield to numbers and were forced to abandon their Greek and adopted the Spanish or Ladino as their everyday language, with the exception of a few towns in Greece like Yanina, the island of Corfu, etc., who still use the Greek language. These *Romaniotes* resisted, at the beginning, to mingle with the newcomers, and clung to their customs, and for a long time they had their own synagogues with their own separate daily and holiday prayer books.

According to the Sephardic historian Solomon Rosanes (see p. 42), this prayer book contained quite a few differences from the Spanish ritual. Mr. Rosanes tells us that in his day, there remained only one such synagogue which they called Kahal Kadosh Romanya, and these prayer books were already not available. He had a copy, however, although it was worn and torn. Among many variations he cites were the following examples: On *Hoshanah Rabbah* they used to recite *Nishmath* in the morning prayer; on the second day of *Purim* (*Shushan Purim*) they used to take out a *Sefer Torah* and used to read the *Megillah* in Greek; on days that we read the *Hallel* they did not repeat *Hodu*.

The Sephardim of Turkey still use some first names or family names that are a leftover from these native Jews. Names like Kalo, Kalomira, Hursi, Galimidi, Zafira, Kalimera, Bula or Policar. Besides these names we still use words of Greek origin like *trandafila* (rose), *eskularichas* (earrings), *papu* (grandfather), *vava* (grandmother), *tarapapu* (great-grandfather), *papasni* (priest) and *nikochera* (a capable housewife).

To realize how ancient this *Romaniote* community really was, we only have to read the book written by the famous Spanish traveler Rabbi Benjamin de Tudela, who, in 1176, visited Constantinople and found there about 2,000 Jews and 500 *Kara'im* (Karaites). He says in this book that he saw many of these Jews in various businesses and some of these were extremely wealthy.

G-d willing, in the next article, I will describe the magnificent job these *Romaniote* Jews and their leaders did to provide these refugees with food, lodging and jobs. (See p. 30.)

March 1975   Adar/Nisan 5735

Early Constantinople

Today, I would like to write a few additional facts about Rabbi
Moshe Capsali, the first *Haham Bashi* (chief rabbi) in Constantinople.
(See also p. 30 and p. 55.) In 1453, when the Turkish Sultan
Mehmet II conquered that city from the Byzantine Empire, he selected
Rabbi Moshe to guide the affairs of all the Jews living in the vast
Ottoman Empire, most of whom were Greek-speaking Jews known as
Romaniotes.   This was thirty-nine years prior to the Sephardim's
arrival in Turkey after the Spanish Expulsion of 1492.

At this time (1488) the Ottoman ruler, Sultan Bayazid, was
waging a war against a certain Chief Melek Bey of Egypt, who
rebelled against Bayazid.   Through a long siege, Melek Bey got
possession of the holy city of Jerusalem.

This long siege on Jerusalem caused the small and poor
community of that city to send a *shaliah* (emissary) to different world
Jewish communities to collect funds to help the destitute families.
One of these *shaliahs* came to Constantinople in 1488 to collect such
funds. His name was Moshe Arba Veesrim. Some say that was his
name. Others say he was given this name to indicate his education
was limited to the knowledge of the twenty-four books of our Bible.
Arba Veesrim, in Hebrew means twenty-four. This emissary, on his
arrival in Constantinople, contacted the *Haham Bashi* for permission
to go to the various synagogues and make his appeal.

Unfortunately, Rabbi Capsali could not allow this because the
Ottoman government had just issued a royal decree that no one was
allowed to raise or transport money to Jerusalem because of the war.
Even though Rabbi Capsali's hands were tied, he helped the *shaliah* in
many other ways. But this emissary, being of a low and ungrateful
character, contrived a plot, accusing the *haham* of many false
accusations, even going as far as Italy in spreading rumors about the
haham. This *shaliah* convinced four other prominent persons in
Constantinople to write a letter to Rabbi Yoseph Colon, chief rabbi of
Mantua, full of unfounded charges against Rabbi Moshe Capsali.

Rabbi Yoseph Colon, on hearing and believing the *shaliah*, and
on reading the grave charges contained in that letter, hastily issued a
rabbinic order to the effect that from now on Rabbi Capsali's authority
as chief rabbi in Constantinople is invalidated.   Fortunately, the

Haham Bashi had a number of good and sincere friends who came forward and defended him, both on the complex issues involved, and as to Rabbi Moshe's impeccable character. When Rabbi Colon realized his mistake, he quickly made a very personal and intensive campaign, this time to the effect that he was sorry that he had acted too hastily. He sincerely wished to rectify any wrong or any damage that he might have caused to Rabbi Capsali.

In 1490, when Rabbi Yoseph Colon was on his deathbed, he called in his son Peretz. He made Peretz promise him that he would go to Constantinople to ask Rabbi Moshe Capsali for his personal forgiveness for all the unjust and offensive accusations that he, Rabbi Colon, had charged him with. The *Haham Bashi* was so generous in his actions that he not only welcomed Peretz Colon to his house, assuring him of his complete forgiveness towards his father, but also took him in and treated him and protected him like a loving father.

May 1972   Iyar/Sivan 5732

Jewish Community In Istanbul

The Turkish government in Istanbul decided to have a census count of the entire population of the city. The date: Sunday, October 20, 1935.

In order to finish the whole count in one day, they came out with a city ordinance to the effect that absolutely no one was allowed to leave his or her house until the census count was completed. That same year, our Jewish holiday of *Simhath Torah* fell on Sunday, October 20, the very same day of the census counting.

The Istanbul rabbinate found itself in a quandary as to what to do. They knew that this government order applied to everybody, and they were not able to change the law. At the same time, the rabbis wanted to fix it so the Jewish population of the city would not miss the religious services of such an important holiday as *Simhath Torah*.

The problem was carefully studied by the rabbis. They came up with the solution of combining the reading of the *Sefer Torah* of the two days, Saturday itself being *Shemini Atzereth*, which is always the day before *Simhath Torah*, and *Simhath Torah* itself, thus taking out four *sefarim*.

The following public communique was issued by the Istanbul rabbinical court to all the synagogues in the city. This announcement was issued in Ladino, which we reproduce here.

El onorado publico - Ya esta al koriente ke el 20 Octobre proximo fue consacrado por el governo al resensamiento de la populasion. Esta data corresponde al dia de alhad, Simhath Torah. Sera dunke emposivle a nuestra populasyon de salir de kaza for azer nuestras orasyones en este dia, en la sinagoga. Nozotros beth din, aviendo estudiado este kazo, desidmos ke las orasyones del dia de Shabbath, Shemini Atzereth, seran selebradas como sigye: Se devran kitar kuatro Sifre Torah. En el primero se devra meldar perashath Kol Abehor empesando de asser teasser, y azer yamar syete olim, y se devra dizir kaddish.

En el sigundo se devra meldar perashath Vezoth Aberaha, en yamando kuantos olim ke les plaze, y sigun el uzo de kada anyo, y devra suvir hatan mesayem y eskapar la perashah entera, y no se deve dizir kaddish.

En el tresero devra suvir hatan mathil y meldar perashath Bereshith y devran dizir kaddish.

En el kuatreno devra suvir el maftir y meldar bayom ashemini, y devra dizir kaddish y meldar la aftara Vayii Kehaloth Shelomo y despues Vayii Ahare Moth Moshe.

La tadre en la minha devran meldar perashath Bereshith.

Todos lo sinyores sheluhe tzibur son tenidos a konformarsen, estriktamente, a estas enstruksyones religiosas.

El Beth Din Atzedek. 20 Elul 5695

Translation:
Honored public - The public is advised that this coming 20th of October was consecrated by the government to the count of the population. This date corresponds to Sunday day of *Simhath Torah.* It would then be impossible to our population to come out from the house to make our prayers on that day in the synagogue. We the *Beth Din* (religious court), having studied this case decided that the prayers of Saturday *Shemini Atzereth,* should be celebrated as follows: You must take out four *Sifre Torahs.* In the first should be read *perashath Kol Abehor* starting from *Asser Teasser,* and call seven *olim,* and then say *kaddish.*

On the second, it should be read perashath *Vezoth Haberaha*, by calling as many *olim* as they please, and according to the custom of every year, and go up to *sefer Hatan Mesayem*, and finish the *perashah* entirely, and you must not say *kaddish*.

In the third *sefer* the *Hatan Mathil* goes up and should read *Bayom Hashemini*, must say *kaddish* and read the *Haftarah Vayii Kehaloth Shlomo*, and then *Vayii Ahare Moth Moshe*.

In the evening in the *minha* they must read perashath *Bereshith*.

All the leaders of the congregation must strictly conform with these religious instructions.

The Righteous Jewish Religious Court
September 18, 1935

This was an emergency regulation which applied only to the taking out of the *sefer*. As far as the holiday morning prayers were concerned, everyone was required to say them at home privately.

February 1973   Adar 5733

Tekirdag (Rodosto)

Situated some seventy miles southwest of Istanbul, on the Sea of Marmara, is the city of Tekirdag, on a beautiful seashore. It was the city in which I grew up, from about ages four to sixteen. I remember when we used to go swimming at the beach, the water was so pleasantly warm and so shallow that we had to go out quite a distance before we reached deep water.

In the old days the city was called Rhodestus which evolved into Rodosto. Historical authorities explain this name Rhodestus to mean Little Rhodes, and that Rodosto was named after the Island of Rhodes, because of its resemblance. I'm inclined to believe this explanation because I have some Hebrew legal documents in my possession in which the name of the city is recorded as Rodoschik, meaning Little Rhodes.

Benjamin of Tudela, the famous traveler from Spain, visited Rodosto in 1173. He reports in his famous travel book that he saw in Rodosto about 400 Jews, mentioning names of some rabbis who lived there at that time.

Around the year 1450 the city was overrun by the Ottoman Empire, and the Turkish name Tekirdag was given to it sometime later. In 1912, during the Balkan war, the city was occupied by the Bulgarian army. Many Tekirdalis (people who live in or are from Tekirdag), fearing the Bulgars, fled the city. I remember my family was among the *majires* (refugees). We spent nine months in Istanbul in various communities until the Bulgars vacated the town. We returned to Rodosto along with other families, but some families remained in Istanbul. Before the Bulgars came, the city contained a Jewish population of 2,800 members. Ever since then, the number of Jews in Tekirdag started diminishing, what with emigration to the United States and Cuba and later to Israel.

When we visited the city a couple of years ago (1970), they told us there were only eighteen families left. The beautiful synagogue was knocked down to make way for a highway.

After the First World War the Allies, as a punishment to Turkey, gave the whole region of Turkey called Thrace to the Greek government. I remember one morning we woke up and heard a lot of guns and bombardment coming from the harbor. We found out later that the Greek fleet, along with some British warships, was shelling the rear of the town, taking the precaution of chasing away any remnant of Turkish troops that might still be around. The next day we saw the Greek king in Rodosto, with thousands of Greek soldiers that disembarked from the warships. This Greek occupation lasted two and a half years.

At the end of that period, the Turkish National Army, under the leadership of Mustapha Kemal (later known as Ataturk, Father of the Turks), was able to reconquer that part of Turkey from the Greeks. I remember it was in the summer of 1922 that once again Tekirdag was under Turkish rule.

November 1977   Heshvan/Kislev 5738

The Jews of Rhodes

In the June 1888 edition of the bulletin of the Alliance Israelite Universelle, there appeared a report on the Jews of Rhodes, written in French by a certain Mr. Paryente, then director of the Jewish schools of Izmir. Rabbi Avraham Danon, the famous Sephardi scholar translated this long article into Ladino. I'm here translating it (only in part) into English for our *La Boz* readers.

Mr. Paryente says: The Rhodes Jewish community has existed since ancient times. One of the fascinating items about the island of Rhodes was the Colossus of Rhodes, one of the seven wonders of the world. This was a huge bronze statue of the Greek idol Apollo which was built in the city's harbor. Then, around the year 282 before the Christian era, a severe earthquake shook the island and the Colossus collapsed, and large chunks of the bronze toppled over and were scattered all over the waterfront. This debris lay there for hundreds of years, until a Syrian Jew, in the year 656, bought the rights to all this metal. History tells us that the Jewish merchant had to hire 900 camels to move all this copper and bronze, transferred it to Marmaritza, twenty-seven miles away.

The island of Rhodes was ruled by, among others, the knights of the Crusades, who used the island as the jumping off place to Jerusalem. In 1523 Sultan Suleiman captured it, and it continued under Turkish rule until 1912 when Italians ruled it. At present, the island of Rhodes is under Greek rule.

In the year 1840, the Jews of Rhodes suffered from a very tragic incident of which, Mr. Paryente says, many of the elderly Jews of Rhodes still remembered in 1888. The story goes that a certain English businessman from Izmir dispatched his agent, a Sephardic Jew by the name of Eliya Calomete, to Rhodes to purchase a large shipment of sponges, a commerce that still flourishes in the Greek islands. The Greek merchants of Rhodes were not very happy with the arrival of Mr. Calomete figuring he would be an unwelcome competitor. So these Greeks developed such a fierce and bitter hate for all the Rhodesli Jews, that they devised a vicious plan in order to wreak their revenge against the Jews.

They accused a certain half idiot Jew, by the name of Elyakim de Leon Estanbulli, with the charge that he did away with a Greek youngster (probably as a blood libel accusation). And so, these Greeks had the Turkish authorities arrest him and put him in prison.

On the promise of the Greek merchants to Elyakim that they would give him a good paying job, Elyakim confessed and said that he handed this Greek youth to a local Jewish man by the name of David Mizrahi. Based on the confession of this idiot Elyakim, a group of *jandarmas* (Turkish law officers) descended on the Jewish district on the afternoon of *Purim* and arrested ten of the island's civic leaders, one of whom was the grand rabbi Yaakov Yisrael. These Jewish leaders were taken to various dungeons and tortured. Rabbi Yaakov was forced to give his gold ring to the jailer in order to make him stop the terrific beating the jailer was giving him.

The whole Jewish community was terror stricken and no one dared to go out of the Jewish district. The Turkish governor of Rhodes Yusuf Pasha, as well as his advisors, believed this absurd story, so he gave orders to institute a search through all the Jewish homes for the Greek youth, naturally without result. A certain Rabbi Avraham Amado succeeded in running away to Izmir where he presented the case againt this false accusation. Then the ten Jewish leaders were released from prison after spending fifteen days in the foul Turkish jails. Meanwhile the Greek youth that disappeared was found alive and well in the island of Shera.

Finally the royal *firman* (decree) arrived from Istanbul. (It was the same type of *firman* which was obtained for a similar case in Damascus, Syria, against the blood accusation. This *firman* was obtained by the internationally known French Jew Adolph Cremieux with the help of Count Camondo and Sir Moses Montefiore). The Turkish governor Yusuf Pasha was dismissed and banished. This incident among others led to the formation of the Alliance. (See p.104)

An interesting item in the same report by Mr. Paryente says that even to this day (1888) the descendants of the civic leaders that were imprisoned and tortured gather every year on the night of *Purim* in one of their family homes and sing a special song of thanks composed in Ladino for this occasion.

The report says that in one of the Rhodes synagogues, called El Kahal de Shalom, there was, on one corner, a little flask of oil to which, according to tradition, they assign many miracles, and "now" (1888) they use the oil to ease the *dolores de paridas* (birth pains). It also mentions the fact that in one of the doors of the *hehal hakodesh* (ark for the Torahs) of the synagogue, there's one board or panel missing. This was due to a general belief that whoever will add this panel may not live too long.

The Jews of Rhodes used to call the Colossus by the name *Arapula*. This word is an abbreviation of the two Turkish words *arap oglan* (meaning, the black valiant youth) a name assigned to the Colossus of Rhodes.

December 1977   Kislev/Teveth 5738

Salonika

I have a book I borrowed from Eli Almosnino called *Salonika, Ir Vaem Beyisrael* (*Salonika, City and Mother in Israel*). This fantastic book, written in Hebrew, records in great detail the history of Salonika since its beginning, including its customs, institutions and other pertinent information. The book is written by a group of ten Selanikli writers of renown, all of them expert in depicting their subject matter in a masterly fashion.

Salonika was founded in the year 315 B.C.E. by the Macedonian king Cassandra, who named the town after his wife Thessaloniki, the sister of Alexander the Great. It's recorded that the apostle Paul visited Salonika in the year 50 and delivered his sermon, in a synagogue, to an assembly of Jewish residents. In the year 1160, the famous Sephardic traveler Benjamin of Tuleda, visited the Jewish community of Salonika and he recorded in his book the names of the civic leaders and the situation of the Jewish congregation at the time.

Salonika was conquered by the Ottoman Empire in 1430. Turkish rule continued until 1912 when the Greek army entered the city. Salonika at present is part of Greece. In 1492 and 1497, thousands of our Sephardic brethren exiled from Spain and Portugal settled in Salonika where they built new homes for themselves and their families. Since the majority of the town's population was Jewish, all commerce, banking and other business were in the hands of the Jews. So when *Shabbath* came, all the stores and other activities in town were closed. No ship was ever loaded or unloaded in the Salonika harbor on *Shabbath*.

In the year 1923, when the Greek government imposed a compulsory Sunday closing of all business activities, a large number of Selaniklis who wouldn't comply with this law, started leaving Salonika. There was a massive wave of emigration to Israel, among them a great number of port workers like stevedores, fishermen, sailors, etc.

Yitzhak Ben Zvi, who later became president of the state of Israel, made several trips to Salonika to recruit and make deals with a large number of these port workers to emigrate to Israel with their families and work in the ports of Jaffa and Haifa. These Selanikli fishermen and stevedores were very helpful in aiding thousands of "secret *olim*" to *Eretz Yisrael* during the British Mandate. Even today the majority of Haifa port workers are descendants of these Selaniklis.

The German Nazis came to Salonika in 1941. By 1943 they had managed to confiscate most of the Jewish wealth and they shipped thousands of Salonika Jews to the concentration camps and the gas chambers of Poland and Germany. From a Jewish population of nearly 50,000, Salonika today has barely 2,000 Jews left. So the word Holocaust has a very bitter meaning and is a word filled with horror for those who were lucky to survive.

The book contains many chapters on different customs. I would like to mention here what I thought was a fascinating custom on *paridas* or future *paridas* (women who had babies or will have them soon).

A couple of months after the marriage, the mother-in-law would look for any signs of pregnancy in the recent bride. If these signs were positive, the young lady was treated with tender care. One custom they had was that they left all the doors and windows open. This, they believed, would help the future *parida* have a painless delivery.

If the young lady did not show any signs of pregnancy within a reasonable time, then the *vizinas* (neighbors) would offer many homemade *remedios* (remedies). One popular *remedio* was based on the belief that on the night of *Tu B'shvat* (*Las Frutas*) also called *Hag Ha'ilanoth* (Festival of the Trees), all trees would hug each other and make love on this night. So the *vizinas* would fill a pitcher of regular drinking water, mixed with rosewater and water from a well. They took this pitcher to some orchard and placed it in between the trees. In the morning they gave this girl to drink from this blessed water with the hope and prayer that the effect of the fruitful trees would work on this girl to enable her to have children.

Another *remedio*: A magic potion concocted by some elderly lady. This potion was drunk by both the young lady as well as her husband. These potions were made from a variety of exotic spices, some mysterious herbs and drugs. All these were designed to induce the desire for the sex drive. Other potions were made from the egg of a black chicken, herbs and spices. (See p. 189 for similar practices.)

November 1981   Heshvan/Kislev 5742

Gallipoli

A few weeks ago, our friend, Mrs. Fortuna Calvo, called me on the phone. She said she and her husband Shaya had seen the movie "Gallipoli" the night before and Shaya remembers quite a bit about the war in Gallipoli. I said to her that I also remember those days.

Some time before, I happened to have had a similar conversation with Mrs. Matilda Mezistrano. She remembered the time her family had to run away from Gallipoli, where she was born, to seek safety from the fierce bombardment during World War I.

Gallipoli is a seaport town in European Turkey, 135 miles southwest from Istanbul. In 1908 there were 1,200 Jews living in Gallipoli. The Sephardic traveler, Benjamin of Tudela, visited Gallipoli in the year 1162. He reports in his book of travels, published in Spain, that at that particular time Gallipoli contained 200 Jews. The Ottoman Turks captured Gallipoli in the year 1365. When our Sephardic brothers were exiled from Spain in 1492, a large number of these refugees settled in Gallipoli. The chief rabbi then was a prominent scholar, Rabbi Yaakov Ben Habib, the compiler of the famous book, *Ein Yaakov.*

As is well known, the body of water called the Dardanelles Straits serves as a dividing line between the two continents, Asia and Europe. On the Asiatic side, right at the entrance of the straits, stands the city of Chanakkale. Going north and across the straits, on the European side, and up a few miles stands the city of Gallipoli.

After the outbreak of the first world war, by 1915 it became evident that the Allies had definite plans to go through the Dardanelles, across the sea of Marmara, and finally invade Istanbul, which was their main goal. The British captured part of the straits, pouring naval bombardment, and constant artillery fire reaching to the very outskirts of the city of Gallipoli. The British used troops named Anzacs, which is short for Australians and New Zealanders. That's when the population of Gallipoli was forced to evacuate the town. Some families left their homes, businesses, etc., and settled in various towns in Turkey. A few families came to Tekirdag (Rodosto) where my family lived. I remember Ben Habib, a classmate of mine in Tekirdag, who originally came with a number of others from Gallipoli.

It was at that time that Mustapha Kemal, later called Ataturk, was finally able to take full control of the Gallipoli front, and was successful in defeating the Allies. My uncle David Maimon, a younger brother of my father's, spent years in the Turkish army, a large part of the time around the Gallipoli front. We hadn't heard from him for over two years, when one day we got a letter from him which contained four Turkish words: *Para yonder chigara isterim.* (Send me some money, I need cigarettes.) The conditions in the Turkish army then were so terribly low, it was unbelievable how they survived. When my uncle came back, he looked so emaciated we couldn't even recognize him. He used to tell us incredible stories about the war. He told us how day after day for months on end, his job was digging new trenches for the Turkish troops, literally walking and trampling on dead Turkish soldiers -- *bar minan* (may it be far from us).

The Turkish name for Gallipoli is Yelibol or Yeribol. The Sephardim called it Galipo for short. All the Mezistrano family, and all the Varon families (except Becky Souriano's family from Izmir) are from Galipo. People called them Yelibollis. Also from Gallipoli are the following Seattle families: the Condiotys, the Abolafias, the Habibs, Nessim Eskenazi's family and the late Shelomatchi Levy.

I haven't seen the movie "Gallipoli," but I understand it deals with a story about two Australian friends and their World War I adventure during the time they were with the British troops in the battle of Gallipoli. It was produced (not in Hollywood) by an Australian movie maker and has hardly anything to do with the town. This movie maker could have been a little more obliging to our members from Galipo and could have included some familiar scenes or familiar streets or places in Galipo. These would have afforded the ones born there with a few tidbits of reminiscing, and could have brought them some fond memories of their native town, making it more enjoyable.

My brother, Rabbi Maimon, on one of his more recent tours, took a group and visited the city of Gallipoli. Not many Sephardim live there any more. They either moved to Israel or to Istanbul and other places. I borrowed a book from my son-in-law, Dr. Eugene Normand. The book is a biography of Ataturk, (see p. 51) in which the author describes, in minute detail the battle of Gallipoli. There is an item in this book which I would like to mention here.

In short, the author of this book writes that at the height of the battle a piece of shrapnel had hit the breast pocket of Mustapha Kemal's shirt, shattering a watch he had inside the pocket and leaving only a superficial wound. After the war, Kemal would look at this watch, saying, "Here is the watch that saved my life." That is fate!

August 1973   Av/Elul 5733

Jerusalem Visits

I often wonder why it was that the Turkish Sephardim did not affiliate themselves with Theodore Herzl and Zionism as much as our brothers the Ashkenazim. Perhaps the following incident will shed a rather tiny light on the reasons why.

When we read the history of Jerusalem and its leaders, we find that the Kaiser Wilhelm of Germany visited the Holy City in October, 1898. At the head of the religious community of that period were the two saintly rabbis - Yaakov Shaul Elyashar for the Sephardim and Shmuel Salant for the Ashkenazim. (For more on these two rabbis, see p. 40.) Since the Holy Land was under Turkish rule, Rabbi Elyashar was the only officially recognized chief rabbi because he was a Turkish subject or citizen.

It happened that Dr. Herzl was visiting Palestine at the same time. Some accused Rabbi Elyashar of deliberately ignoring Herzl during the royal reception ceremonies, but the truth was, that just before the royal visit, the *Rishon LeZion* (title of Sephardic chief rabbi in Israel), Rabbi Elyashar, received a very confidential letter from Istanbul, from the *Haham Bashi* (title of Sephardic chief rabbi of the Ottoman Empire), Rabbi Moshe Halevi. It advised him to act discretely during the Kaiser's visit and to avoid any display of excessive cordiality to Herzl, which may suggest to the Sultan, through his spies, that the Jews are demonstrating an attachment to Herzl's ideology. The letter went on to say that the Sultan had announced his opposition to Zionism. Consequently, any such display might cause and create an anti-Jewish reaction which could reflect badly on and harm all the Jews living in the Turkish Empire.

In addition to this, another consideration forced Rabbi Elyashar to act cautiously with regard to his relationship to Dr. Herzl. It was because of the well known anti-Jewish attitude of Tevfik Pasha. This pasha was the Turkish ambassador to Berlin, so for purposes of diplomacy, he was the one who was sent to Jerusalem by the Sultan to make all preparations for the Kaiser's royal visit to Palestine.

In one of his talks, Tevfik expressed his intense opposition to Zionism by saying the following: "When we settled our account with the Armenians, it only took us three months, and with the Jews, I'm sure we can settle and finish it in just one day." It was for these reasons of trying to avoid trouble for the Jews of the Turkish Empire, that Rabbi Elyashar did not dare offer a more personal, warm welcome to Theodore Herzl.

This historian I'm quoting, the very reliable Avraham Almaleh, says also, that some newspaper accounts of the period, told of the two Sephardic rabbis, Rabbi Moshe Halevi and Rabbi Elyashar, conspiring to proclaim a *herem* (a religious ban) on Herzl. This report, Almaleh asserts, was absolutely unfounded and a malicious lie.

Now, this incident, I think, is an indication that the Jews that lived in Turkey, at least at that period, had to watch their step in regard to their affiliation to the ideology of Zionism lest their enthusiasm be misconstrued as being against the Turkish government. At a later date, when the Turkish empire started losing some of its territory, we find a different story. For example, the Sephardim of Salonika, freed from Turkish rule in 1912, started to form Zionist clubs, with hundreds becoming ardent supporters of Zionism.

December 1975   Kislev/Teveth 5736

The Chuetas of Majorca

Majorca (or, in Spanish, Mallorca) is one of the Balearic Islands in the Mediterranean Sea close to Spain. From the year 797 it had belonged to the Moors, but in the year 1229, Jaime I of Spain captured it and annexed it to his kingdom.

Jews had lived in Majorca for centuries. When first it came under Spanish rule, they were granted liberty and were treated with fairness and tolerance. This lasted only until 1391 when a fierce mob sacked the Jewish homes, killed hundreds of Jews and forced most of them to abandon Judaism and accept Catholicism under the penalty of death.

These *conversos* or *marranos*, kept their Jewish faith in their hearts, privately and in secret, meeting and observing Jewish customs.

They were harassed occasionally, but they managed to keep and transmit this type of secret Judaism to their children for more than 250 years. Of course, this double life was not easy. In 1673 a servant-girl described to a priest, in great detail, the Jewish ceremonies she had seen in the house of a Majorcan *converso*. This *marrano* was brought before the Inquisition tribunal, was judged guilty and all his property was confiscated.

As for the name given to these Majorcan *marranos*, known as "*chuetas*," historians give different meanings to the origin of the name. Some say the term "*chuetas*" means the diminutive of the word Jew with the Majorcan dialect and means simply "little Jew." Others maintain it means "pork chops," meaning that these *conversos* were forced to eat pork chops publicly, to prove that they were faithful Catholics.

Ever since the fourteenth century, untold suffering was inflicted on them. At one time or another they tried to run away from the island to some other parts of Europe where they could live without persecution, but to no avail.

For example, in 1691, one of their leaders by the name of Raphael Valls, together with a group of these *marranos*, hired an English vessel and started on a journey to another destination. Unfortunately, due to a terrible sea storm and unfavorable winds, they were forced to return to the harbor of Palma, where the government imprisoned them and all their property and possessions were confiscated.

Today, hardly any Jewish customs are practiced by the *chuetas*. They are full Catholics, practicing Christianity and yet they are distinct from the majority of the rest of the Majorcan population in that they are known and are pointed out as having Jewish ancestors. Among the things that identify them as separate from the rest, are two items proving that they're discriminated against. First, at church, they sit apart from the other congregants. Second, even in the cemetery, their bodies were buried in an entirely separate section.

The majority of these *chuetas* today refuse to speak to strangers, claiming that all this was in the past, and that at present there are no differences between them and the rest of the Catholics, most probably out of fear of being discovered and being rejected. Some prominent Jewish authorities, among them the late Professor Cecil Roth and Professor Raphael Patai, made visits to Majorca. They both met a very few of these *chuetas* who expressed the desire to move to Israel so they could practice the Jewish faith openly again.

All the silversmiths or jewelry shop owners of Majorca are descendants of or themselves *chuetas*, even today concentrated in the "*Calle de Plateria*" (Street of the Silversmith) or as it used to be called the "*Juderia*" (Jewish section). It would be very interesting to know what the Israeli rabbinate would do, when confronted with the problem of admitting these *chuetas* as Jews again.

August 1981   Av/Elul 5741

The Sephardic Prince from Atlanta

Every man, woman and baby in the Atlanta Sephardic community should rush and plant a kiss on the proud face (and lips) of Mr. Sol Beton as gratitude for his creating this fascinating book which made them all instant celebrities. I call him a prince because he was instrumental in carrying their proud banner for all Sephardic communities to emulate.

The book to which I refer is the same book given to me by my brother Rabbi Maimon who said to me, "Here, Bension, write a book review on it." The book's title is *Sephardim and a History of Congregation Or Veshalom*. It is an extraordinary book, compiled, arranged, organized, coordinated by our prince Mr. Sol Beton.

Some time ago we had the pleasure of meeting Mr. Benatar from Atlanta. He is married to Mrs. Ralph Varon's sister. We had a very enlightening conversation with him. He indicated that he would donate a few copies of this book by Mr. Beton to our synagogue library. The book consists of two distinct parts. Part one deals with the general history and origin of Sephardim in various articles written by several historians and scholars. Mr. Beton himself writes some interesting articles on a variety of subjects dealing with early Sephardic history. All this takes the first ninety-two pages of the 256. Readers will find many fascinating new facts on the early origin of our Sephardic beginnings. It all makes very worthwhile reading.

An objective comment, if we are allowed to make one, is that in compiling all these writings, Mr. Beton gets a little too sentimental and emotional in delineating life in the vivid Sephardic community on the island of Rhodes to the partial exclusion of other centers of Sephardic life.

Part Two of this impressive book recounts in minute detail how the first Sephardim settled in Atlanta. It is so similar to the early history of our Seattle Sephardic beginnings that you could substitute Atlanta for Seattle or vice versa, and you would have a general idea of the chronicles and annals of each town's founding of the community.

When, in 1907, there were enough members to form a *minyan* (a religious quorum), they held religious services on *Yom Kippur* in a large room of a hotel owned by an Ashkenazi Atlantan.

The first families hailed from Rhodes, Bodrun, Izmir, Istanbul and Melas. Later on they formed two groups. One was called Ahavath Shalom; the other group was called Or Ahayim. In 1914, after due deliberations by the leaders to the two groups, they came to a cordial and successful decision to merge and form one united organization. They came to a clever decision, by combining the two names, creating the present name Or Veshalom, using the name *Or* from Or Ahayim and *Veshalom* from Ahavath Shalom. Voila! One name, Or Veshalom. The first president was Victor Avzaradel who later came to Seattle to live with his family.

Mr. Beton, with a group of helpers whom he names in gratitude, managed to collect literally hundreds of photographs of all segments of Atlanta Sephardim, going back to the early pioneers, and showing pictures of every Atlanta Sephardic family.

At first, they obtained the services of knowledgable individuals to conduct religious services, until, in 1934, they engaged the services of Rabbi Joseph Cohen who also acted as director of the Atlanta Sephardic Talmud Torah. Rabbi Cohen, who was born in Istanbul, had emigrated to Cuba in 1920 where he served as hazan and Hebrew teacher. Then in 1934 the Atlanta Sephardic community engaged him as spritual leader and director of their religious school.

Before Rabbi Cohen arrived in Atlanta, the Sephardim there needed to organize a religious school, so they contracted the services of a certain Reverend Mordehay A. Gabay who tried his best, from 1925-1927, to make a success of that project. Unfortunately, due to some dissension, he had to resign. Reverend Gabay was a native of Istanbul, where he had taught in the Istanbul Alliance school.

After Rabbi Cohen, there came the present rabbi of the Sephardic community of Atlanta, Rabbi Robert Ichay, a native of Soussa, Tunisia. Rabbi Ichay obtained his rabbinic education under Haham Solomon Gaon in London, first serving the Sephardic community of Manchester, England for a while. He later held the post of rabbi in Salisbury, Rhodesia, from whence he came to Atlanta in 1968.

The Atlanta Sephardic community's new synagogue was dedicated in 1970. The exquisite stained glass windows were designed by our prince, Mr. Sol Beton, who employed his professional talents in creating a magnificent job.

In 1973, a group of our young men and women from Seattle visited the Atlanta Sephardic community as guests, on the occasion of the convention of the American Sephardic Youth Conference. Members of both cities still talk about the good, friendly relationship which was formed at that gathering.

There is so much more we can say about this book. My advice is if you are interested, go ahead and read the book!

September 1975   Elul/Tishri 5736

The Falashas - I

Two famous Sephardim made trips, at two different times in history, to study the origins and history of this group of Ethiopian people known as *Falashas*, who claim to be descendants of Jews who were exiled at the time of the destruction of the First Temple and the capture of Israel.

The first one was the famous Orientalist Yoseph Halevy who set out from France in the year 1877. Besides bringing back an enormous amount of information about the *Falashas* and their history, he brought with him to Paris a prayer book in *Falasha* language, which he published with a Hebrew translation.

Again, later, in 1906, the Alliance (see p. 104) had Rabbi Haim Nahoum make a trip to Abyssinia to gather further information. Rabbi Nahoum was able to befriend King Menelik who supplied him with guides to the interior, thus enabling Rabbi Nahoum to bring back and publish a lot of valuable facts about *Falashas*.

This was two years before Rabbi Nahoum was elected as *Haham Bashi* (chief rabbi) in Istanbul. The former chief rabbi, Rabbi Moshe Halevi, had to resign due to the political turmoil in 1908, which resulted from the granting of *huriyet*, the Turks' constitutional freedom.

Who are these *Falashas*?

As for their origin, very little is certain. Some authorities are of the opinion that they are descendants of the Jewish prisoners driven from Judea when Jerusalem and the Second Temple were destroyed by the Romans.

Today they study the Bible. They specially prefer the book of Psalms, and when they recite their prayers, they employ their own dialect which is called Falashin. The Hebrew language is unknown to them. They observe the *Shabbath* very strictly. It is not permitted to them to light a fire. They are also very careful to slaughter animals according to *shehita* rules.

In modern times a few of these *Falashas* emigrated to Israel. The question of whether these *Falashas* are considered as Jews, and therefore have the same rights and privileges in relation to the law of return in Israel, has been debated and discussed pro and con for many years. Israeli rabbinic authorities have not come to a definite conclusion about them as yet.

An interesting case happened about three years ago in Israel when a young *Falasha* man fell in love with an Israeli young lady and he expressed the desire to marry her. Rabbi Ovadia Yoseph, who was at that time Sephardic chief rabbi of Tel Aviv, was approached with this problem. After considerable and extensive study and examination of their history and the *halachic* sources, he came to a conclusion that this doubt that exists as to their Jewishness is because of a lack of communication for many hundreds of years. He concluded that those that came to live in Israel and wished to be converted according to *halacha* should be helped. And so Rabbi Ovadia Yoseph granted the request of that young man and offered him the right of conversion. The report that gives all this information says that forty of these Falashas have been granted conversions, and this caused quite a bit of discussion and strong opinions by other authorities.

April 1979   Nisan/Iyar 5739

The Falashas - II

A few years back we reported about the sect of Ethiopian Jews and whether they could be considered as full fledged Jews, as citizens of Israel, with all the privileges granted to all Jews who emigrate to Israel.

At that time, we mentioned how Rabbi Haim Nahoum (of blessed memory) was sent by the Alliance Israelite Universelle (see p. 104) to make a thorough study of this group and deliver his findings to a committee of the Alliance. The report contained many interesting details, noting that the leaders he met claimed to be Jewish, but nothing much was ever heard of them since the destruction of the First Temple. They are acquainted with the Bible but they are not aware of the Talmud and other rabbinic literature.

Before this report by Rabbi Nahoum, other great authorities had expressed their views. In particular we read of the opinion of the eminent Sephardic scholar and rabbi Rabbi David Ben Zimra, (see p. 88) around the year 1530. Rabbi Ben Zimra was thirteen years old during the Spanish Expulsion, and he achieved such a high position in the knowledge of Jewish law that he is still quoted by rabbinic authorities to this day. He had this to say on the question of the *Falashas*: "After an intense study, based on eyewitnesses, and other reliable evidence, I am of the opinion that these *Falashas* are indeed of the seed of Israel, and are descendants of the tribe of Dan. In the event one of these *Falashas* wished to marry a Jewish girl, he's permitted to do so as long as he accepts upon himself certain conditions and obligations to fulfill the more recent practices of rabbinic Judaism . . ."

After Rabbi Nahoum, in December 1921 the most revered Ashkenazic chief rabbi Rabbi Abraham Isaac Kook, commenting on the status of these *Falashas*, strongly urged world Jewry to "save our *Falasha* brethren from extinction and try to bring their young children to Jewish centers in Palestine and try to rescue 50,000 holy souls of the house of Israel from oblivion."

In 1973, the Sephardic chief rabbi of Israel, Rabbi Ovadia Yoseph, was faced with making a very serious decision on a specific case involving a *Falasha* young man who wished to marry an Israeli girl. He said, "I have investigated and inquired well and after profound research and study I have come to the conclusion, in my humble opinion, that these *Falashas* are indeed to be considered as Jews." Later, the Ashkenazic chief rabbi, Rabbi Shelomo Goren, joined Rabbi Ovadia Yoseph in this important decision, stressing the need to educate them and instruct them in the spirit of our holy *Torah*.

It was based on the statement by Rabbi Ovadia Yoseph that the Israeli government in 1975 decided to recognize the *Falashas* legally as Jews, entitled to automatic Israeli citizenship with full benefits as prescribed under the law of return. Both chief rabbis, however, requested that members of these *Falasha* immigrants undergo a symbolic ceremony called *hidush haberith* (reacceptance of the covenant, renewal) consisting of ritual immersion (*tevila*) and, because the males are already circumcised, they will need only a ceremonial *milah* (circumcision).

One of these recent arrivals, a "*kohen*" *Falasha* who visited the chief rabbis, is reputed to know the whole Bible by heart in their own native tongue, which they call Falashina. They do not know Hebrew. This "*kohen*" asked for the rabbis' blessing, adding, "Please, dear revered rabbis, tell us what happened to the Jewish people during these 2,000 years we were in *galuth*."

A great number of these *Falashas* were persecuted for a long period of time, and a lot of them were forced to convert to other local religions, under the threat of the sword. At present, there are still 26,000 *Falashas* living in Ethiopia. [Editor's note: Due to the Operation Moses and Operation Solomon airlifts to Israel in the early and late 1980s, there are at most a few thousand *Falashas* left in Ethiopia in 1993.]

Chapter Two

Events In Jewish History

January 1980   Teveth/Shevat 5740

Jews In Islamic Countries

Since Khomeini's seizure of hostages, an illegal act of terrorism, a question comes to mind: How did our Jewish brethren, who lived in Moslem countries, fare through the centuries past? We know they had their ups and downs. History tells us that ever since Mohammed founded their religion around the year 622, it began with torture, murders, and plundering of Jewish homes, all in the name of their Allah.

Ramban (Nachmanides), who lived in Spain during the 13th century, makes a very astounding observation in his commentary on the *Torah*, in regard to the destiny of Jewish people living under Moslem rule. He said: "Our mother Sarah sinned greatly against Hagar, her servant, by inflicting this pain (of banishment) on her ... But G-d saw her affliction and rewarded Hagar by giving her (a son), a wild man, who would inflict on the seeds of Abraham and Sarah every sort of affliction." Nachmanides, of course refers to Ishmael, the ancestor of all Arabs and most Moslems. Sad to say, it all came true, as we list below a few of the troubles the Jews suffered at the hands of Moslem rulers.

1. One of the caliphs of Babylonia decreed that every Jew must wear a small bell hanging from their neck, so that Moslems would recognize the Jews and look at them with hate and ridicule.

2. No Jew was allowed to build a home or a synagogue on a higher level than a Moslem's home, on threat of death.

3. In the year 1228, upon all Jews was imposed a severe special tax. Even after payment, the Moslem official would smack this

Jew with a horrible slap on the face, shouting: "Pay Allah his due, you infidel dog, dirty enemy of Allah."

4. If a Jew and a Moslem had a lawsuit, the Moslem judge would find the Jew guilty, despite evidence to the contrary.

5. In 1676 in Yemen, the Moslem rulers issued a proclamation to demolish all synagogues, prohibiting all Jewish prayer in public - all under threat of death.

6. When walking the city's streets or bazaars, a Jew was restricted to walk only on the side, as a thief; any Jew walking in the middle of the street was put in jail.

7. All Jewish women had to tie a small bell on their shoes when walking in town, pointing to them, in shame and humiliation.

8. Any object that was touched by a Jew was declared "defiled."

9. In Bokhara, the Moslem government issued eighteen restrictions against the Jewish community there, all intended to point them out as "degraded and disgraceful members of their country." [Editor's note: Bokhara is a city in Central Asia whose Jews had been known for the splendor of their costumes and fabrics; today it is part of Uzbekistan.]

A few years back, the famous French Jewish novelist Albert Memmi, had occasion to meet with the Libyan leader Khadaffi, at a public symposium in Paris. Khadaffi was boasting about the fact that the Moslem religion is more liberal and freedom-minded than the Jewish religion, and bragging that Jews always enjoyed great freedom in Islamic countries. Mr. Memmi, who's an expert in this phase of Jewish history, arose and successfully refuted Khadaffi's statements. Mr. Memmi began by saying that, no doubt there were some times when there were some bright spots, but Jews had mostly a rough time in Moslem countries. He said, "In the early times in Marakesh, Morocco no Jew was allowed to live in the city proper because all Jews were regarded as contaminated."

After mentioning a multitude of persecutions and massacres at different times, Mr. Memmi asked: "How can you claim about your good treatment of Jews, when as recently as 1912 all Jews in Morocco had, under threat of imprisonment, to take off their shoes on leaving their Jewish quarters (ghettos)?" Memmi continued, "The rulers in North Africa imposed an exorbitant and merciless special tax on all Jews. A large portion of these Jews, who found it impossible to raise this enormous sum, were forced to take to the hills, there to live in subhuman circumstances, even to this day."

Mr. Memmi continued, mentioning also that in 1945 a large group of Arabs in Libya began spreading a vicious and unfounded rumor, that the Jewish Zionists were killing Palestinian Arabs. This false rumor caused an unruly mob to wreck a number of synagogues, killing many saintly rabbis, and looting a large number of stores owned by Jews. Mr. Memmi went on to prove his point to those present which included many journalists, authors and other intellectuals.

There are a number of books written on this sad, but true portion of Jewish history, and the list of atrocities is practically endless, proving Ramban's prediction. This, by necessity, can only be a very small sample.

May 1974   Iyar/Sivan 5734

The Expelled Sephardim

In the last issue of *La Boz* we wrote about the *Romaniotes*, the Greek-speaking native Jews living in Turkey at the time of the Spanish Expulsion in 1492. To continue this story, we find at this time, the *Haham Bashi* (chief rabbi) was a saintly scholar named Rabbi Moshe Capsali, who was so well-liked by the Sultan Bayazid II, that he gave Rabbi Capsali the full power to help out these unfortunate refugees.

Most of these Spanish Jews had undergone quite an ordeal on their trip out of Spain, what with some unscrupulous ship captains taking advantage of their sore plight to cheat and rob them of their meager belongings. The captains often demanded ridiculously large ransoms before they would allow them to land anywhere.

As soon as Rabbi Capsali heard of this, he appealed to the Sultan, obtained money grants from the Sultan, collected contributions from wealthy members of his *kehila* (synagogue), started and founded societies that were called *Kupath Pidyon Shevuyim* (Fund to Rescue the Captives), and many times spent quite a sum of his own personal money to defray the expenses.

He worked very diligently and saw to it that families were lodged together, and formed committees to provide these new arrivals with much needed medical care, and later placed them in schools and *kehiloth* (synagogues). He appealed to some of his members that were owners of fairly large homes to take in, temporarily, a couple of these refugee families, until such time that it was possible for them to find a place of their own. One such member and owner of a large home gives us a very vivid eyewitness account of how his home was used as an initial home for refugees, saying - "this group of poor Spanish refugees were made very welcome in my home. We used to treat them with great compassion, and we were always so anxious to hear all their horrible stories about their departure from Spain, especially the troubles and hardships they endured during their long and arduous sea voyage until they reached this part of Constantinople. We would go out of our way to make their stay as comfortable as possible. They later would move out to their permanent homes, which the various communal organizations found for them, settling in the different districts of Constantinople - such as Ortakoy, Kuzgunjuk, as well as Haskoy, Balat."

After these refugees were able to settle down and install themselves, they proved very useful to their new country. Among these Sephardim were men experienced in all kinds of industry, as well as doctors and other important professions.

A very interesting development that the historians of those times like to relate is that a group of these Sephardic Jews were men who were experts in the skill of manufacturing ammunitions and gunpowder, which they were able to teach to some Turkish engineers. It thus developed that these Spanish Christian persecutors, in chasing the Jews out of Spain, literally placed military arms in the hands of the Turkish Army, which inflicted such humiliating defeats to those responsible for throwing them out of Spain.

When Sultan Bayazid II saw all these refugees that were so efficient and so knowledgeable in the ways of the world, he is quoted as making that very famous statement, "People say that Ferdinand considers himself a wise and a smart king. He is the one that impoverished his own kingdom and made ours a rich one."

Rabbi Moshe Capsali died three years after these first refugees arrived in Constantinople, and after his death, this very important work was continued by his successor as *Haham Bashi*, who was Rabbi Eliyahu Mizrahi. In 1497, when the kingdom of Portugal also expelled all of the Jews, it befell on Rabbi Mizrahi to make these converted or Portuguese refugees welcome and comfortable.

September 1978   Av/Elul 5738

The First "Keaya"

Keaya is a Turkish word meaning an administrator, or a general manager in charge or in control of the affairs of a group or people. The Levantine Sephardim incorporated this Turkish word into the Ladino idiom. One would usually hear the expression: "*Keayalik no se quiere.*" As if to say: "We don't need anyone to boss us around."

The great Sephardic historian, Solomon Rosanes (see p. 42), writes about the first *keaya* who functioned in Constantinople. When the Sephardim were expelled from Spain in 1492, thousands of the refugees began to establish new homes for themselves and their families in various cities of the Turkish Empire. We read how the first *Haham Bashi* (chief rabbi) Rabbi Moshe Capsali, and after him, Rabbi Eliyahu Mizrahi, spent precious hours to help these exiles to provide them with food, lodging and attended to their needs.

In order to lighten the burden from these overworked spiritual leaders, they appointed a man by the name of Shaltiel Hanagid to act as top administrator, a *keaya*, so he could supervise the affairs of the newcomers. Shaltiel was chosen for three reasons. First, he was a highly capable administrator acting as a representative or liaison between the office of the *Haham Bashi* and the Turkish government. Secondly, he spoke the Turkish language fluently and thirdly, he was personally acquainted with a great number of Turkish government officials with whom he would have to deal to achieve his various missions.

For quite a long time, this *keaya* Shaltiel was extremely helpful. Due to his expertise in getting things done, he was able to assist these newcomers in opening different businesses and shops, buying and renting houses for them, and finding suitable employment for them. He even kept some out of prison. However, in the course of managing all these affairs, it was of course inevitable that he should disappoint or displease some individuals. As a consequence, some of these malcontents started vicious rumors against Shaltiel accusing him of improprieties. They charged him with being an arrogant dictator, too proud and too "bossy." Some of these dissidents developed such an intense hatred for him, that they called, on their own, a general meeting in one of the large synagogues in Istanbul, in which they succeeded to invoke the terrible and dreadful *herem* (a community ban) against him. This *herem* is an appalling weapon. It stopped the *keaya* from functioning at his job. A great number of the community members avoided him and wouldn't even communicate with him.

Not very long after this, a group of respectable members of the Constantinople community came to realize how much Shaltiel's services were missed, and how much the small merchants began to suffer for lack of adequate representation with the Turkish government. A panel of these civic leaders approached the *Haham Bashi*, Rabbi Eliyahu Mizrahi and respectfully requested that he do something to void the *herem* so Shaltiel could function again.

And so, Rabbi Mizrahi called Shaltiel and the dissidents to a general meeting, and read out loud a long *responsa* (rabbinic ruling). He explained in great detail that the *herem* was not binding because the original charges were proven to be without any basis, and therefore ridiculous. Rabbi Mizrahi also stressed the point that Shaltiel's services were very essential to the community at large in that the entire Jewish population benefited enormously from this *keaya* Shaltiel's expertise. All this happened in the year 1517.

October 1978   Elul 5738/Tishri 5739

The Semiha Controversy - I

Semiha is a Hebrew word meaning rabbinic ordination. This is equivalent to a college degree or a diploma which is presented to a candidate at the conclusion of his studies in a rabbinical academy. It authorizes him to assume the office of spiritual leader of a given congregation or community.

However, when we speak of *semiha* in this article, we refer specifically to that traditional authority that was awarded to a group of scholars and judges called "the *Sanhedrin*," which had jurisdiction over the entire Jewish nation, including the power to judge capital punishment cases and such. Moses was the first one that ever gave this *semiha* when he ordained Joshua to become his successor. Joshua in turn, ordained others in *Eretz Yisrael* (Israel), who in turn ordained others throughout the generations, comprising an unbroken series or chain, which was abolished when the *yeshivoth* in *Eretz Yisrael* were destroyed (5th century of the common era).

An attempt was made to re-introduce this original *semiha* principle, by a great Sephardi in 1538. This was done by Rabbi Yaakov Berab who was born and educated in Spain before the expulsion. After leaving Spain, he emigrated to North Africa, Salonika, and other places in Turkey, and finally settled in Safed, in 1524, where he became the dean of one of the rabbinical academies there. A large number of students came to Safed from all over Turkey.

Rabbi Yaakov states that he, along with many prominent scholars, undertook this gigantic *semiha* enterprise for three reasons:

First, renewal of the *semiha* would be a step towards the spiritual unification of all Jewry, having *Eretz Yisrael* as the central focal point of authority, to which all Jews would direct their questions they wished to resolve.

Second, Rabbi Yaakov quotes the Rambam who said that before we can expect the *Mashiach* (Messiah) who is to redeem our people, it's necessary for our Jewish leaders to re-establish the *Sanhedrin* in *Eretz Yisrael*. This can only come about by assembling all Jewish scholars in *Eretz Yisrael* to agree on the renewal of the institution of *semiha*, which is a prerequisite for the establishment of the *Sanhedrin*.

Third, Rabbi Yaakov felt that, at that particular time in history, thousands of *marranos* continued to emigrate to Turkey from Spain and Portugal to re-embrace the Jewish faith. It was pointed out to these *marranos*, that the only way they could ever obtain full atonement from their former status as Catholics, was through the official authority of rabbis who had the authentic original *semiha* giving them full power to cleanse *marranos* from their sins.

And so, Rabbi Yaakov set out to accomplish this gigantic and difficult task. After two years of planning, consulting and having serious discussions with other scholars, he was able to assemble twenty-five prominent rabbis who agreed with him that the time was ripe to vote for this extremely important project. These scholars selected Rabbi Yaakov as the one to be endowed with the title of the bearer of *semiha*, granting him the power to ordain others whom he deemed competent for this high office. Rabbi Yaakov granted *semiha* to four qualified rabbis. These were: Rabbi Yoseph Caro, the famous author of the *Shulhan Aruch* and other important works; Rabbi Moshe Mitrani; Rabbi Yoseph Sagues; and, Rabbi Moshe Cordovero.

All this was very well, but this project met with some formidable opposition from some *yeshivoth* in Jerusalem, causing a real obstacle in the path of this ambitious project.

November 1978   Heshvan 5739

The Semiha Controversy - II

In last month's *La Boz* we saw how Rabbi Yaakov Berab, the
recognized head of the Safed Jewish community, tried to re-introduce
semiha in *Eretz Yisrael.* This unfortunately, did not last too long. He,
in fact, did consult a large number of Safed's prominent scholars, but
he neglected to take in the *hahamim* of the holy city of Jerusalem.
These *hahamim* maintained that because of the dignity and the sanctity
of their city, they should have been called in from the very start.

During this period, (1538) the leader of the Jerusalem rabbis, was
an eminent scholar by the name of Rabbi Levi Ben Habib. Born in
Spain, he settled in Jerusalem after living in Safed and in Salonika for
a time. He was the son of Rabbi Yaakov Ben Habib who was the
author of the famous book called *Ein Yaakov.*

Rabbi Yaakov Berab quickly realized that he had overlooked
including the Jerusalem rabbis in his project, so he immediately
composed a letter of apology. Together with a *semiha* especially
bearing the name of Rabbi Levi Ben Habib, he sent both by a special
messenger, the *haham* Shelomo Hazan, to Jerusalem, thus granting
Rabbi Levi that distinguished honor of being a rabbi with an authentic
semiha. In the letter, Rabbi Yaakov Berab explained that the reason
he chose the city of Safed to launch this project was that Safed
contained a large number of prominent Jews involved in wool
manufacturing and other industries, while   Jerusalem was an
impoverished city. Because of Safed's prosperity, there were many
more *yeshivoth* with prominent scholars attracting hundreds of
students from many Jewish communities.

Many letters were exchanged between the Safed and the Jerusalem
rabbis, who still maintained that they should have been consulted
about the *semiha* project, or at least an attempt should have been made
to obtain their consent before the finalization of the project. The Safed
rabbis argued back saying that what was done was done, and the
superior number of scholars in Safed was enough to counteract and
overcome any opposition to this undertaking.

In one of the letters Rabbi Levi Ben Habib pointed out in no
uncertain terms, that the holy city of Jerusalem, with its historic
prominence in all matters of momentous *halachic* (Jewish legal)
decisions, could not accept a secondary position in such a solemn

enterprise. However, he continued, because the issue was so vital to the very unity of the entire Jewish people, he would agree to arrange an assemblage of rabbis representing both cities, to discuss the question thoroughly. In the event the Jerusalem rabbis were convinced beyond any doubt as to the legality and viability of the project, then they would vote to offer their full consent to have the *semiha* institution re-introduced in *Eretz Yisrael*.

Unfortunately, other obstacles arose in the path of this *semiha* project, when Rabbi Yaakov's son Moshe, got involved in a disastrous lawsuit regarding a parcel of real estate which was in litigation. Rabbi Yaakov Berab was forced to run away from Safed secretly at night, when his son's opponents succeeded in convincing the *pasha* (governor) of Safed, charging Rabbi Berab with an absurd and false accusation. Thus an interesting chapter in our history came to a close forever.

Of course, there are intricate points of law and *halacha* relating to this *semiha* enterprise. I do not pretend to understand their full meaning. The reader should understand that this is just a superficial look at the historical aspect of this fascinating episode.

January 1979   Tevet/Shevat 5739

Sultan Murad's Revoked Edict

The first hundred years after the 1492 Spanish Expulsion, the Sephardim who settled in the Turkish Empire were fortunate to build new homes for themselves and their families. This was especially true during the life of Don Yoseph Nassi, whose close friendship to Sultan Selim helped these exiles to establish several industries. They enjoyed complete religious freedom, resulting in a definite cultural advancement.

However, when Sultan Selim died and his son, Murad III (1574-1595) came to the throne the picture changed drastically. Eyewitnesses report, that on the day of Murad's coronation, the first words he uttered were "I'm hungry, give me something to eat." Intelligent onlookers took this as a symbolic forecast of Murad's rule. The Jews of Turkey came very close to a disastrous catastrophe during Murad's rule. Specifically, the historian Solomon Rosanes (see p.

42) refers to the following episode that took place around the year 1590.

The second and third generation of Sephardim became very prosperous. The wives and daughters of these wealthy Sephardim began to wear expensive clothes and fancy jewelry. This was very unfortunate, because it tended to arouse the envy of the Turkish people. Some of these Sephardic women ignored this threat, and started to overdo this over-display of affluence. They began parading around in the streets of Istanbul in dresses made from *seda, atlas y katife*(silk, satin and velvet), and wearing very expensive jewelry.

As if this was not stupid enough, Mr. Rosanes tells of one of these matrons in particular wearing an extra fancy dress embroidered with gold *bin dali* (multi-colored gold leaves). She was also bedecked in an enormous gold chain set with the most exquisite precious stones estimated to cost 40,000 Turkish gold liras, a sum considered a large fortune in those days. Murad's attendants would, from time to time, report to him of these unwise displays of luxuries by these insensitive Jewish ladies. One time, in demonstrating his displeasure and his disapproval of these displays, he went into a hostile rage. Happily, people around him were able to contain his anger. But when they reported to him about this particular Jewish lady parading around Istanbul wearing that chain worth 40,000 liras, he couldn't hold back his fury. In a moment of violent rage he came out with a royal decree to the effect that all his Jewish subjects living in the vast Turkish Empire were to be put to death on a given future date.

One can understand the feelings of sadness, grief and confusion that befell all the Jews of Turkey. At first, they tried to dismiss it, saying it could be a momentary decision, but to their great consternation, they discovered that Sultan Murad was quite serious about carrying out his proclamation. Unfortunately, the man that possessed the capability to defend the Jewish people and help them avert this dreadful calamity, Don Yoseph Nassi, had just died. There was another influential Jew, a physician by the name of Dr. Shelomo Ben Nathan Eskenazi, who, although very close to the Sultan, did not have the same clout on behalf of his coreligionists. He did try to convince Murad to change this evil decree, but he couldn't make him change his stubborn mind.

Dr. Eskenazi didn't get discouraged. He, together with several other Jewish communal leaders, approached Murad's mother, the *valide hanum* (sultan's mother) who was known to be friendly towards the Jewish people, to beg her to intervene with her son on behalf of the Turkish Jews. Dr. Eskenazi had, years before, saved the Sultana from a very serious illness. Dr. Eskenazi, through a large and generous bribe, also obtained the services of the chief of the *yenicheris* (Janisarries). These two, the *valide hanum* and chief Janissarry, were successful in changing the decree. The new decree stated that no Jewish woman was allowed to wear gaudy clothes or jewelry. It also stated that from now on all Jewish males shall wear a different type of headdress, the *kaook* (it looked like a dunce cap), but later, this was changed into a fez. Mr. Rosanes quotes an *haskama* (communal decision) from a book written by the eminent Rabbi Yoseph Mitrani, the chief rabbi of that period, to the effect that *b'not Yisrael* (the daughters of Israel) shall wear very modest and conservative clothes and issued a stern warning against wearing expensive jewelry on the streets. The *haskama* contains all the details of this near-tragic episode, thanking the Almighty for saving the Turkish Jews from that disastrous calamity. May He always preserve us from all our troubles. Amen.

June 1973   Sivan 5733

The Donmehs

We'll take it for granted that the majority of our readers are acquainted with the part of Sephardic history which deals with the false Messiah, Sabetai Zvi. Born in Izmir in the year 1626 on *Tisha B'Av*, and educated in the famous *yeshivoth* in that city, after a stormy and controversial journey to Jerusalem and Egypt, he returned to his native city and was declared Messiah by his many followers.

Our story of the *Donmehs* begins in 1666 when he was forced by the Sultan in Istanbul to either prove his title to Messiah, or be put to death. Not being able to do that, Sabetai Zvi changed his religion and converted to Islam, explaining to the Turkish monarch that he would have all his followers convert to the Turkish religion.

With the help of his brother-in-law, Jacob Querido, thousands of Sephardim became converts. These people were known as *Donmehs*, Turkish for apostates or converts.

At the beginning, these "believers" were only outwardly Turks, secretly observing quite a few of the Jewish laws and holy days such as *Yom Kippur*, etc. They were scattered in a number of towns in Turkey, like Istanbul, Izmir and other cities. But the biggest concentration of

Donmehs was in Salonika. For over two hundred years they lived there, not quite like Turks and not like Jews; they had their own peculiar customs. At the beginning they used to circumcise their sons on the eighth day of their birth, like all other Jews, but later they changed and they circumcised them on the child's third year.

They used to read Hebrew and Ladino and some of their scholars were even known to study the *Zohar* (book of Jewish mysticism). One peculiar custom they used to have was that they would gather at the seashore, all of them praying to Sabetai with the words: *Esperamos a ti.* (We are waiting for you.)

In the year 1912, when Turkey lost Salonika, and it was occupied by Greece, it was estimated the *Donmeh* population in the city to be approximately 15,000. After that date some of them left the city. It was in the year 1923 that the great exchange took place. As a result of the Lausanne Treaty, Greece and Turkey agreed to exchange populations. This meant that all Turks in Greece were compelled to leave and move on to some part of Turkey. This, of course, made it necessary for all those *Donmehs* in Salonika to migrate to various towns in Turkey. This migration obviously caused the weakening of their customs, and losing their identity.

Solomon Rosanes (see p. 42), who wrote the most complete history of the Sephardim, made a trip to Salonika in 1915. A certain Ahmed Efendi, a good friend of Mr. Rosanes, took him to the *Donmeh's* archives, where he saw a lot of their religious books that they had accumulated for about 250 years.

Among these books, Mr. Rosanes saw a book of *Zohar* translated into Ladino and another book called *Sefer Dinim*, which Rosanes says, is nothing but a condensed *Shulchan Aruch* on the laws of Jewish holidays, like *Rosh Hashanah* and *Yom Kippur*, and many books of *derushim* (sermons) that their *hodjas* (religious leaders) composed.

Abraham Galante, the modern Sephardic historian, in writing about *Donmehs* of Salonika reports that some attempts were made by some *Donmehs* to return to traditional Judaism. The Salonika rabbinate refused to admit them, citing some very valid reasons.

These *Donmehs* were called many other names; one funny one that comes to mind is *Sazanicos. Sazan* is a Turkish word meaning a certain type of fish we used to eat in Turkey. They say about this fish that it changes colors while still in the water, making allusion to the fact that these Donmehs changed their religion at random - or whenever convenient.

October 1981   Tishri/Heshvan 5742

The Telegram

This is a true story that happened during the time that Rabbi Yaakov Shaul Elyashar was Sephardic chief rabbi of *Eretz Yisrael*. This important position is more popularly known as *Rishon LeZion*.

Rabbi Elyashar was elected in 1893. He served until his death in 1906 at the age of ninety. Three days before his death, Rabbi Elyashar received a telegram which read as follows:

I, being *rav* (rabbi) in the city of Novominsk, respectfully appeal to your eminence, in the name of the entire congregation, that we are in terrible danger, because a prominent member of our Warsaw government, by the name of Nazalink was murdered here a few months ago.

The police arrested five non-Jews who were brought to trial and judged guilty of this murder, solely on the testimony of three Jewish people, two brothers, Eliezer and Noah Horwitz, plus a woman by the name of Mottel. These three Jews have since moved from here and are living at present in Jerusalem. Some people here in Novominsk believe that these three Jews testified against these five out of an intense hate for the accused.

And now, we plead with your eminence to summon these three, Eliezer and Noah Horwitz and the woman Mottel, to appear before you, so that you will extract an admission from them, and retract their testimony. This will help the Jewish community of Novominsk tremendously, in that it will spare us the agony and tortures of possible pogroms.

We beg you to convey these facts and the retraction, to the Russian consul in Jerusalem. The consul, in turn, will send an official wire to the Warsaw authorities.

Signed:
Rabbi Rabinowitz
of Novominsk in the
Province of Warsaw

The moment Rabbi Elyashar was notified of this telegram, he was very puzzled at the contents. He immediately summoned the three named people to appear at the *beth din* (tribunal), and after due inquiries, discovered they were telling the truth. Rabbi Elyashar was convinced that those five non-Jews that were accused were indeed guilty.

Rabbi Elyashar then called a meeting of the twenty communal and religious leaders to decide on a plan of action which would not tend to compromise the office of the *haham's* views. After due deliberation this body of prominent leaders concluded to dispatch a wire in answer to the telegram.

All through the deliberations, Rabbi Elyashar did not utter a word, but just as the decision was to be announced by the secretary, he stood up and said, "My dear brethren, it's my solemn duty to advise you of my own personal opinion. It's my belief that this telegram we received from Rabbi Rabinowitz is an absolute forgery. It's very possible that this telegram was a plot by the friends and family of the five non-Jewish accused criminals, in order to impress the trial judge to extend mercy to these five murderers. And, if we dispatch this telegram you gentlemen decided on, it might incriminate us in this whole scheme. And, who knows, this might result in terrible consequences against our fellow Jews living in that region."

The leaders present in the assembly then asked Rabbi Elyashar, "What do we do now?" To which he replied, "There are two options. One is to ignore this telegram completely and the other alternative we have is we dispatch a wire to Warsaw telling them as follows: As the *Haham Bashi* of *Yerushalayim*, I'm bound by Turkish government regulations which forbid me, categorically, to intervene in the affairs of a foreign state." Rabbi Elyashar added, "This reply will neither support nor deter the effect of the issue at hand."

Not everyone in this special assembly was in accord with this curious opinion of Rabbi Elyashar. Right then, Rabbi Elyashar determined to consult his colleague, the Ashkenazic chief rabbi, Rabbi Shemuel Salant, without disclosing Rabbi Elyashar's suspicion as to the authenticity of the telegram, nor his decision as to the type of reply to send the Warsaw authorities. It was already very late at night and they awakened Rabbi Salant to advise him of the contents of the Warsaw telegram.

After Rabbi Salant studied the issue, he addressed the notables present, saying, "My dear friends, in my humble opinion, this Warsaw telegram is definitely a forgery, composed and dispatched at the behest of those five non-Jews who are the real criminals. It could be that the signature of Rabbi Rabinowitz was invented and those friends of the accused are playing a trick on us." Rabbi Salant was then asked,

"What do we do?" To which he replied, "The best thing to do in this case is to dispatch a telegram to Warsaw saying that the *Haham Bashi* is not authorized to interfere in the internal affairs of another country."

All those present were amazed at the similar opinions offered by the two chief rabbis without the one seeing the other. As events proved, indeed the rabbis were right in their wise decisions.

Some time later, the Hebrew newspaper *Hatzefira* reported the whole plot in full detail. The editor wrote the following, "Thanks to the wisdom and the shrewd detection of our two rabbis in *Yerushalayim*, we here in Russia were saved from what could have proven a terrible catastrophe perpetrated by our enemies against all the Jewish people here."

January 1975   Teveth/Shevat 5735

A Quest For Sephardic History

A young Sephardic student from the University of Washington, met me not long ago and said, "I want to write a term paper on Sephardic history. Where can I obtain the necessary material to do this?" I had to answer him that there is an abundance of books, pamphlets, and articles around, but most of these writings are in either Hebrew or French, and these are not so readily available around here in Seattle.

It's our fervent hope that some day a capable and energetic person will gather all these writings, and write a comprehensive history of the Sephardim in the English language. For example in French there's Moise Franco's *Histoire des Israelites de L'Empire Ottoman*. Also in French, Abraham Galante's *Documents*, and many others, scattered through various publications.

However, the most important work written specifically as a Sephardic history is the six-volume *Koroth HaYehudim BeTurkia* by Solomon A. Rosanes. This superior and valuable work is very difficult to obtain, because it is out of print. The set I use belongs to my brother, Rabbi Maimon, who had to pull some influential strings on some VIP in Israel to obtain it.

At any rate, I mention the historian Rosanes so many times, that I decided to write a few biographical notes on him. Mr. Solomon A. Rosanes was a Sephardic Jew born in Roustchuk, Bulgaria in the year

1862. His father, a very learned scholar, sent young Solomon to school in Constantinople, where he attended the newly organized Alliance school. He tells us that his teacher in his secular studies was the renowned Nissim Behar, who instilled in Rosanes a special love for knowledge and literature. (See p. 104.)

His teacher in religion and Hebrew was Rabbi Haim Babani who instructed him in the language of our great biblical prophets, thus acquiring a skillful mastery of our holy tongue. After he finished his schooling, he returned to his native Roustchuk, where he became a businessman, namely a *saraf* (a dealer in silver and gold coins) and a jeweler.

In one of his poems that he wrote in Hebrew, he takes us into his confidence and tells us what exactly prompted him to write his history. He says, "One day, while in [my] jewelry shop, some robbers came in to hold [me] up, threatening [my] life with a large and ominous knife. In fighting off [my] assailants, [I] got hold of the knife and in the commotion, [I] lost some of [my] fingers. Somehow, miraculously, [I] regained the use of [my] hands. [I] was so grateful to *Hashem* for saving [my] life, that [I] took a solemn oath that from that moment on, [I would] consecrate [my] time to writing the history of [my] people, the Sephardim."

He devoted all of his leisure time in gathering precious material from numerous sources for this gigantic work, so much so that experts agree, had it not been for Rosanes, all this information would have been definitely lost to us, because most of the books he had access to, are either forgotten, too rare to find, or out of print.

In addition to extracting material from these reliable sources, he started a campaign to visit a great many archives, libraries, and museums in Europe, such as Paris, St. Petersburg, etc. Whenever he found related information, he would sit and copy it, day after day. Also, he obtained much valuable information from sages, professors, and many knowledgeable elders of different communities, that had something to contribute to his vast collection of historical facts.

Mr. Rosanes died in 1938 at the age of seventy-six.

Yehi zihro baruh. (May his memory be blessed.)

Chapter Three

Sephardic Life In the "Old Country"

September 1974   Elul 5734/Tishri 5735

Fifty Years

Our family recently celebrated the fiftieth anniversary of our arrival in Seattle from Tekirdag, Turkey. (See p. 11.) As is normal in such get togethers, all of us remembered a lot of stopovers in Marseilles, Le Havre and Ellis Island, New York.

Our family was originally from Brusa, in Asiatic Turkey. How did my father become the *haham* in Tekirdag? In the year 1912, the *haham* of Tekirdag (previously called Rodosto), the very respected Rabbi Yom Tov Cordova had taken ill. Mr. Shelomo Altaras the *gabay* of Rodosto came to Istanbul to search for a man to replace Rabbi Yom Tov, whose family still lives in Seattle. The family consists of three grandsons, Tom, Alfred and Albert Cordova; a daughter, Mrs. Rebecca Halfon, and her three children, Sol N., Tom and Esther Halfon. After an interview with my father, Mr. Altaras liked what he saw and heard, and engaged Rabbi Abraham Maimon to fill the position of *haham* of Rodosto. He moved his family to Tekirdag where subsequently three more members of our family were born, namely my sister Rachel Benoliel, and brothers Morris and Rabbi Solomon Maimon, who was five years old when we arrived in Seattle.

In 1924, the committee of the Sephardic Bikur Holim Congregation in Seattle entered into negotiations with my father (sometimes known as Haribi Avraham), and as a result my father was brought over to Seattle, with his family to be the *haham* of our synagogue. At that time the synagogue was situated at 13th and Washington Street, but it later moved to 20th and Spruce Street. A great number of Seattle *Tekirdaglis* (people from Tekirdag) knew my Dad personally and remembered him both for his *hazanuth* and his ingenuous and charming personality.

I remember on the train coming over from New York to Seattle, I repeatedly asked my father, "How will we do in Seattle, we don't know the language?" and such questions. His answer was "*Yerahem Ashem, ijo,*" which became his trademark in later years in Seattle. Loosely translated it means "G-d will be very kind to us, son." As it happened, the night we arrived in Seattle it seemed like the whole membership was there at King Street railroad station to greet us, and we all had a treat to ride in long fancy limousines, at that time driven by Mr. Benny Cohen and his chauffeurs.

The committee had prepared and furnished for us our first home, which was at 15th and Yesler Way, but they did not take us home right away. As many of the group that could fit, assembled at Mr. Joseph Caston's house where my father was bombarded by questions from the audience till the wee hours of the morning, quite a few of them wanting to know about their relatives back home in Tekirdag. Some of those relatives had given my father a gift to hand over to their sons, daughters etc., that they had in Seattle. Some gave a *kolana* (necklace), an *aniyo* (a ring) or a pair of *eskularichas* (earrings). All these gifts were called *amanet*. My Dad made all these gift senders write down a few words on a little notebook he had purchased for this purpose.

We arrived in Seattle the night before *Erev Kippur* (day before *Yom Kippur*, the Day of Atonement). As was the custom in those days, on *Rosh Hashanah* and *Kippur* they used to call to *sefer* from thirty to forty people, and each one of these members that first *Kippur* donated generously to the new *haham*. I remember, Albert Moshcatel donated *dos cashas de mansanas* (two cases of apples). Mr. Caston donated *una casha de melones, y patatas, y sevoyas* (a case of melons, potatoes and onions) and many more too numerous to mention. The most unusual gift was by the late Mr. Yuda Benezra. Being a barber, he donated *arapar los kaveyos para la famiya entera por un anyo entero* (haircuts for the entire family for a year). His usual "thank you" was *gustozos, y dovletlis* (greetings of happiness and prosperity).

Later, in some gatherings like *meldados* (memorial services, see p. 178) and others, people used to ask my father a lot of questions, because they knew, that besides the regular logical answers, he had an arsenal of clever ones. Like the time someone asked him "How come they serve raisins (*passas* in Ladino) after a *meldado*?" He said in

Spanish, "*Y esto va a pasar*," loosely translated as, "Raisins will help us forget all sad incidents."

I could go on and on, but this is enough for now.

January 1978   Teveth/Shevat 5738

Brusa

Brusa (now called Bursa) is a city of real natural beauty, at the foot of Mt. Olympus of Mysia, about fifty-four miles from Istanbul across the sea of Marmara in Asiatic Turkey. It is the city where I was born and the city in which my family had lived for generations. Jews have lived in Brusa many centuries as confirmed by the Epistle of St. Peter who recorded finding there an old tombstone with Jewish symbols. The late Sephardic historian Professor Abraham Galante tells us of a trip he made to Brusa in 1938 when he visited some ancient ruins called Zindan Capusu. There was a large ancient monument with seven huge rocks on which were some Hebrew inscriptions, and a Jewish date corresponding to the year 820. He saw also some other ruins left over from Byzantine times.

Solomon Rosanes (see p. 42) tells us that an Ottoman sultan in the seventeenth century had a number of Jewish families brought over to Brusa from Egypt and Damascus. These Jews brought with them their expertise in various trades, among which was the silk manufacturing industry. They imported a large number of mulberry trees to feed the silk cocoons.

I have no documentary proof for this but it wouldn't surprise me a bit if our family immigrated to Brusa during this transfer of population to Brusa, as my family was engaged in silk mills in Brusa. Perhaps they came to Brusa from Egypt where the Rambam's descendants lived.

Professor Galante says that the yeshiva of Brusa had some very eminent rabbis, some of whom authored some important Hebrew books. He mentions the famous Rabbi Avraham Ben Yaesh, a descendant of Don Yahya Ben Yaesh, treasurer to the first king of Portugal.

Mr. Meir Benayahu, formerly the director of *Mahon Ben Zvi* (the Sephardic Institute located at Hebrew University of Jerusalem -- see p. 210) showed me a large number of rare books and manuscripts from the Brusa yeshiva. Some of these books had the seal of the *Hida*, the acronym for the famous Sephardic rabbi-author Haim Yoseph David Azulay. When I asked the reason for this seal on those books he told me that a great grandson of the *Hida*, was a *haham* in Brusa, and these books were part of this *haham's* library in Brusa. Rabbi Moshe Halevy and Rabbi Rephael Saban, both *Haham Bashis* (chief rabbis of the Jews of Turkey, see p. 191) were born in Brusa and educated in the *yeshiva* of Brusa.

Because Brusa had natural sulphur baths and hot springs a great number of Sephardim from Turkey and other parts used to go to Brusa to cure their rheumatism, and other ills. They used to call them *los banyos de Brusa* (the baths of Brusa).

From a substantial community of over 3,000 Jews that lived in Brusa before the First World War, now there are only sixty to seventy Jews left. There are a number of explanations but the principal one is the same reason that the rest of the Sephardim left Turkey. This is the horrible *varlik verguisi* (a tax on wealth) which was put into effect in November of 1942. This very unfair and exorbitant tax (example: an increase in taxes from 700 to 7,000 liras) was placed on property owners, on business people, merchants or any who, since 1939, had any business at all. Farmers were exempt from this *varlik* tax and eighty-five percent of the Turkish population were farmers. Those really affected by this atrociously high tax were the Jews and a few others from the minorities. If a person was unable to pay his assessment, his furnishings were removed from his home and sold at public auction. One man in Brusa was sent to the forced labor camp in Anatolia (Asiatic Turkey) for nine months because he couldn't pay his tax. This law was fortunately abrogated in 1944, when the Turks realized that Germany was losing the war.

Of course there were many other reasons for the Jewish people's exodus from Turkey. Among these was the fact that a wave of anti-Jewish propaganda caused very severe hardship on the Jews. Some say these waves were caused by the natural tendency in most Turks of being terribly fearful of foreigners. They have a morbid fear of control by foreigners. Some say this fear goes back to the fierce nationalism that led to the founding of the modern Turkish state in 1923. Even today, in the 1970s, when Turkish Jews talk to us in public, they are constantly looking over their shoulders as if they are afraid of being overheard. What a change from the situation of years gone by.

May 1980   Iyar/Sivan 5740

Childhood Memories

When Turkey was dragged into World War I, in 1914, the mighty
Ottoman Empire had already dwindled down to nearly half of its
former magnitude. The incompetent government officials looked after
their own personal gains, thus endangering the soundness and security
of the whole nation.

The Turkish army was one of the worst in the world. I had an
uncle (my father's younger brother) who served four years in the
Turkish army, and the horrible tales he told us about the shabby army
conditions made us shiver (how the soldiers existed in filth and disease
for most of the time). It was a real miracle how he survived.

The first terrifying experience I recall of World War I, is when,
one night, a British airplane bombarded the Post (Tekirdag's post
office building), which was situated right in the center of our *Mahle
Judiya* (Jewish District).   The objective was to knock out all the
telephone and wireless communication lines. The British bomb not
only accomplished its mission, but also shattered all windows in the
neighborhood. The ensuing days and nights we were scared out of our
wits because of a possible repeat of the bombing. Thank heaven, it
didn't happen again.

Our town of Tekirdag, because it was a seaport (on the sea of
Marmara) and was situated in the center of European Turkey, was
used as the Army dispatch point. We were told at one point in time
that Tekirdag and the surrounding area accomodated nearly 200,000
troops. Of course, all these soldiers had to be fed and provided with
lodging. In order to accomplish this, the Turkish military officials
confiscated almost all wheat, barley and other food commodities that
were available in our region, leaving the civilian population to fend for
themselves.

Somehow, we survived for a couple of years, availing ourselves of
any type of grain with which we could bake any bread. As time
passed, our hopes of getting any help in the wheat situation was
getting dimmer every day, simply because there wasn't any available in
the whole of Turkey.

At one point, in the later years of the war, conditions got so bad,
that the city government instituted a sort of rationing to distribute
whatever the government could obtain. At one period when things

went from bad to worse, someone found a warehouse full of *kush uto* (birdseed). But this birdseed was still uncleaned; that is, it was still full of dirt and rocks. We took this uncleaned birdseed to the flour mill, had it ground and we baked bread. I can still feel the rocks and dirt scratching in my teeth.

The military officials appropriated for the army all school houses in town, including our beautiful Alliance school, and converted them into hospitals for the wounded soldiers.

All school children were moved to a dilapidated *meldar*, and some students were transferred to the top floor of the town's synagogue, which was situated on the seashore, with a full view of the harbor.

One day, someone found out that a boatload of sacks of wheat was expected to arrive in town. You can imagine the joy of the townspeople. I remember this ship was approaching the *escala* (pier), when one of the students sighted a pole-like object in the far side of the harbor, and he screamed: *Mira, el palico de la sumarin!* (See the pole of the submarine!) All of the students went to the windows to see. It was the periscope of a British submarine. Just a few moments later, we sighted a torpedo projecting from this spot where the submarine was, and traveling swiftly towards our "savior" ship. This torpedo blasted a direct hit on our ship, sinking it and our hope for ever expecting any help, because our town was constantly blockaded and surrounded by land and sea. *En bueno contarlo.* (We should tell this story on good occasions.)

June 1980   Sivan/Tamuz 5740

More Childhood Memories

Oy vamos a Panados. (Let's go to Panados today.) A little distance from our town Tekirdag there were some small villages populated entirely by Greeks. On a nice day we would go walking on a one-day excursion. Beyond Panados there were also Koonbaos, Ganos, Hora and Miryofto, also populated by Greeks mostly.

These Greeks were almost self-sufficient, a very sturdy stock. They grew their own food and, living close to the beautiful seashore, they all had *sandalicos para peshcar* (fishing boats), catching a variety of delicious types of fish, including the tasty *barbunyas* (a type of fish).

These Greeks, who had lived in our region of *la Trakia* (Thrace) for hundreds of years, were later the victims of the "population exchange" when Greece and Turkey made a deal in 1922 or 1923 to have Turks who lived in Greece exchanged for these Greeks who lived in Turkey.

We also had another minority. These were the Armenians or the *Erminis*, as we used to call them. Most of these *Erminis* were decent and very industrious. Quite a few of us remember Kirkor who was an *Ermini* born and raised in Tekirdag. He emigrated to Seattle along with some of our early pioneers. Later on he ran a grocery store on 17th and Yesler Way. He spoke in Ladino with us.

However, there were some *Erminis* that turned out rotten. Because of their lack of scruples and their greed, they caused a lot of grief and aggravation to our Sephardic businessmen.

As I mentioned in last month's *La Boz*, the British submarines plying the sea of Marmara caused a lot of damage to our towns. The Turkish government realized that somehow these submarines were receiving supplies from within our shore, because the straits of the Dardanelles were all mined.

After many months it was discovered that a few of these *Erminis* had turned out to be traitors. They would sail a *kayik* (sailboat) in the dark of the night, not far from Tekirdag, load them with benzene in five-gallon cans, and furnish the enemy, the British submarines, with all types of supplies, including food, tobacco and other commodities.

The Turkish secret agents finally had these bad *Erminis* apprehended, tried and sentenced to be hanged. I actually remember witnessing the hanging of two of these traitor *Erminis* in our *meydan* (town square). It was quite a gruesome experience, a very unpleasant childhood memory.

In referring to these *Erminis*, we used to call them by the name of *Aymem*. The explanation is that these Armenians were reported to be direct descendants of Amalek, the biblical archenemy of the Jews. In fact, any Jew haters, like Haman or Hitler were labeled as Amalek or from the stock of Amalek. The first two Hebrew letters of Amalek are *ayin mem* or, for short, *Aymem*. Some of our old ladies would also call these bad Armenians as *Ermini gursuz* (damned or cursed Armenian).

Not far from our *Mahle Judiya* (Jewish Quarter) in Tekirdag, they used to point out to us an Armenian church in which was displayed a very large nail. To the Armenians, this nail was a very precious and sacred relic because they claimed that this particular nail was salvaged from the boards of the crucifixion. That's the reason some people called Tekirdag *la sivdad del clavo* (the city of the nail). Who knows?

Believe it or not. I wonder whatever happened to this "sacred" church and this celebrated *clavo*? It would be very interesting to find out.

July 1980   Tamuz/Av 5740

A Reply -- Tekirdag Under Turkish/Greek Control

From time to time some of our readers tell me how much they enjoy an article of mine in *La Boz*. This is all very gratifying. Who knows? Some day we'll gather all of them together. [Editor's note: Unfortunately, the author did not accomplish this before his death.]

In a letter I received recently, Mr. Murray Shiff [Editor's note: At the time, executive director of the Jewish Federation of Greater Seattle] expressed not only his keen interest, but he also adds that he has a good friend in Canada to whom Mr. Shiff mails our *La Boz*. This Canadian friend made a couple of comments on my last month's article. One is about the "Greeks from Thrace who left Turkey in the population exchange." He asks, "How could Greeks who lived in Thrace be the victims of the population exchange?"

The simple answer to this "puzzle" is that our region of European Turkey is called by historians eastern Thrace, as distinguished from western Thrace, which is in Greece proper (see *Ataturk, the Rebirth of a Nation*, by Lord Kinross, page 357).

The second comment our Canadian friend made is regarding my calling the Tekirdag local merchants as "Sephardic businessmen." He asks, "Did the Sephardic Jews in their native habitat refer to themselves as Sephardim?" He adds, "It's possible the writer is influenced by diasporic conditions . . . to distinguish themselves from the rest of us."

Perhaps he has a good point there, but there was no such intention on my part. I admit it sounds a little provincial with a dash of prejudice. The only reason I can give is perhaps this was provoked by my desire to achieve a little more recognition. Besides, to me Sephardic is synonymous with Jew, never forgetting the fact that all of us are first and foremost Jews, and then Sephardim and Ashkenazim.

I witnessed and recorded the departure of these Greek refugees from our towns. A writer, writing on the arrival of these Greeks says, "They came to Calonica [*sic*] and other parts of Macedonia, hundreds of thousands from Trakya and Asia Minor." He continues, "It was thanks to the efforts of an American Jew, Henry Morgenthau, who collected large sums of money to help these newly arrived refugees to help them settle down."

This historian of the Jews of Salonika continues, "It was these very same refugee victims who, a few years later, joined the anti-Semitic Three Epsilon Society in 1931 when a large portion of the Jewish district of Salonika was set to flames during the barbaric and infamous Campebella episode. Hundreds of Jewish homes were burned down, including synagogues, schools and other important buildings."

Backtracking a little, one of my most vivid recollections is of a morning when we woke up to a spectacular sight. The entire Tekirdag harbor was covered with Greek and British warships. After Turkey lost the war (World War I), the Allies allowed the Greeks the right to occupy a large chunk of Turkish territory, including our town, Tekirdag. The Turks were forced to flee, and Greeks took over. That same afternoon we saw the Greek King Constantin arrive in Tekirdag in his royal yacht.

The local Greek VIPs gathered on the pier to give the king a royal welcome. A reception was held at the local plush ballroom called the *sylogos*, followed by a parade. Then they held religious services in one of the Greek *eglysyas* (churches). My father, Z"L, (may his memory be for a blessing) being the *haham*, attended these services where he represented the local Jewish population.

For over two years our town was ruled by the Greeks: a governor, Greek police and Greek schools. They made a lot of improvements, some streets were paved, new parks built, etc.

Our "Sephardic businessmen" who had shops or boutiques were required by a special Greek ordinance to leave a *fenerico* (kerosene lamp) lit every night when they closed the shops.

One amusing episode I can never forget is that on one occasion, when there was a three-day Jewish holiday, the merchants were unable to go and light the *fenericos*. On the following Sunday, when these merchants opened their shops, they were all hauled away to jail for violation of the *fenerico* ordinance. My father, Z"L, had to go to the governor to explain the merchants' failure to leave the lamps lit, thus securing their release from jail.

January 1977   Teveth/Shevat 5737

Old Country Education

For a long time in Turkey, the Sephardim living there had to be content with a very low level of education for their children, both in Hebrew and in secular studies. We can break down the system of education into three levels.

The first was what was popularly known as the *maestra* (or *mestra* or *mestrica*). This was the place or the home of some woman or young girl that acted as combination "babysitter" and teacher-nurse to three or four year old children who lived in the *mahle* (district). These young children were delivered to her house where she would have them sit on *esteras* (straw mats), or a long bench around a table. On cold winter days these children would sit around the *ogar* or *mangal* (a brazier-like stove), to warm themselves on the charcoal-made glowing fire. (Remember we had no central heating there.) Naturally, when the *maestra* felt that a child needed personal attention like wiping a nose or other bodily needs, she would take care of it promptly.

Then, when the child got to be older, he would be sent to the *meldar*. That's where a child would learn to *meldar* (read) the *aleph beth*, *ajuntar* (join the letters to form distinct words) and then *apretar* (exercise in fast reading). Some families that had the means used to have a party the day before the child would enter the *meldar* and all the invited guests would chant the following poem:

La Torah, La Torah, mi ijico ala hevra,
Con el pan y el kezo, el livrico en el pecho.
Ande vas ijico del Dio, a meldar la ley del Dio.
El Dio que te guarde a ti y a tu madre.
Y a tu senyor ke es un buen judio,
Y a la comadre ke te aresivyo.

Translation:
The Torah, the Torah, my small son to the Talmud Torah,
With the bread and the cheese, the book in his pocket.
Where are you going G-d's son, to read G-d's Torah.
G-d should protect you, you and your mother.
And your father who is a good Jew,
And to the midwife that received you.

When these boys would attain a good command of Hebrew reading, then they learned the weekly portion of the *Torah* in *Lashon* and Ladino, meaning in Hebrew and translated into Judeo-Spanish. This *perashah* (*Torah* portion) would be taught accompanied with its *taamim* (musical notes).   Then the boys would learn the weekly *haftarah* (portion from the Prophets) also with the *taamim*.   Then the boys would learn *berahoth* (blessings) and *tefilah* (prayers), and on different holiday times of the year, they were taught appropriate songs of the liturgy.   For example, on *Purim* time they would learn *Mi Kamocha* (story of Purim in poetic form written by Rabbi Yehuda Halevi, see p. 78, *Purim* article) in Hebrew and Ladino; close to *Pesach* they would learn the *Hagadah* in Hebrew and Ladino.

It wasn't until the Alliance Israelite Universelle established its schools, that secular subjects like history, geography, math, and French literature, were introduced.   All these subjects were taught in the French language.

In our town of Tekirdag (Rodosto) the Alliance built a nice school building in the year 1905, consisting of a number of classrooms where girls were given an elementary education for the first time, along with the boys. It was truly an innovation.

During the First World War, Turkey entered the war on the same side as Germany against the European Allies.   Tekirdag was a city in which the soldiers gathered to be sent to the different battle fronts. The Turkish government found it necessary to confiscate a lot of buildings to accomodate the thousands of soldiers coming to town.   So among other buildings, our Alliance school building was taken over by the army and it was converted into a *kishla* (army camp.)   And so all the children were transferred to a dilapidated place called the *meldar* (school for Hebrew studies) and the higher classes were taken to a place on the top floor of our synagogue, the *azara* (ladies' section in the balcony), which overlooked the Tekirdag harbor.   I remember one day while we were learning in the *azara*, we saw a cargo ship approaching the dock, and soon after that, we saw the periscope of a British submarine.   A few minutes later, we saw that cargo ship go up in flames in a terrific explosion from the British torpedo.   Everyone was so painfully dejected, because that ship carried a load of wheat and other supplies to relieve the hunger we had endured for nearly three years.

En bueno contarlo. (We should tell this story on good occasions.)

June 1981   Iyar/Sivan 5741

Religious Leaders in Turkey - I

Around eighty years ago, a group of dedicated Sephardim in Istanbul commissioned a history student to make a study and formulate a comprehensive list of all the chief rabbis (*Haham Bashis*) that existed in the Ottoman Empire up to fairly recent times, giving names, places of birth and the dates. [Editor's note: See Appendix I.]

This student came up with the approximate number of thirty-two, adding to our knowledge many historical facts and other valuable information.

At that time, there was already some small history written by a certain Mr. Moise Franco who wrote, in French, *Histoire Des Israelites de l'Empire Ottoman*. Mr. Franco was principal of the Alliance school in Shumla, Bulgaria. He was also a contributor to the Jewish Encyclopedia [Editor's note: Published c. 1905] on articles pertaining to Sephardic personalities and history.

The first *Haham Bashi* was a venerable scholar, Rabbi Moshe Capsali, a native of Greece and leader of the local Jews which we call *Romaniotes*. When Sultan Mehmet II conquered Constantinople from the Byzantine Empire, in 1453, more than half of the Istanbul residents had run away. The Sultan had Rabbi Moshe act as an agent to bring these citizens back to repopulate the country. Rabbi Moshe was able to find these refugees and get them to return to their homes, their jobs and their synagogues.

Thirty-nine years later, it was Rabbi Moshe Capsali's arduous task again, this time under the Sultan Bayazid II, Mehmet's son, to receive all those thousands of refugees from the Spanish exile in 1492. Again, he had to find them homes, jobs and regulate their lives until such time as these exiles could settle and rebuild their homes in the various cities of the Ottoman Empire.

The sultan had so much respect and admiration for Rabbi Moshe Capsali's judgment, that he invited the rabbi to sit in the royal council chambers right next to the mufti, the Mohammedan religious leader, a great honor. Rabbi Moshe was so strict in the discipline of the unruly youth of the capital, that some of these youths perpetrated a secret plan to have the rabbi murdered, all this in the name of revenge. Thanks to some dear friends, Rabbi Moshe was able to escape from these rowdy rioters in 1481. Rabbi Moshe died in 1495.

The next *Haham Bashi* in the line of succession was an eminent scholar by the name of Rabbi Eliyahu Mizrahi, whose *responsa* literature is still being studied, and which provides historians with an enormous amount of facts regarding the condition of the Jewish communities of that period.

He was a venerable leader and rabbis and communal leaders were continuously seeking his advice on matters of religion as well as matters dealing with Turkish government rules and regulations. Many times he was able to act in the capacity of reconciler and averted many a dispute between individuals, as well as between the leaders and their synagogues.

After the death of Rabbi Eliyahu Mizrahi, the office of *Haham Bashi* lost some of the privileges originally given to that high office, for the following reason. Before 1492, the Jewish population of Constantinople consisted of Greek-speaking (Byzantine) Jews called *Romaniotes* and *Kara'im*. However, with the mass arrival of the Sephardic Jews from Spain, it changed the whole picture of the city's Jews, the Sephardim becoming the majority. So, after the death of Rabbi Eliyahu Mizrahi, the local Jews demanded that the spiritual leader be one of their own, from their own ranks, a *Romaniote*. They actually elected as their chief rabbi a scholar by the name of Yehoshua Candioty, a native of that region and a former student of Rabbi Mizrahi. The Sephardim did not agree to this choice and insisted on electing one from their own ranks. Even then the Sephardim did not agree to elect one chief rabbi of Spanish origin, but instead each synagogue chose one of their own. This was due to the fact that each synagogue in their new home had a spiritual leader from their own home town, that is, from the different cities and regions of Spain, like Castilia, Aragon, Catalan, etc.

This disagreement among the various Sephardic communities, and their failure to come up with one central authority, resulted in the curtailing of many privileges formerly afforded to the high office of *Haham Bashi*.

Although the government of Turkey continued to collect a certain tax called *rav akchesi* for the mere privilege of Jews having the right to elect a chief rabbi, that split in their ranks caused the office of *Haham Bashi* to be reduced in power. Later the chief rabbis of Turkey were called *Haham Bashi vikili* or *kaymakam efendi*, meaning a position of a lieutenant to the original high office of *Haham Bashi*.

July 1981   Sivan/Tammuz 5741

Religious Leaders in Turkey - II

Last month we covered some of the early religious leaders in the Ottoman Empire, that is, the *Haham Bashi* in Constantinople. There existed so many, that it is virtually impossible, in the limited articles in *LaBoz* to cover as many as we would like. So we will confine this month's article to two scholars who left a fascinating imprint on the history of the Sephardim in Turkey. Material for this is taken from the writings of S. Rosanes (see p. 42) and A. Galante (see p. 46).

Around the 1660s when that messy confusion caused by the false messiah from Izmir, Sabetai Zvi, was getting out of hand (see p. 38), the action of one religious leader by the name of Rabbi Yomtov Ben Yakar stands out. He was capable of not only bringing order out of the chaos, but of answering hundreds of letters directed to him from a great number of places as far as Amsterdam, Leghorn and even from Germany and Poland. Rabbi Ben Yakar, along with his colleagues in Istanbul, was instrumental in averting what could have been a devastating massacre of Turkish Jews. Jewish people all over the world were so hungry for news from a reliable source. One can imagine how busy he was.

It seems a crime to pass over so many scholars and sages who acted as *Haham Bashi* between 1660 and 1860, but we must. These others left us so many worthwhile books, that are still studied and referred to relating to Jewish problems. However, I have to remind you, this is only a selective reading. The one *Haham Bashi* who fills an interesting chapter in Sephardic history is a charismatic sage by the name of Rabbi Yakir Gueron. He was chief rabbi of Edirne at first. His full name was Rabbi Yakir Astruc Gueron. Most of his friends and relatives used to call him Haribi Preciado. (*Haribi* is a word constructed from the words *haham* and *ribi* meaning sage and rabbi; *preciado* is the Spanish translation of the Hebrew *yakir*, both meaning precious.)

Professor Abraham Galante tells us the way Rabbi Gueron became *Haham Bashi*. El Conde (Count) Abraham de Camondo, a very wealthy Jew, decided to open up in Istanbul (during the 1850s), a modern school where local youth could obtain a formal education, besides their Hebrew and talmudic subjects. Mr. Camondo obtained the approval of the then *Haham Bashi*, named Rabbi Yaakov Avigdor.

Meanwhile there arose a group of enthusiastic opponents of the school, who claimed that this type of school would damage the quality of religion in the youth attending school.

These antagonists, after a fierce campaign, gathered enough forces, and demanded from the Vizir Fouad Pasha to have Rabbi Avigdor removed from office. Being a fair and equitable man, Fouad Pasha refused to act on his own, and instead, invited three eminent Jewish scholars to form a panel, or rabbinic tribunal, to resolve this disturbing issue, and so put an end to this dissension. This distinguished panel consisted of Rabbi Haim Palachi of Izmir, Rabbi Yakir Gueron of Edirne and Rabbi Menahem Cohen chief rabbi of Sheres. [Editor's note: city about forty miles northeast of Salonika; today it is Serrai, Greece.]

These three rabbis got together and, after long deliberation rendered their decision to the Vizir. The verdict was in favor Rabbi Avigdor and El Conde de Camondo. Fouad Pasha was extremely impressed with Rabbi Yakir Gueron's intelligent and prudent presentation of the issue, so after a few years when the office of *Haham Bashi* became vacant, the Vizir joined the electoral college of Istanbul in naming Haribi Preciado Gueron as the next *Haham Bashi*. Fouad Pasha dispatched one of his generals to escort Rabbi Gueron from Edirne to Istanbul, carrying a personal letter on the occasion of his election to the high office of *Haham Bashi* to all of the Turkish Jews.

Rabbi Gueron gained great popularity, and because he was respected, he established a great number of rules and improvements in the affairs of the Ottoman Empire's Jewish population. Professor Galante, because of his close association with the Turkish government's official documents, tells us that in one *defter* (legal document) he found two episodes which demonstrate that Rabbi Yakir Gueron took advantage of his office and acted very unfairly with two *hahamim*. One was Rabbi Shabetay Fresco, who disagreed with Rabbi Gueron on a certain issue, so he used his influence and had Rabbi Fresco exiled to Demotica in 1863. He did the same thing with a *haham* from Edirne by the name of Rabbi Haim Mevorah who was exiled (*surgun*) to Youmuljina.

When Rabbi Gueron reached advanced age, he resigned the post of *Haham Bashi* and went to Jerusalem where he opened his own *yeshiva*. He passed away in February 1874. The next *Haham Bashi* was Rabbi Moshe Halevi who ministered for thirty-six years. He had to resign as a result of the changes that took place in 1908 with the new Turkish constitution. Rabbi Haim Nahoum succeeded Rabbi

Moshe Halevi. Many of our elders in Seattle remember when Rabbi Nahoum visited Seattle in 1923 to collect funds for the Alliance (see p. 104). In 1925 Rabbi Nahoum accepted the post of chief rabbi of Egypt.

The present *Haham Bashi* is Rabbi David Asseo who obtained his rabbinic ordination in the rabbinical seminary of the island of Rhodes. Rabbi Isidore Kahan [Editor's note: Rabbi Kahan was rabbi of Congregation Ezra Bessaroth in the 1940s and 1950s.] was one of Rabbi Asseo's teachers before Rabbi Kahan came to Seattle in the late 1930s.

August 1982   Av/Elul 5742

Communication Director

Once in a while, after all the regular household chores are done, along with some reading, some viewing on the tube, a person sits down to pause and reflect a bit. One of my periodic reflections is looking back over the years and comparing the modern lifestyle with the way it was in the old country. One that did cause a chuckle is the topic we will discuss in this month's *La Boz*.

To start with, this topic has to do with the manners of communication in past years, as compared with modern methods. Whenever there is something that the authorities or our synagogue need to notify the residents or the members of, we get fliers through the mail. However, at the turn of the century in some small towns in Turkey, where the art of printing was not yet developed, the city officials had to find another means to notify the public on some important civic news. The only means available in our town of Tekirdag was to employ the services of a competent town crier, who was qualified to make these periodic announcements so everyone in town would be sure to be duly notified.

Such a qualified crier we had in Tekirdag. His name was Arap Selim. "Selim" was his given name and "Arap" because he had an extremely dark complexion. (*Arap* means black in Turkish.) The reason he was chosen for the job was because he possessed an extremely loud and thunderous voice. When he started - *Ehali !!!* (Listen, everybody!) - he could be heard for dozens of blocks around.

All this was all right, but wait! There was one hitch. The man could not read!

Although he looked like a Turkish *hodja* (clergyman), dressed in a regulation clergy outfit and he probably could recite parts of the Koran by heart, he never learned to read. He probably memorized this by attending the *namas* in their *jami* (liturgy in their mosques). Not being able to read, how did he manage to read an official document? How did he broadcast it to the local residents?

Although he was an illiterate, he was a shrewd and a resourceful person. What he did was find a Turkish man who knew how to read the legal document. This Turk would stoop right behind Selim, almost invisible to onlookers. The Turk would read to Selim one word at a time and Selim would blast it and shout it out. In order to present the image that he was the one that was reading it, Selim would hold in his hand a copy of the announcement. Everyone got the message.

At the end of the proclamation, he had a cute habit of clicking his tongue, which sounded like the blast of a trumpet. He expended so much energy that when he was through with the proclamation he would be absolutely exhausted, both physically and mentally. He would rest on one of the large rocks close by. Then he would give a big smile to the people around and would end the ritual by injecting a little humor of his own by saying, in Turkish, *Ishittik, ishitmedik, demeyelum*, implying the following: Let no one come forth with the pretext claiming "I did not hear the proclamation."

On those days when there were no official documents to be announced, he would also be employed by the local steamship company to notify the people on the times of departure of such and such boat leaving the Tekirdag harbor for different ports like Istanbul, Silivriya, Pandurma and other cities close by.

This would be preceded by the same word - *Ehali!!!* Then he would blast out the news, "*Bu aksham, saat sekizde, vapor kalkiyor.*" (Meaning: Such and such a boat is leaving tonight at exactly 8:00 p.m. sharp.)

Scores of people would gather around Arap Selim to hear what he had to say. That was the main purpose. Yet, there were a number of people who would gather around him to watch him and his antics and to see how he operated. It was just like a show, like a circus without tickets, and everyone had a lot of fun.

June 1977   Sivan/Tamuz 5737

Our Turkish Neighbors

We Sephardim who lived among Mohammedans know quite a bit about their form of worship. Many of their *jamis* (mosques) were situated right in our Jewish neighborhood, and we couldn't help but observe their daily practices. First, the *muezin* (cantor) would climb the spiral steps up to the *mishkita* (minaret tower) and he would chant their *Alayin Pana* and their *Allah Akhber*. Some of these *muezins* had excellent voices.

Right after these calls, we used to see the Turkish worshippers, one by one, enter the courtyard of these *jamis* and make a dash straight to the *fuentizicas* (fountains) to take their *aptes* (ritual washings) washing their hands, their feet and their faces, before they would go into the mosque to *kildear namas* on the *tapetes* (pray on the carpets).

It was such a marvelous sight to see a *sunnet* (circumcision). They have a custom to circumcise their young men when they reach the age of thirteen. This is because they're descendants of Yishmael who was circumcised by his father Abraham at the age of thirteen. We could tell which one of these young men was circumcised recently by the way he was dressed, in a loose multi-colored nightgown, and also by the way they used to walk (like an American cowboy).

Some of us who attended their schools, would be taught the *Koran*, which is their sacred scripture. In addition to the *Koran*, they have   their other literature, which they call *hadit*, and which they claim came out of the mouth of Mohammed, and therefore is taken as official.

Many of these additional sayings can be traced straight to our Hebrew literature like our *Talmud* or *Midrash*. We know that Mohammed had many Jewish teachers, some of whom were forced converts, and they introduced many of these *Talmudic* sayings into their literature. Of course in many instances, their clergymen changed the content and tone to suit their belief and ideology.

Professor A. S. Yehuda, the famous Hebrew lexicographer, made a very deep study of many of these sayings and stories. He discovered that almost all of them had their origin in our Jewish sources.

One of the sayings that Professor Yehuda was having difficulty in tracing to our literature was the following: Mohammed says that their Allah promises any Moslem who fulfills certain precepts that he would be provided with 310 virgins daily when he reaches their Gan Eden (paradise).

What gave Professor Yehuda a broad hint to discover the origin in our Talmud was the number 310. Our Talmud contains the following passage. Rabbi Yehoshua Ben Levi says: The Biblical verse which says *leanhil ohavay yesh* (I have a good inheritance for my friends) is traditionally interpreted to the effect that *Hashem* (G-d) promises to all righteous Jews that they will inherit 310 *olamoth* (worlds), because the numerical value of the Hebrew word *yesh* amounts to 310.

Now the convert that transmitted this into the Moslem literature was probably an educated Jew, and knew the rabbinical method of applying "*al tikre*" (don't call it...) which allows rabbinic scholars to substitute a certain word in order to give the meaning an instructive sense and a deeper meaning.

So this convert substituted the word and changed *olamoth* (worlds) into *alamoth* (young ladies), which destroys the whole intent of Rabbi Yeoshua's reading in the Mishna of *shay olamoth* (310 worlds) by promising their men *shay alamoth*, 310 virgins, which would entice them to be good much quicker than mere worlds. This may sound ingenious, but you can detect the immoral tinge to it.

August 1979   Av/Elul 5739

Missionary Schools In the Old Country

How cunning and tricky were the Protestant missionary schools in the old country (the Ottoman Empire)? In this article I will cite particularly the situation in Jerusalem in the late 1800s. Mr. Avraham Almaleh, of blessed memory, describes the events in his excellent articles.

Mr. Almaleh explains how the missionaries would approach some unfortunate Sephardi father and offer this poor man some financial help if he would agree to enroll his children in one of the missionary schools. At the beginning these children had to study the New Testament, attend their religious services, and then obtain their secular education. But, gradually, these teachers would lure the children to agree to accept baptism, foresaking their Jewish faith forever. These missionaries spent millions of golden Turkish liras to achieve their treacherous goal.

It was at this particular time that the well known Nissim Behar (see p. 104) was sent by the Alliance to organize and open up a school in Jerusalem in order to combat the missionaries' damaging influence. When Mr. Behar was almost ready to open up the first of the Alliance schools he was confronted by a wave of violent opposition. This conflict was initiated by a group called *Chassidim-Kanayim* (pious and zealous ones) who were opposed to any type of secular education as being foreign to the Jewish faith. This group went as far as declaring a *herem* (religious ban) against both Nissim Behar or any father who would allow his child to attend this school. They even threatened Nissim Behar with bodily harm. Mr. Almaleh, who discovered the entire correspondence in the archives of the Alliance, quotes from letters of Nissim Behar: "I deplore the general attitude of *Kanayim*, but I will never give in to their threats because of the importance of the project of saving these youths from being deprived of their Jewish heritage."

Finally, through the tenacity of Nissim Behar, the first of these schools was opened on the ninth of April, 1882. By the middle of May the school had over fifty students, among them some of the children of well known Sephardi leaders and rabbis. Only one Ashkenazi father disregarded the ban and enrolled his son, as a result of which he was criticized severely. The school program consisted of Bible studies, general education, both religious and secular, plus some classes in various manual skills in order to prepare some of these youngsters to obtain employment.

As an illustration of the struggle, Mr. Almaleh cites a particular incident when a measles epidemic struck some of the Jerusalem school children. A group of the *Kanayim* made a personal appeal to the Sephardi *beth din* (religious court) to have this school closed up because, they maintained the measles epidemic was due directly to the existence of this dreadful school.

The *Rishon LeZion* (chief rabbi) at that time was a scholar by the name of Rabbi Refael Meir Panijil. He was a staunch supporter of the Alliance school. In answer to the group's appeal, he tried to convince these *Kanayim*, saying that on the many times he had occasion to visit this school, he examined the situation and talked to many students. He gave the *Kanayim* his personal assurance that the school was run according to our traditional faith. On his many recent investigations of the school he had never found an iota of evidence that this school had ever deviated from our sacred *Torah*. On the contrary, he assured them that these school children are fed healthy meals and are taught well, instead of wasting their time in the streets of Jerusalem learning to live off charity.

Four years later, through the encouragement and support of Rabbi Panijil, his colleague, the then Ashkenazi chief rabbi Rabbi Shemuel Salant, convinced fully of the school's sincerity of purpose, applied to the Alliance school to admit a few Ashkenazic youths as students.

Nissim Behar later became director of Alliance and many other communal *Talmud Torahs* in Jerusalem. I can safely say that Nissim Behar was instrumental in saving hundreds of Sephardi school children from becoming victims of the overzealous Protestant missionaries. Mr. Behar later came to New York with the goal to organize some segment of Sephardim. Unfortunately, due to his advanced age, failing health and other severe disappointments, he died a very lonely and destitute man in New York in the early 1930s. (See also p. 104)

September 1979   Elul 5739/Tishri 5740

Missionaries In Istanbul - I

In last month's *La Boz* article we wrote about the tricks that were used by missionary school teachers in Jerusalem in order to trap some poor Sephardic youngsters, to entice them into converting to the Christian faith and accept their baptism.

There was a similar Protestant society in Istanbul. They tried different tactics in that they duped some Istanbul *hahamim* into promoting some innocent sounding books containing hidden and undetected references to the Christian creed.

The man who was at the helm of this society was an ardent missionary by the name of William Gottlieb Schauffler. He had thousands of dollars at his disposal, funds provided mainly by missionaries with headquarters in London and other European cities.

Mr. Schauffler had come to Istanbul pretending to be a friend of Hebrew and Sephardic culture. After years of hard and laborious work, he mastered the Ladino language to such a degree that he knew the definition of every word of Hebrew that occurs in our holy Bible. He compiled and published a Hebrew-Ladino dictionary in the year 1855. Unfortunately, the words that he manipulated and changed the meaning of, to suit his purpose, were not discovered until years later. (We have a copy of this dictionary in our synagogue library.)

Before he published this dictionary, however, he prepared for publication a new edition of the Hebrew Bible, in two volumes, which he translated into Ladino. When he was ready to put this work to the printing presses, he brought a sample to the then chief rabbi Rabbi Shemuel Haim for his approval and official approbation. When Rabbi Shemuel saw this sample, he was fascinated by the excellent quality of both the paper and the clear readable print. A further consideration for Rabbi Shemuel's ready recommendation of the books was that Bibles with Ladino translation were getting very scarce. Jewish printers found it very difficult to produce Bibles because of the tremendous cost of paper, labor and printing. Moreover, Mr. Schauffler made it so attractive by offering these sets of books at a very nominal, inexpensive price. Unfortunately, in retrospect, we can say that Rabbi Shemuel did not examine the contents very thoroughly, falling for the smooth talking and deceptive Mr. Schauffler. This first printing was dated 1838.

Five years later, in 1843, all these books were sold out. Mr. Schauffler wanted to go into a second printing. Rabbi Shemuel Haim had passed away, so Mr. Schauffler presented his petition to the Istanbul *beth din* (religious court) for their approval.

Recently, Mr. Albert S. Adatto showed me a copy of this second recommendation, dated 1843. It is a full page consisting of enthusiastic praises of Mr. Schauffler's benevolent attitude towards Hebrew works and his generosity in offering such highly splendid books at such a nominal cost. This document, approving the second printing, is signed by three very prominent *hahamim*, namely Rabbi Eliezer De Toledo, Rabbi Yaakov Behar David and Rabbi Abraham Gabay.

Obviously, this panel of religious leaders did not deem it necessary to examine the books, in detail, perhaps because they relied on the previous approval given five years before by the very revered Rabbi Shemuel Haim who was taken in by the crafty Mr. Schauffler.

Mr. Avraham Yaari, the famous bibliographer, who saw copies of the Bible in the Hebrew University library in Jerusalem, says that Mr. Schauffler's Ladino translation was actually the translation published by Rabbi Avraham Assa in Constantinople in the year 1744. Mr. Yaari says that Schauffler's is the exact copy of the Assa edition, with the exception of some places where Mr. Schauffler changed some words to suit his Christian ideology.

In next month's *La Boz* we will write how the *hahamim* of the next generation discovered Mr. Schauffler's shifty alterations, and how they exposed him as a deceitful schemer.

October/November 1979   Tishri/Heshvan/Kislev 5740

Missionaries In Istanbul - II

We continue our last month's *La Boz* article in which we tried to report the attempt on the part of Mr. William Gottlieb Schauffler to attract readers for his two seemingly innocent works, his Hebrew-Ladino Bible and his Hebrew-Ladino dictionary. Both were extremely useful works for Ladino-speaking Sephardim in Turkey. These two books by this famous missionary were endorsed by the *hahamim* after a cursory examination.

However, on further examination, some alert readers began to point out that these two works contained unacceptable definitions which were intended by Mr. Schauffler to entice the readers into accepting meanings to suit his missionary motives.

I will cite here two illustrations to prove how Mr. Schauffler altered the meanings of some words to fit his Christian doctrines.

One is found in the Book of Psalms, Chapter 2, Verse 12, which contains the two Hebrew words *nasheku bar*. Our traditional Ladino definition of these two words is *armadvos de limpyeza* (arm yourselves with purity). Mr. Schauffler changed the Ladino translation into *bezaldo a el ijo* (kiss the son). Any student of the Hebrew language can realize how ridiculous and contrived Mr. Schauffler's translation is, and can detect his inference, that our Bible bids us Jews to pay homage and adoration to his Christian faith.

The second illustration, also in the Book of Psalms, in Chapter 22, Verse 17, is another proof of juggling Hebrew roots to suit his purpose. This is the same psalm that we recite on the night of *Purim* before *Arvith*. The Hebrew phrase in question is *kaari yaday veraglay*. Our traditional Ladino translation is *como el leon, mis manos y mis pies* (like a lion, my hands and my feet). Comes Mr. Schauffler and he translates the word *kaari* as "they pierced," filling a whole page in the dictionary to prove his point.

Looking through my own copy of Schauffler's Hebrew-Ladino dictionary on page 161, I discovered and noticed a very interesting footnote, written in purple ink in our Sephardic Ladino cursive. This was obviously written as a refutation of Mr. Schauffler's absurd rendering of the word *kaari* to mean "they pierced."

This anonymous critic explains Mr. Schauffler's tricky way of maneuvering the key word *kaari*. I will quote here below this footnote in the original Ladino and I shall translate it into English for our non-Ladino readers.

Ditto sinyor, siendo protestan, esplica este biervo (kaari) dela sorte: siendo este salmo (22) lo attribuen ke fue dicho por el Cristo en ora ke lo mataron. Y azer remez ke buracaron sus pies y sus manos. Ma, en verdad, el pasuk es kaari yaday veraglay, "Como el leon mis manos y mis pies."

Translation: Due to the fact that the author of this dictionary is a Protestant (Christian) he defines the word *kaari* to mean "they pierced." Since they (the Christians) maintain that this whole psalm was said about Christ on the day he was executed, casting a direct implication that the executioners pierced his hands and feet. However, in reality, this verse *kaari yaday veraglay* is simply translated as "like a lion, my hands and my feet."

It's surprising to notice that this word *kaari* is also translated as "they pierced" in the 1916 edition of the Hebrew Publishing Company's Hebrew-English Bible. I'm not able to explain how this slipped in there.

When people became aware of Mr. Schauffler's intentions, (he was also printing other pamphlets and brochures to promote his missionary ideas), the religious lay leaders of Istanbul began an intensive campaign to expose Mr. Schauffler for his deceptive motivations. These leaders appealed to our Sephardim to get rid of all this literature, or at least erase the pages which contained these unacceptable meanings. They wrote articles and inserted ads in the Ladino newspapers of the times like *El Telegrafo* or *El Tiempo* and others to unmask Mr. Schauffler's motives. The effect of this campaign was very satisfactory. A few copies are still in existence, but the so-called harmful and damaging sting was removed.

June 1976   Sivan/Tamuz 5736

Yerushalayim Of Old

One of the best known Sephardic books in Hebrew to come out during the last century is the one called *Pele Yoetz* written by Rabbi Eliezer Papo who ministered as *haham* to various Sephardic communities in the Balkans. This book contains many pointers on proper behavior called in Hebrew *musar*.

In many small communities in the old country, the *haham* of the *kahal* (synagogue) would read a chapter out of this book every *Shabbath* just before the taking out of the *Sefer Torah*.

Rabbi Eliezer Papo wrote this book in Hebrew. In order to have it available to the vast majority of Sephardim who did not understand Hebrew, came his son, Rabbi Yehuda Papo and translated it into a beautiful and easy to read Ladino.

I met Joseph Papo, Rabbi Yehuda's grandson, in Sacramento, California, where he showed me an autographed copy of this book *Pele Yoetz* in Ladino with his grandfather's personal remarks.

Now this Rabbi Yehuda, who originally lived in Sarajevo, later on moved to Israel, and settled in Jerusalem with his family, some of whom were later to become famous in the north of Israel where they specialized in scientific farming.

From time to time, this Rabbi Yehuda Papo used to write certain articles which he called *iggeroth* (letters), describing conditions in the Jerusalem of his time.

One of these articles which Joseph Papo from Sacramento showed me is written in such quaint Ladino, with a large number of picturesque Ladino expressions, that I would like to share with you some of them. The article itself is very long, but I'll just include a few excerpts, first in Ladino, and then with my translation into English. The reader will note what a change in conditions from then, to modern Jerusalem where we meet a vibrant atmosphere all around.

> *"Yerushalayim es la sivdad capitala de la proveza, siegos y koshos y sakates vienen a Yerushalayim para mantenersen de sedaka: ke dizen?*
> *Negro por negro, shema Yisrael. A lo manco desharemos muestros guesos en akeya tiera santa"*

"En Yerushalayim, gente ke se mantengan de entrada de mulkes (cazas), no ay

"De mujeres se topan en Yerushalayim tresdoblado de lo ke se topa de ombres, el rov de eyas son proves. De guerfanos y guerfanas ay mucho bereket. ashreem Yisrael, todos keren bien a Yerushalayim, ma el aniyuth traye al ombre a pecado. Y ay malavlantes ke aze descayer a Yerushalayim. De una pulga azen un gameyo. Ya dizen la gente: De lo ke ves, creyete la mitad, y de lo ke syentes, nada."

"De rogar es, el shem yithbarah ke aserke los corasones de muestra nacion, y azer lo derecho para ke tengan a Yerushalayim en la onor y la estima ke yakisheya."

Translation:

Yerushalayim is the capital city of poverty. Blind people, lame people, crippled people come to *Yerushalayim* to live off public welfare or charity. These people say to themselves: "What could be worse. *Shema Yisrael* and G-d help us. At least, when we die, we leave our bones in the Holy Land."

"There are hardly any people in *Yerushalayim* who live off the income of property.

"The number of women living in Jerusalem are three times as many as there are men, and the majority of these women are very poor and there's a surplus and an abundance of orphans - boys and girls.

"To the credit of the Jewish people, everyone loves *Yerushalayim*. However, because of this tremendous poverty, a person tends to engage in malicious gossip, therefore causing a disservice to *Yerushalayim*. These people exaggerate so much, they make a small insect seem as big as a camel. People have a popular saying: Of what you see, you can only believe half, and of what you hear, believe nothing."

"We appeal to the Almighty that he will bring the hearts of our Jewish people closer together, and act in a sensible and proper way so that people will hold *Yerushalayim* in the reverence and esteem that is coming to it."

Chapter Four

Jewish Religious Practices

February 1980   Shevat/Adar 5740

Ribi Akiva and the Orphan's Kaddish

This is not an essay explaining the *kaddish*. That's beyond my capacity and beyond the scope of this article. Readers have to look elsewhere for their answers. [Editor's note: See *The Kaddish Prayer*, N. Scherman, Artscroll Mesorah Series, Mesorah Publications, Ltd., 1980; or, *The Old Jewish-Aramaic Prayer, the Kaddish*, D. de Sola Pool, 1909.]

However, one of the essential facets of reciting the *kaddish*, is when we pay respect to the memory of a dear departed, so it deals with the spiritual world. Its main theme, though, is to sanctify the name of G-d, even in time of bereavement, when humans are prone to question G-d's divine judgment.

In this connection, I read a fascinating story about Rabbi Akiva, the famous sage and martyr, which I would like to share with the readers of *La Boz*.

The story goes that one day Rabbi Akiva was taking a stroll in the cemetery. Suddenly, he saw a figure of a man reeling under a huge load of wood which looked beyond human endurance. Rabbi Akiva told the man to stop, saying to him, "My son, why are you working so hard? You're exhausted. If you're a slave, let me pay your ransom, so you can regain your freedom. Or, in case you're a poor man, I will show you a way to gain your livelihood in a more dignified manner."

The man replied, "Please let me be - don't detain me. I'm afraid my supervisor will be angry at me." Rabbi Akiva asked him: "My son, what forces you to carry on like this?" The man answered: "My name is not recorded in the Book of the Deceased yet - and every day they order me to cut down some trees, and all this accumulated firewood might be used, someday, to burn my body."

Rabbi Akiva was amazed, asking,"What was your occupation in the human world?" To which the man said:"I was a tax collector in a certain town, and I was considered as one of the leaders in that community. But I showed a special treatment to the rich and I made the poor suffer terribly."

Rabbi Akiva said, "Perhaps you can offer to do penance, to atone for your injustice." The man answered, "I did overhear my superiors saying: If this unfortunate man had a son who would devote his life to the study of *Torah*, as well as reciting some prayers, then the heavenly ministers might recommend a merciful solution." The man continued saying: "I never had a son, but I left my wife pregnant when I passed on. Even if my wife had a son, who would bother to raise him, to teach him *Torah*, because as I told you, I never left a friend in the world." At that moment Rabbi Akiva decided to go and search after this man's family, to see whether his wife had possibly given birth to a son. But before he left, Rabbi Akiva asked this man his name. His name was Arkavta, and he said his wife's name was Shoshana Keviya, and the name of the town was Dukia.

When Rabbi Akiva arrived in Dukia, the people of the town spoke very bitterly about Arkavta. When he inquired about the man's wife, the townspeople had nothing but curses for her, and she did give birth to a son, but he was so bad, he was never circumcised.

However, Rabbi Akiva was not discouraged, he took the young man to the academy and tried to teach him *Torah*, but all to no avail, until Rabbi Akiva fasted forty days with prayers, saying, "dear Heavenly Father, I hereby place all the responsibility of this youngster's future in Your hands."

As in a miracle, G-d opened up this lad's heart and understanding, learning *Torah* diligently, until Rabbi Akiva had the boy ready to stand before the congregation, reciting the mourner's *kaddish*, and the people responded *amen*. Later Rabbi Akiva taught him the mysteries of our religion, the lad growing up to be very proficient in profound matters.

After this happened, one day, Arkavta, the boy's father appeared before Rabbi Akiva, thanking him for having saved him from the tortures of *gehinam*, and Rabbi Akiva, in turn, recited an appropriate chapter from the book of Psalms. A happy ending to a sad story.

March 1972   Adar/Nisan 5732

The Prayer Alenu Leshabeah

The prayer *Alenu Leshabeah*, with which all Jewish worshippers end their daily religious services, has a story of its own.

When and by whom was the prayer composed? Many authorities, among them the ancient prayer book called *Kol Bo*, say that the author of *Alenu* was Joshua, who composed it at the time of his victorious entrance into the promised land after his battle with numerous kings and his triumph at Jericho. Other scholars maintain, that it was composed by Ezra and the Great Assembly. While others assign the authorship of *Alenu* to the famous Babylonian Rabbi Aba Ariha, founder of the Rabbinical Academy of Sura.

Alenu was first recited only and especially, as introduction to the first part of the *Mussaph* of *Rosh Hashanah*, known as the portion of *malhioth* (kingdoms). It was only after quite a few centuries that it also came to be incorporated into the conclusion of our daily services as we know it today.

None of our great liturgical authorities like Rambam (Maimonides), Abudraham, or Rav Amram Gaon, mention the *Alenu*, as far as saying it at the end of the daily prayers. The book known as *Kol Bo* composed over 450 years ago is the first authority that mentions the *Alenu*, citing its importance, and therefore, requiring it to be recited while standing. This prayer expresses beautifully the faith of the Jew in one universal G-d and the hope that all the nations of the world will some day in the future proclaim G-d as the only Ruler of the World.

A great amount of absurd accusations were spread about in connection with one phrase contained in the *Alenu*. In the year 1399, an ingrate Jew, named Pesach Peter, who converted to Christianity, was the first to charge the Jewish people of secretly insulting the founder of Christianity. He maintains that the phrase "*shehem mishtahavim lahevel varik*", which, translated means "that they (the pagans) bow down to vanity and folly," the Hebrew word *varik* (folly) surely alludes to *Yeshu* by virtue of the fact that both words *Yeshu* (Jesus) and *varik* have the same numerical value amounting to 316.

This evil man also offered the unfounded and utterly ridiculous statement that the Jewish rabbis required all Jews to spit when they came to the word *varik*, claiming the word was derived from Hebrew word *rok* which means spit. This, he claimed, was done as a mark of impudence toward the Christian deity. The critics all overlook one simple fact. This prayer was originally composed, for the *Rosh Hashanah Mussaph*, long before Jesus was born. So it could only refer to the idol worshippers and pagans.

In order once and for all to shut the ugly mouths of these accusers from spreading their poison, the rabbis of Germany asked the printers of Jewish prayer books to omit entirely the phrase "*shehem mishtahavim*," etc., from this prayer. Consequently, our brothers the Ashkenazim, do not use this phrase. Some other books contain this phrase, but in parentheses. Our Sephardic rabbis never agreed to this omission so it was left intact. Perhaps because most of the Sephardim lived in Moslem countries, they did not have this problem.

Nevertheless, we came under fire by some Moslem anti-Semites, with the following charges in connection with this same phrase "*shehem mishtahavim*," etc. The word *hevel* (vanity) in Hebrew is composed of three letters: *he*, *beth*, and *lamed*. They claim the letter *he* (five), alludes to the Moslem religious rite of washing their hands and feet each time before their fifth daily religious service (*aptes y namas*). And the letter *beth* which we use also to mean two, refers to their two major holy days (*Bayram*), and the letter *lamed*, in our numerical figure thirty, refers to the thirty days of *Ramadan*, which is their thirty-day period of fasting and prayer.

It is very unfortunate that all this ingenuity was employed "*para mal*" (for bad purposes).

September 1972   Elul 5732/Tishri 5733

Havdala

The Prophet Isaiah, speaking about *Shabbath*, tells us that those who observe the day of *Shabbath* with genuine sincerity will be aware of it as a day of pure delight. At the conclusion of such an important day, our sages have instituted a small ceremony, to be recited both at the synagogue and at home, as a way of saying farewell to the *Shabbath*.

This ceremony is called *havdala*, meaning separation or distinction. First, they inserted a paragraph called *Ata Honantanu* into the fourth *beraha* (benediction) of the *Amida* (silent prayer of the

Saturday night *Arvith* (evening service). The *Amida* contains nineteen benedictions, each with a separate theme.

The theme of this fourth *beraha* is that we bless G-d for endowing us with the faculty of intelligence and understanding. That's the reason they placed this *havdala* paragraph in this *beraha*, to indicate that without intelligence we cannot distinguish between the holy *Shabbath* and the rest of the week days.

Then at the conclusion of the *Arvith*, the *hazan* says a *beraha* over a cup of wine followed by another *beraha* over some spices (like cloves, etc.) or some good smelling plant like myrtle or romero or a lemon. This is followed by another *beraha* over a freshly kindled light (usually a candle). Then he says a special *havdala* paragraph in which we thank G-d for having distinguished the holy *Shabbath* from the days of the week, as He distinguished Israel from the rest of mankind.

In order to remember the order of this *havdala* ceremony, which of the four *berahoth* come first, the wine or the spices, etc., the rabbis have given us a very good sign. This sign is the Hebrew word *yavne*. This word in Hebrew is written with four letters -- *yod, beth, nun, he*. *Yod* stands for *yayin* (wine), *beth* stands for *besamim* (spices), *nun* stands for *ner* (candle) and the letter *he* stands for *havdala*, the recitation of the special paragraph.

The following reasons are cited by the rabbis for the *havdala* ritual. The blessing over the wine is because we feel sad at *Shabbath's* ending, so we drink some wine to help us forget this sad feeling. The reason for the blessing over the spices some rabbis hold, is that the enjoyment we derive through the sense of smell acts as a small compensation for the departing "additional spiritual soul" (*neshama yetera*) which we receive on *Shabbath*. The reason for the blessing over the light is because light was created by G-d on the first day of Creation, and we're now entering the first day of the week.

When the blessing over the candle is recited, we're told to bend our fingers and gaze at our fingernails. In the Sephardic Ladino we call this *mirar las ounyas*. There are a number of reasons for this. One simple reason is we're not allowed to say a *beraha* on the light unless you derive some benefit from it, by seeing the fingernails with the light beaming on them. Another reason is that the fingernails grow continually and growth is a symbol of blessing.

Another reason is for purposes of humility. When you bend your fingers, they become equal in size. This causes you to remember the day of death where everyone is equal and no one is superior to the other.

Some customs that are connected with *havdala* include a popular belief that after the blessing, the hands are placed upon the eyes, or some take some of the wine in their fingertips and pass the fingers over the eyes for its mysterious healing power, or some put their hands in their pockets as a symbol of *beraha*, blessing and prosperity.

Buena semanas; semanadas buenas y claras. (Have a good week.) *Salud y vida.* (Health and life.)

April 1977   Nisan/Iyar 5737

Un Cavretico

The Passover *seder* is the grand scene, when we relive the events that led to *zeman herutenu* (time of our freedom), the birth of our people and the forming of the beginning of our national free life.

On the two first nights of *Pesach*, when we conclude the *Hagadah* (Passover service), where we express our gratitude to *Hashem* for our deliverance from slavery to freedom, we then have a few traditional songs that we sing. Among these hymns, we have the merry rhyme called *Had Gadya* (A Single Kid), or as we Ladino speaking Sephardim call it: *Un Cavretico*. It's so named after the first two words of this folk-song, recurring as a refrain at the end of the ten verses.

This *Had Gadya* was written in Aramaic; it's not Hebrew. Our Sephardic scholars translated it into our own Ladino language and they even set a tune to it. The origin and composer of this song is unkown. Some sages say it was modeled after a very early French song and that the famous Rabbi Yehuda Halevi who lived around the 1100s wrote a beautiful commentary for it. The first time it ever appeared in print was in the Prague *Hagadah* published in 1570. Although it sounds like a nursery rhyme, our *hahamim* say that it's a very serious piece demonstrating that after centuries of suffering under different nations, Israel survived and those nations perished. I will now explain the various verses.

Un cavretico ke me lo merco me padre por dos levanim. (A kid that my father bought for two coins.) The *cavretico* (the kid) represents the Jewish nation. The father represents our Father in Heaven, *Hashem*, who redeemed Israel through the two leaders, (the two *levanim*), Moses and Aaron in Egypt. Then start the eight verses, representing the eight nations that subjected us to all the terrible and brutal suffering and persecution throughout the many centuries.

Y vino el gato y comio a el cavretico. (And then came the cat and ate the little kid.) The cat represents Assyria and Sennacherib their king, who exiled and dispersed the ten tribes of Israel from their land of Israel to all parts of the world.

Y vino el perro y mordio a el gato. (And then came the dog and bit the cat.) The dog represents Babylonia and Nebuchadnezzar their king, and the loss of our first commonwealth.

Y vino la vara y aharvo a el perro. (And then came the stick and beat the dog.) The stick represents Persia, where the story of Esther happened and the Jewish people were still in *galuth* (diaspora).

Y vino el fuego y kemo a la vara. (And then came the fire and burned the stick.) Fire represents the *Yavanim*, the Greek-Syrians, who almost succeeded in annihilating us. The story of *Hanukah* happened during this period.

Y vino la agua y amato a el fuego. (And then came the water and put out the fire.) Water represents the Roman Empire and their burning the city of Jerusalem and with it the destruction of our second Holy Temple.

Y vino el buey y bevio a la agua. (And then came the ox and drank the water.) The ox represents Saracens, i.e., Moslems, who conquered and plundered Jerusalem.

Y vino el shohet y degoyo a el buey. (And then came the slaughterer and killed the ox.) The *shohet* (ritual slaughterer) represents the Crusaders who caused so much bloodshed and suffering to our people.

Y vino el malah hamaveth y degoyo a el shohet. (And then came the Angel of Death and slew the slaughter.) The Angel of Death represents Islam and the Ottoman Empire which, at the beginning of their conquest, told all Jews, "You either convert to Islam or you die by the sword." They are still persecuting Jews today in some Moslem countries.

Y vino el santo bindicho el, y degoyo a el malah amaveth. (And then came the Holy One Blessed be He and killed the Angel of Death.) Finally the Most Holy One arrived. We have the *avtaha* (certainty) He will save us again, and show that He stands for the principle of mercy and justice.

March 1973   2 Adar 5733

Purim - I

In reference to the feast of *Purim*, the Talmud says *"Mishenihnas Adar marbim besimha,"* meaning, "beginning with the Jewish month of Adar, we should get involved in happy occasions."

The *Shabbath* before *Purim* is called *"Shabbath Zahor"* by all Jews. However, we the Sephardim have added another two names to this *Shabbath*. One is *Shabbath De Mi Kamocha*. On this particular Saturday we recite that beautiful poem *Mi Kamocha* composed by the illustrious Sephardic poet, Rabbi Yehuda Halevi, skillfully relating the story of *Purim*.

The other name is *Shabbath De Folares*, referring to the type of pastry we Sephardim call *folares*. This consists of baked dough shaped like a hangman's tower, with a hard-boiled egg inserted in the middle. The egg, some say, represents Haman in jail ready to be hanged.

On the eve of *Purim*, Jewish people congregate at their synagogues to hear the *Megillah*, which is a scroll, on which is written the Biblical story of Esther. On this night, children usually bring their various types of noisemakers to *kahal* (synagogue), and when the *hazan* reaches the episode that mentions Haman's hanging, etc., they create quite an uproar.

Remember in our *kahal* on 20th and East Fir? When we finished the *Megillah* we used to go to Behor Condioty's store to buy various sweets such as *mavlatches, halva de susam, soujouk, pitas de susam, pitas de kaymak, loucoum,* and other candies that only Mr. Condioty knew how to make. All this so we could go home and greet our families with a hearty *"Purim alegre and dulce."* (Happy and sweet *Purim*.)

On the afternoon of the day of *Purim*, it is customary to have a family *Purim* party, at which time we're bid to indulge in a few drinks. All this to express our joy and our thanksgiving to the Almighty who redeemed us and turned our sorrow to joy and our mourning to holiday. The rules also command us to remember the needy on this day, as well as sending gifts to one another.

Some people used to play at deciphering riddles. The *Midrash* quotes one riddle that the Queen of Sheba asked of Solomon to test his wisdom:

One woman said to her son:
Your father is my father;
Your grandfather is my husband;
You are my son;
And I'm your sister.

King Solomon's answer: This mother is one of the daughters of Lot who were with child by their father. (Read the whole story in the book of Genesis, chapter 19).

Riddle number two (the Queen of Sheba asked King Solomon)

Seven depart;
Nine enter;
Two pour;
One drinks.

King Solomon's answer: Seven days of woman's uncleanness, nine months of pregnancy, two breasts of the mother, at which the one child is nourished.

February 1975   Shevat/Adar 5735

Purim - II

All of us humans, regardless of any religious affiliation, are supposed to show our gratitude and appreciation to our Maker for any favors or miracles that He has made happen for our benefit.

However, the Jewish sages, understanding human weakness, did not want to leave this duty of saying "thank you," to chance. So they made it mandatory, incorporating certain prayers in our liturgy, and in the case of *Purim*, they made it a very solemn duty to listen to the *Megillah* reading, both night and morning.

In celebrating *Purim*, which represents our deliverance from our archenemy Haman, we Sephardim evolved certain customs. Before *Purim* we sing:

Purim, Purim lanu,
Pesach en la mano,

Ya vino Enverano,
Para ir al kampo.

Translation:
It is our *Purim,*
Passover is at hand,
Spring is coming,
Time to go to the country.)

The *Shabbath* before *Purim* is officially called *Shabbath Zahor,* because on that Saturday in *kahal* (synagogue), we take out an additional *Sefer Torah* in which we read a portion that starts with the word "*zahor.*"

However, we Sephardim have two other names for this particular Saturday. We call it *Shabbath De Folares,* and *Shabbath De Mi Komocha.* For the word *folares,* ask your grandma to make you some (see p. 77). (*Folares* is a Ladino word for some dough shaped like bars of a jail with a hard boiled egg in the middle, baked. We have Haman (the egg) stuck right in the middle of these bars and he can't get out. He's in jail.) The reason we also call it *Shabbath De Mi Kamocha* is that we read, on this particular Saturday before *Purim,* a beautiful poetic composition by the Sephardic philosopher Rabbi Yehuda Halevi. This composition starts with the Hebrew words *mi kamocha,* and in a very masterful way recounts the story of Purim. What makes this work more fascinating is that the author ends every sentence with a quotation from our Bible that ends with the Hebrew word "*lo,*" skillfully weaving and fitting it into the story. In years past we used to read this *Mi Kamocha* in Ladino.

How many of you remember, when we came out of *kahal,* we used to run over to Behor Condioty's candy store on Yesler Way, and buy *mavlatches, halva de susam, halva colorada, dulce de sharope,* take it home and say "*Buen Purim, buenos anyos*".

Some families would get together on the night of *Purim,* others for *Seudath Purim* (*Purim* dinner) on the next day in the afternoon, and start singing from a little Ladino book called *Alegriya De Purim* (*Happiness of Purim*), which is full of humorous poems and compositions. One very popular song started like this:

Empesar quero contar echas Del Dio Alto
De lo que quero mentar, nada yo no falto.
Con rizo y canto, y kon gran plazer
Porque Haman el mamzer

Mos cujo mataromos
Tambien atemarmos.

Translation:
To start I wish to recount deeds of the Almighty G-d
With what I wish to curse, there's nothing missing.
With laughter and song, and with great pleasure
Because Haman the illegitimate one
He wanted to kill us
And also to annihilate us.

Then the refrain:
En Shabbath lunforkaron,
Alhad lonteraron. Hey!

Translation:
On Saturday they hanged him,
on Sunday they buried him. Hey!

Then this book contains the very hilarious and comical *Ketuba De La Ija De Haman* (The Marriage Certificate of Haman's Daughter), *Hashkava De Haman* (Haman's Memorial Service), *El Ashugar De La Ija De Haman* (The Bridal Dowery of Haman's Daughter).

Among other *komplas de Purim* (songs of *Purim*) in the book, *Alegriya De Purim* (*Happiness Of Purim*), you will find a long poem which starts on Page 67. Here are a few samples

#53
La vizindad adjuntavos,
Beveh y enborachavos
A bayla alevantavos,
Ke ansina es el dever.

Translation:
The neighborhood gets together,
We drink and get drunk,
Get up to dance,
For thus it is our duty.

Refrain:
Biva el Rey,
Biva yo,

Bivan todos los Judios,
Biva la Reyna Esther,
Ke tanto plazer mos dyo.

Translation:
Long live the King,
Long live I,
Long live all the Jews,
Long live Esther the queen,
That she gave us so much pleasure.

#56
Beve el vino a okas,
Muchos biscochos y roskas,
Ke no esten kedas las bokas,
De komer y de bever.
Refrain: Biva el Rey . . .

Translation:
Drink the wine by the gallons,
Many biscuits and pastries,
That the mouths should not be still,
From eating and drinking.
Refrain: Long live the King . . .)

#58
Purim y blanco
Muy alavado,
No lo deshesh de bever.
Refrain: Biva el Rey . . .

Translation:
Purim and white
Are greatly praised,
Do not quit drinking.
Refrain: Long live the King . . .)

#63
Los Francos uzan pidrizes
Buen tabaco de narizes
De afeda bilibizes,
Que es meze para bever.

Refrain: Biva el Rey . . .

Translation:
The French use small stones,
Good tobacco of noses,
From nauseating dried chickpeas,
Which is an hors d'oeuvre for drinking.
Refrain: Long live the King . . .

Buen Purim - Buenos Anyos. (Have a good *Purim* and good years.)

December 1976   Heshvan/Tevet 5737

Hanukah - The First "Entebbe"

Haneroth halalu. . .(These candles we light . . .--*Hanukah* prayer)
We light these candles to commemorate the wonderful miracle *Hashem* (G-d) worked for us during the period of the *Hashmonaim* who defeated the *Yavanim* (Greek-Syrians) and restored the Holy Temple service to its full glory again.

The story of *Hanukah* dealing with the *Maccabees'* victory over the *Yavanim*, who wanted to impose their ungodly will and their lifestyle on the Jews is very well-known by all. But not everyone is familiar with the personal and very private reason why the five *Hashmonean* brothers were aroused to action.

Rambam mentions it when he says: *Upashetu yadam bivnotehen*, meaning that the *Yavanim* not only took away all the property belonging to the Jews, but they also "dominated and mistreated their Jewish daughters." Rashi, in his commentary on the *Talmud* (Sab. 23) adds a couple of details and says, "Whenever a Jewish bride was ready for marriage, the immoral high officers of the *Yavanim* would capture this young lady and would force her to have relations with them the night before the wedding." We still need to be enlightened further, so we find a complete story in a book called *Ma'ase Hanukah*.

During this struggle, this book says, the *Yavanim* enacted the above immoral law, and this indecent and vicious practice went on for three years and eight months.

Then it happened that the daughter of Matatya (Matathias), the high priest, got engaged to be married, and when the governor heard of this coming wedding, he sent some of his officers and she was brought to the govenor's mansion. When her five brothers heard of this, they just couldn't bear this disgrace to their sister. So they formulated a super-secret Entebbe-like scheme to rescue their sister from the Greek soldiers. This plan worked perfectly, and after a daring and heroic raid on the palace, they not only freed their sister, but they also rescued many other Jewish young brides.

People are still talking about the Entebee affair that was heroically carried out this last Fourth of July by our Israeli supermen. All of us are very proud of the fantastic way they executed their strategic plan.

The same type of miracle happened during the Hashmonayim period of Hanukah. And so we call it "the first Entebbe."

The Saturday before Hanukah, we read the perasha called *Miketz* (not this year, though). This *perashah* tells the story of Joseph who was elevated to the high office of prime minister in the court of Pharaoh. So our Sephardic humorists in Turkey composed a nice little ditty to suit the occasion.

Vayi Miketz Birmuelos Con Miel
Paro' Los Aziya, Yoseph Se Los Comiya.
Hanukiya - Bayla Tu Tiya
Hanuka - Bayla Tu Vava

And it came to pass, fried doughnuts with honey
Pharaoh made them, Joseph ate them
Menorah - your aunt dances
Hanukah - your grandmother dances

Children play the "dreydel" (four-sided spinning toy) on *Hanukah*. This dreydel is a purely Ashkenazic custom. We Sephardim in America adopted it. This "*furuldac*" contains four Hebrew letters (one on each side) *nun, gimal, he* and *shin*, reading *Nes gadol haya sham*, which means "A great miracle happened there."

Some have a custom of playing cards on *Hanukah*. According to some authorities, this custom came about when the *Yavanim* issued a decree prohibiting any Jew to study the *Torah*. Some people who couldn't tolerate a life without *Torah*, devised a plan whereby they studied and discussed *Torah* while holding some playing cards in their hand. If the "Gestapo" soldiers would drop by on this group, they would pretend they were playing cards.

January 1973   Shevat 5733

Burying Holy Objects
(Yevar La Ley)

Aside from burial, there are several other occasions at which time Jewish people go up to the cemetery, referred to as *beth ahayim* (house of the living). For example, such as going to unveil a tombstone, or going to make a "visit" to our dear departed, or going to say prayers on *Erev Rosh Hashanah* or *Erev Yom Kippur*.

One such special event that was prevalent in the early days of our Seattle Sephardic community was the custom of making a pilgrimage to the cemetery for the purpose of *yevar la ley*, literally "to carry the law." This was done probably once every three years, and most often coincided with the Sunday or the week of *Lag La Omer*.

To understand this practice, we would do well to review, in short, the rabbinical rule that anytime any religious object got worn out or became unusable, rather than throw it in the junk heap, we are bid to put it away in the *geniza* (a small storeroom or a cupboard). This is done to avoid the desecration of the name or names of G-d that these objects might contain. A torn out page from a Bible, or an old *mezuza* contains the name of G-d. It's our duty to treat these names of G-d with dignity and respect and not to discard them wantonly, without regard to its sacred contents.

Every synagogue has a *geniza* where members bring in their worn out leaves from *tefilah* (prayer) books, old *taleths* (prayer shawls), *mezuzoth* (small parchment with biblical passages affixed to doorpost), *tefilin* (phylacteries), etc. When these storerooms or cupboards get too full, all these contents of the *geniza* were gathered and taken to the *beth ahayim* to be buried in a special grave set aside for this purpose.

In our Seattle Sephardic community, when the men in charge had determined that there was enough *ojas de ley* (torn pages from sacred books, etc.) to warrant such a pilgrimage to the cemetery, this *geniza* material was filled up in several gunny sacks. The general public also accompanied this procession, which included singing and dancing. People today still talk about this as a very unusual and happy occasion.

When the people reached the cemetery, the chairman then would announce that there were so many gunny sacks filled with *la ley* and that each gunny sack was to be auctioned off, the highest bidder thus acquiring the privilege of accomplishing the *mitzva* of *enterar la ley*, or burying that particular sackful in the appropriate "grave," and so the chairman would sing, "*Kuanto dan por el primer saco de la ley?*" ("How much is offered for the first sack of the law?") Each gunny sack that was sold was accompanied to the place while the audience would sing appropriate songs including *Bar Yohay*, a song which Jewish people usually sing on *Lag La Omer* in tribute to the memory of the saintly *tanna* Rabbi Shimon Ben Yohay who died on *Lag La Omer*.

After this ceremony, naturally, delicious refreshments followed, including *raki* (licorice-flavored raisin brandy), *guevos haminados* (hard-boiled eggs), *azitunas* (olives), *pishcado salado* (pickled fish), *pishcado frito* (fried fish), and most times *portucales* (oranges) for dessert.

Somehow, we haven't seen this custom lately. Is it because we haven't got enough "*geniza* material" or not enough *ley*?

Chapter Five

Sephardic Personalities

May 1977   Iyar/Sivan 5737

The Ramban

The title Ramban stands for Rabbi Moshe Ben Nahman. He was an illustrious Sephardic scholar who was born in the city of Gerona in Spain in the year 1194 and passed away in *Eretz Yisrael* in 1270. Just as other scholars refer to the Rambam as Maimonides, the same way they refer to the Ramban as Nahmanides because his father's name was Nahman.

This article doesn't pretend to be a real biography of our famous Rabbi Moshe. That would take a whole book to cover his colorful life. I read a few interesting facts about his life and so I would like our *La Boz* readers to read about it.

Rabbi Moshe Ben Nahman is very well known for his disputation with the apostate Jew Pablo Christiani in Spain. As an aftermath of that famous debate, Rabbi Moshe was exiled from Spain for two years. He decided not to return to his native land, but instead he would go to *Eretz Yisrael* to spend the rest of his life there. That was his fondest wish, to live in the Holy Land.

Despite his advanced age (he was already seventy-three years old at that time), and despite the dangers of a long sea and land voyage, he arrived in Israel on the ninth of Elul in the year 1267. He was very astonished and very saddened to find the city of Jerusalem in shambles. There were no Jews left. They had all run away in the year 1240 when the Mongols and Tatars plundered the city and nearly burned it all down.

After looking around, he found only two Jews (brothers) who were dyers by trade. He made contact with some Jews who lived in other nearby towns in *Eretz Yisrael*. He invited some of them to come back to Jerusalem and establish themselves there and so, gradually, he was able to form a small community. First there was no *Sefer Torah*, no synagogue. He was able to obtain some *sefarim* from the city of Shehem from some Jews that fled there from the Jerusalem massacre. He also found a vacant building which he converted into a temporary synagogue where they held services for some time. Later on he opened up a school and established a *yeshiva*.

As soon as some young men heard about this *yeshiva* that was headed by our Rabbi Moshe, they flocked to hear his lectures, from as far away as Baghdad and other places. Of all the other cities in *Eretz Yisrael*, he chose to live in Jerusalem because, as he says in his commentary, "anyone who prays in *Yerushalayim* is considered as if he prays directly in front of the Throne of Glory, because the gates of heaven are open there to hear the prayers of the Jewish People." Later on, for some reason, he moved to the city of Acco (Acre).

Although he wrote many important works on *halacha* such as *Torath Ha'Adam*, *Hiddushim* (novellae) and others, his popularity was widespread with the lay Jews because of his superb commentary on the Pentateuch. This commentary was recently translated into English. Our synagogue has this English two-volume work, which besides being an excellent explanation of the *Torah*, it also contains many lessons which make one understand our religion much more clearly and fully.

A *derasha* (sermon) he delivered when he lived in the city of Acre has been preserved and has been published. Also a very beautiful and interesting letter he wrote to his son Nahman in Spain has been preserved and published along with his other writings.

Recently, someone found a gold ring, with a Hebrew inscription, near the city of Acre in Israel. After careful examination, experts determined that this gold ring (or signet) belonged to the Ramban. They also figured, since Rabbi Moshe lived in the city of Acre or near that area, and the inscription on the ring was close to his signature, he must have lost it around there during one of his walks. This ring was donated to the Sephardic Museum in Jerusalem and is on display there now for all those interested to see.

Zehuto yagen alenu, amen. (May his merit protect us, amen.)

November 1973   Heshvan 5734

The Radbaz

When my son in-law, Eugene Normand, visited Seattle last Pesach with his family, he presented me with a very fascinating book, in English, entitled *The Life And Times Of Rabbi David Ibn Zimra* (Radbaz, for short). This book was written by Dr. Israel M. Goldman of Baltimore, Maryland.

Rabbi David, a Sephardi, was thirteen years old when Spanish Jews were cruelly uprooted from their native Spain in 1492. After short stays in Fez, Morocco, Safed, and Alexandria, he finally settled in Cairo, Egypt. When Sultan Selim conquered Egypt in 1517, Rabbi David was officially named as chief rabbi of Cairo.

In rabbinical circles, Rabbi David is widely known and recognized as a great authority, because of the thousands of *responsa* or *sheeloth uteshuvoth*, meaning "questions and answers." These answers had the weight of authority as final legal decisions. These decisions were later compiled and published by either the family of the author, or by his students or admirers. The questions were mailed to Rabbi David from many communities and from many rabbis that were confronted with some problem to which they wanted legal decisions.

The answers to these queries most often contained a maze of complicated reference to Talmudic and rabbinic writings. This, obviously, is beyond our aim in this short article. We'll confine ourselves to other benefits that are derived from these *responsa*, and that is, the historical tid bits and information that are incidentally contained in these questions and answers.

It seems that Jewish authors very seldom wrote books that were dedicated, specifically, to history as such. There are some, of course. That is why Dr. Goldman, in writing this book, deserves all our admiration. Dr. Goldman examined literally thousands of these long and intricate decisions to glean some pertinent historical information to fit into its rightful topic on their own right. It will suffice to name but three of his correspondents. The well-known cabalist, Rabbi Yitzhak Luria, who later became known as the famous Ari, Z"L, was one. Another was the very great Rabbi Bezalel Ashkenazi, who became one of the greatest Talmudists of his time. Another of Rabbi David's students was a certain Rabbi Shemuel Halevi, who later got a position as rabbi of the island of Rhodes. From the hundreds of questions that this   Rabbi   Shemuel asked of Rabbi David, Dr. Goldman was able to write in his book, a whole chapter on the social and religious conditions that existed and related to the Jews of Rhodes in the 1500s.

A certain Rabbi Yitzhak Akrish (see p. 93, v 34) lived in Rabbi David's house for ten years and in speaking of Rabbi David's library, he says, "whenever I would earn some money, I would hire scribes to copy some of his choice books, among them volumes which neither my father nor my father's father had ever seen. It would almost be unbelievable to recount all of them." These were in addition to the regular books.

Rabbi David Ben Zimra lived to a ripe old age of ninety-six. May his memory be a source of blessing to all the world. Amen.

March 1982   Adar/Nisan 5742

Rabbi Eliyahu Capsali - I

Thanks to the concerted efforts of Rabbi Maimon, our Sephardic Bikur Holim Scharhon Library is being filled with the most valuable books, both in Hebrew and English. It is a terrific opportunity for those members who are so inclined to come and borrow some. There is a large variety to satisfy everyone.

The latest addition is a two volume set named *Sefer Eliyahu Zota* written around the middle 1500s by a very fascinating scholar. His name was Rabbi Eliyahu Capsali, born in Candia in the island of Crete. He hailed from the same family as Rabbi Moshe Capsali (see p. 55) who was the first *Haham Bashi* when the Turks captured Constantinople in the year 1453. Incidentally, Candia is the city of origin of all the Candioty family who later came to Turkey, mostly in the city of Gallipoli, and some eventually came to Seattle.

These two books I mentioned above contain a history of the Jews of the Turkish Empire as well as a section on Spain and Portugal. Rabbi Eliyahu personally saw many of the Spanish-Jewish refugees and he recounts their sad plight. There is enough material to report in these *La Boz* articles for many, many years. However, I will just select a couple of startling facts for today. Perhaps in our later editions I will continue with a few more.

For instance, most historians claim that the Sephardic Jews first settled in Spain after the destruction of our second *Beit Hamikdash* (Holy Temple), after the year 70. They were taken captives by the Romans, marching from Jerusalem through North Africa and then going across to Spain. (See p. 3)

Not so, Rabbi Capsali says. He claims that some exiles, belonging to the tribe of Judah, along with the Levites and Cohens, left Jerusalem during the destruction of the first *Beit Hamikdash* by the Babylonians around the year 568 B.C.E. and, instead of going to Babylonia, they set out in the opposite direction. After years of wandering through Libya, Algeria, Tunisia and Morocco, they finally made their way across to Spain. In fact, he says, when the Persian King Cyrus (*Koresh*) gave the Jews permission to return to Jerusalem and rebuild the Second Temple, these Spanish Jews, because they were so far away, never returned to the Holy Land.

Spain was for a long time occupied by *Yishmaelim* (Moslems), until the Christians joined forces and chased these Moors away from Spain. What we call the Golden Age of our Sephardim in Spain, all happened under the Moorish rule.

Rabbi Capsali says that these early Jews who settled in Spain, eventually established congregations. For example, the community of the city of Toledo was originally called by these pioneers Toletola, so called from the Hebrew word *teltol*, meaning "hardship" for the long and arduous journey they had to endure on their way from Jerusalem. Then centuries later, another group of these early Jewish exiles arrived at a town close to Toledo, which they called Makeda, named after a town with a similar name in Israel. And another group established a congregation in a town which they called Lucena, named after a town in Israel called Luz.

After a long time in history, when Christianity had spread throughout most of Europe, including Spain, Christian children were taught by their clergy that the Jews killed their Christ. Centuries of this type of teaching resulted in persecution, torture and terrible devastation against all Jews. However, Rabbi Capsali says, the Jews of Toletola, etc., were, from early times, spared from all this persecution. In fact, he says, other European rulers had imposed a special, unjust and unfair tax on all the Hebrew inhabitants of Europe. But, since the Jews of Toletola, and other early settlements, were not present in Jerusalem at the time of the crucifixion, and therefore did not take part in killing Jesus, the rulers decided that these Spanish Jews should be exempt from paying all these unfair special Jew taxes. But, later in history, when the Catholic clergy, in conjunction with the popes, objected to this exemption, they changed the laws, and all Spanish Jews were subjected to persecution and heavy taxation.

Although Rabbi Capsali's book has been quoted by eminent historians, it was for a long time buried away in manuscripts in the British Museum and such. It was only recently that a committee was formed to edit and publish this two-volume set in Hebrew. The committee consisted of many scholars, including the well-known Meir Benayahu (see p. 310), a prominent and prolific writer from Israel.

There are many fascinating stories contained in these books. We will probably report some in some future issues of *La Boz*.

April 1982   Adar/Nisan 5742

Ribi Eliyahu Capsali - II

In last month's *La Boz* article, we reported the interesting addition to our synagogue library -- that of the two-volume set of books called *Sefer Eliyahu Zota* by Rabbi Eliyahu Capsali of Candia on the island of Crete.

The unique style the author employs is so captivating that one feels he is reading a masterpiece. In retelling these stories Rabbi Capsali displays an enormous knowledge of Hebrew literature, quoting select phrases from the Bible, the Talmud, etc., and yet manages to connect them all and create a very charming and a very skillful narrative.

Today I would like to report a story that was told to him by what he calls *Anusim* (*marranos*) who, on their way to Constantinople or Salonika or other cities, used to stop in Candia. Rabbi Eliyahu realized that these *Anusim*, or formerly secret Jews, were running away from the brutality and the tortures of the Spanish Inquisition.

Rabbi Eliyahu tells us that even thirty years after the great expulsion of 1492, there were whole families leaving Spain to find a free land where they could relax and find new homes, where they could practice their beloved Jewish religion openly, without the constant fear of being burned at the cursed *auto da fe*.

Some of these *Anusim* had achieved a high degree of economic and political reputation. So the stories they told him were not just gossipy rumors but very reliable information, coming from sources that were very confidential -- first hand accounts told by people who saw it happen.

The story Rabbi Eliyahu tells in great elaborate detail is one that proves that the Spanish King Ferdinand was of Jewish ancestry. There was a very beautiful girl living in Spain. Her name was Palomba. Besides her striking beauty she was also highly educated, attaining a degree of aristocratic refinement and an admirable charm. Palomba was eventually married to a very handsome Jewish young man, equally educated, belonging to an aristocratic home. They lived in a high class mansion situated in the suburb of a large city.

One day, Palomba decided to go to the city on a shopping trip. No sooner had she left her home with her servants than a nobleman happened to see her and began to marvel at her exquisite beauty.

The name of this Spanish nobleman was Fadrique Enriques Almirante de Castilia, one of the most loved governors of one of the Spanish provinces, with close official association with the king. Time passed and Almirante could not forget Palomba. He fell madly in love with her, so that one day he managed to trick her to come with him and he finally seduced her.

Palomba, feeling a terrible guilt, told her husband about this sordid affair. Her husband, who could not bear the shame and the embarrassment, left her. Soon, she discovered she was pregnant and subsequently bore a very handsome son.

Word reached Almirante who became sure that this young son was his own flesh and blood. So Almirante took the boy, brought him to live with him at his palace and afforded him an excellent education, fit for a prince.

At first Palomba refused to give up her son, but she was soon compelled to agree. When the young man grew up, Almirante had him marry a princess who bore him four daughters. Three of these daughters were eventually married to princes of the royal family. The fourth daughter was married to the *Rey* (King) *de* Aragon. Out of this union was born a son, Ferdinand.

The leaders of the Spanish Jewish community including the famous Don Avraham Seneor, who knew of Ferdinand's Jewish ancestry, rejoiced at the fact that this King Ferdinand would be very tolerant in his treatment of his Jewish subjects.

Unfortunately, history and fate decided differently, and as it turned out it was this very same Ferdinand and his Queen Isabella, who ultimately were responsible for the cruel and heartless edict of the expulsion of our Sephardic ancestors from Spain. (See p. 30.)

February 1981   Shevat/Adar 5741

Ribi Yitzhak Akrish

Have you ever read a novel where one of the characters in the
story goes through so many terrible ordeals that you start feeling sorry
for him and, instead of things getting better, problems seem to pile up,
one on top of another? That's the exact cheerless feeling I had when I
read the dismal story of Rabbi Yitzhak Akrish. It just grips your heart
and leaves you so depressed.

Yitzhak was three years old when his father, along with the rest of
the family, had to leave Spain in 1492, as victims of the dreadful
expulsion. They landed in Naples, when again, in 1495, they were
forced to leave because of persecution. They moved on and settled in
the great Sephardic metropolis of Salonika (see p. 15), where young
Akrish received a first class Jewish education from the Sephardic
scholars and teachers in Salonika.

After a horrible accident, *El Zavali de Akrish* (Pathetic Akrish)
was left a cripple in both legs. This must have shattered all his dreams
for the future. Others would have settled down to a life of futility. But
not our Yitzhak. He was a man with a tough will. Despite his
handicap, he decided to travel to Cairo which, at that time, contained a
large Sephardic community, where the chief rabbi was a wealthy
gentleman and a revered scholar by the name of Rabbi David Ben
Zimra (see p. 88).

Rabbi David took Yitzhak under his protection and engaged
Akrish to be a private tutor for his children and grandchildren. As
Akrish tells us in an introduction to a book he later published:

> The best ten years of my life were spent at the home of the
> eminent Rabbi David Ben Zimra. He provided me with
> lodging, food and he gave me two gold florins a month.
> Rabbi David had a tremendous and fantastic library
> containing a large amount of important and rare books.
> Whenever I would earn some extra money, I would hire
> scribes to copy some of Rabbi David's choice books and
> manuscripts, among them volumes which neither my father,
> nor my father's father had ever seen. It would almost be
> unbelievable to recount all of them.

When at an advanced old age, Rabbi David Ben Zimra moved to Jerusalem and Safed, Rabbi Akrish left Cairo on his way to Constantinople to try his luck. It seems that he stopped for a time in Candia on the island of Crete.

As his *mazal* (fortune) would have it, he just happened to be in Candia the very year that the church authorities gave strict orders to seize all Talmudic books, and have them all burned in a bonfire. Along with all Jewish books in town, the priests also confiscated Akrish's books. *El povereto de Akrish nasyo sin mazal.* (The poor Akrish was born without any fortune.)

First he approached the local Jewish leaders and asked them to intercede on his behalf to salvage his treasured library, but all to no avail. Then he decided to go himself. Just imagine Akrish limping with a cane, going straight to the governor's palace. As he describes it:

> The palace guards started making fun of me, laughing out loud at the way I was dressed, with a *djube* and *memma* (robe and turban-like headgear), and jesting at my physical condition. Finally I was allowed to see the governor, and with tears in my eyes, I begged, I screamed at the top of my lungs, I fell down on my face imploring, please, give me back my precious books. "My dear governor, you burn my books, you burn my life. Besides, I'm not a resident. I'm only visiting, waiting for the next sailboat on my way to Constantinople." I continued moaning and groaning. Obviously, the governor, filled with compassion and pity at my state of utter desperation, finally returned my books, asking me to leave the island by the next ship, whereupon, I found a Venetian ship owner by the name of Captain Canalete, and with the help of our Creator, reached our destination. Praised be the Almighty who rescues us from bad situations. Otherwise we would have perished long ago.

In Constantinople he got introduced to the very wealthy and influential benefactor, Joseph the Duke of Naxos. Rabbi Akrish was able to convince this kind philanthropist to give him the job of being an editor of a publishing firm, where Rabbi Yitzhak began the publication of many books. He sensed that the Sephardic public was thirsty to read books of historical interest. Among the books he printed was a book called *Kol Mevasser*, recounting the existence of that legendary and mysterious river Sambatyon and the ten lost tribes, as well as a number of letters he had discovered in manuscript. Among them was the very important letter written by Hasday Ibn Shaprut to the king of the Kazars.

He did all this despite his pain and his tremendous hardship. Rabbi Yitzhak would also engage many Christians in dialogue, defending our faith and belief with a great deal of mastery and skill. He died about 1580.

December 1980   Kislev/Teveth 5741

Donna Gracia Nassi

Donna Gracia Nassi was born in Portugal, in 1510, to the aristocratic Sephardic family of Benveniste. For a time she lived the life of a *marrano* (outwardly Christian but secretly observing Jewish practices). She was married to a very rich *marrano* financier, Francisco Mendes-Nassi, the founder of a banking firm in Portugal, with branches in Belgium and France. After her husband died, some members of the infamous Inquisition in Lisbon began to harass the family. This, Donna Gracia saw, as some kind of a bad sign, causing her to fear for her life, so one night in 1536, she left Portugal secretly with her daughter Reyna, arriving first in Antwerp (Anversa), then traveling to Venice.

After many difficulties, the authorities of Venice put her in jail, claiming that she was secretly making plans to run away to Turkey, where she hoped to return to her former religion. Her daughter Reyna had married Yoseph Nassi, Gracia's nephew. He used his influence with Sultan Suleiman to have his mother-in-law released from the Venetian jail.

She came to Constantinople, feeling so grateful to the Almighty, that she began to offer enormous amounts of money to various philanthropic causes. She also built a synagogue in Constantinople which exists to this day, as well as a *yeshiva*. She selected a scholar by the name of Rabbi Yoseph Ben Lev to suggest to her what the communities' needs were. Rabbi Yoseph says in the introduction of a book he wrote, that one day Donna Gracia said to Rabbi Yoseph: "What else can I do?"

Rabbi Yoseph suggested that she establish a Hebrew printing press in Constantinople because there were still a large number of first-rate manuscripts waiting to be published for lack of funds. She agreed, and it wasn't too long before she had a first class printing establishment founded in Constantinople. Rabbi Yoseph selected a good size list of important manuscripts and had them all printed, all at Donna Gracia's expense.

Historians tell us that were it not for Donna Gracia's assuming the responsibility and generosity of paying for a free printing press, many of these important books, would otherwise never have seen the light of day, and would have probably been lost to the Hebrew literary world.

After Donna Gracia passed away, her daughter Reyna continued this great work, and had many more books published at her expense. The *alcunya* (family name) of Nassi is popular in our Sephardic list of family names.

We here in Seattle have the sisters Mrs. Jack Amon, Mrs. Regina Romey, Mrs. Jack Funes, and Mrs. Leo Baroh, whose maiden name was Nassi, and their late brother David Nassi. We remember Mr. and Mrs. Israel Nassi. Who knows? Maybe, if they trace their roots - they could possibly find out they're descendants of that great noblewoman Donna Gracia Nassi.

The above is a very minute portion of the real story of this great generous lady, to give a small taste to those who would be interested in our past Sephardic history. It is our fervent hope that this would kindle some readers' curiosity and induce them to avail themselves of the book that tells the full story of this charming Sephardic lady, who was proud to live as a faithful and dignified Jewess (*Donna Gracia of the House of Nassi*, by Cecil Roth, Jewish Publication Society of America).

July 1974   Tammuz/Av 5734

Ribi Yisrael Najara

A great *haham*, poet and composer, and sweet singer of Israel (*na'im zemirot Yisrael*), was born in Safed around 1530. He moved to Damascus when his father, Rabbi Moshe Najara, was called to that city to fill the important position of chief rabbi and *dayan*.

In one of the books that he wrote, named *Shearith Israel*, he recounts, in poetic form, a brief autobiography and describes the manner and the time in which he got the first impulse to write poetry and the inspiration and love he acquired to write songs. He developed such an intense fondness for the *makams* (Turkish music styles) sung by some Moslem singers in Damascus in his youth, that sometimes he would go to their houses where he would listen and try to get ideas to apply to his own compositions in Hebrew. The rabbis of Damascus were not pleased with these visits so Rabbi Yisrael was criticized severely.

Because of his tremendous talent, he became well-known and he had a great many admirers in different parts of Turkey with whom he corresponded and exchanged poems and letters. One such admirer lived in Brusa, a very important Sephardic community at that time. Rabbi Yisrael was invited to visit Brusa where he stayed quite a while as a house guest of a wealthy friend by the name of Yoseph Ben Muvhar, himself a poet and composer. I am sure they enjoyed each other's company.

Rabbi Yisrael composed over 200 *pizmonim* (Hebrew songs), all original, but as to the tunes that go with the songs, he employed three different methods: 1) some, he adapted existing Arabic melodies to fit the Hebrew words; 2) some, he composed original melodies indicating the exact *makam* and specific tune that this *pizmon* should be sung to; and, 3) some, he composed the lyrics with the instruction that this particular *pizmon* should be sung to the tunes of such-and-such a popular *romansa* or Spanish song. After all, there were still people living who used to hum all these *romansas*. Some of these songs we sing even in our own day on *Shabbath*, one such is *Yoduha Rayonay*. Another is *Ya Ribon Olam*, which was adopted also by our Ashkenazic brethren (sung in their own tune). Also in our own days, there used to be in Edirne, a group of singers called *maftirim* who assembled early every *Shabbath* to sing some of the compositions of Najara and others. Rev. Benaroya [Editor's note: *Hazan* emeritus at Sephardic Bikur Holim Congregation.] can testify to this because he was one of this group in his youth.

Rabbi Yisrael wrote also the original *Ketuba De La Ley* in Hebrew. In this composition, with his fantastic imagination, he portrays the Jewish people as the *hatan* (bridegroom) and he symbolized the *Torah* as the bride, giving a complete list of conditions of marriage in rhymed prose. This was recited on the first day of *Shavuoth* which is the anniversary of the giving of the *Torah* on Mount Sinai. But nowadays we sing another *Ketuba* in Ladino, which was composed about 100 years ago by a *hazan* from Bulgaria by the name of Rabbi Leon Kalai. It begins with the words *es razon de alavar a el Dio*, and it is fashioned very much after the *Ketuba* by Najara, borrowing many of his ideas and terminology.

In his history of the Sephardim, Solomon Rosanes fills (see p. 42) page after page with the writings and compositions of Najara and records quite a few of the names of these *romansas* that Rabbi Yisrael employed to fit to the tunes of the *pizmonim*. Rosanes took pains to employ the talents of his friend Rabbi Eliezer Behar, the chief *hazan* of Roustchuk, Bulgaria, together with the skill of a very fine musician and violinist from Vienna, Mr. Joseph Fleischman. These two artists, the *hazan* and this violinist, set down in musical notes and scales some of the Najara songs. Mr. Rosanes' book contains only two lines of two songs. This, he says, after 300 years of their composition by Najara, just to record them and preserve them for future generations.

Among other works, Rabbi Yisrael wrote also a book dealing with all the *dinim* (rules) of *shehita* (ritual slaughter) in rhymed and poetic form, which not only requires deep knowledge of the subject matter, but also the G-d given talent to fit every rule into a line with perfect rhyme. Unbelievably fantastic!

May his memory be blessed.

November 1975   Heshvan/Kislev 5736

Chelibi Behor Carmona

During their long stay in Turkey, some unique Sephardic personalities had attained great wealth, and some became very prominent in the inner sanctum of Turkish palace affairs. One of these great personalities of the last century was a Sephardic gentleman by the name of Chelibi Behor Carmona. *Chelibi* is Turkish for a man who is given an honorary title, and *behor*, Hebrew for the first-born male child that's born in a family.

His given name was Yitzhak. He was an extremely generous man who helped his brethren, both financially and looking after their welfare in government matters. He even had a *yeshiva* in his home, where a number of *talmide hahamin* (rabbinic scholars) studied daily, Mr. Carmona contributing towards their livelihood.

At first he lived in Haskioy, (a residential district of Istanbul) where he was known as "*shapchi bashi*," meaning that he had full control and an exclusive franchise in the whole of Turkey, in dealing in the business of alum. After a few years, he bought a large mansion near the shore of Bosporus, in the district of Kuru-Cheshme.

However, fate played a very cruel role on him, and his father had warned him of the danger of palace intrigue.

During this time in the history of Turkey, there were some Armenians living in Istanbul who tried to take away from the Sephardim the vast power they wielded in the affairs of the Turkish government. One of these Armenians, by the name of Artin Kazaz, who outwardly showed himself a friend of Carmona, falsely reported to the Sultan that Mr. Carmona was helping the Sultan's enemies. After hearing this report, the Sultan issued a *firman* (a royal edict) to the effect that Mr. Carmona shall be executed for high treason.

So on a Friday night, in the year 1826, while Mr. Carmona and his whole family were enjoying the *Shabbath* meal in his home in Kuru-Cheshme, there came by boat, a Turkish officer with a group of soldiers, at the door, asking to speak to Chelibi Carmona. His younger brother Hezkiah, who was present at this meeting, recounted later, the inhuman and cruel manner that this official killed his brother. After reading the Sultan's order of execution, this officer took a handkerchief from his pocket and choked and killed Chelibi Behor Carmona, right there in the room.

It was a very sad *Shabbath* for the whole Jewish community of Istanbul. Even the *Valide Hanum* (the Sultan's mother), came to pay her respects, because she was a good friend of Mr. Carmona's. The government confiscated all his wealth, his home and all his possessions. His family, most of whom depended on him for their very existence, were forced to seek elsewhere for help.

After many years, Mr. Carmona's grandson moved to London, England, where he became a British citizen. Through the intervention of the Board of Trustees of British Jews in London, and the assistance of the British ambassador in Istanbul, they succeeded in recovering some damages for the Carmona family. Sultan Abdul Mejid published a royal *firman* (proclamation) to have the Turkish government pay 10,000 groshes per month for the maintenance of the remaining members of the Carmona family in Istanbul.

Incidentally, the owner and publisher of the humorous newspaper in Istanbul, called the *Jugueton*, was a son of the nephew of Chelibi Behor Carmona, named Eliya Carmona, who in his autobiography tells some of the story that happened to his grand uncle.

March 1979   Adar/Nisan 5739

Ribi Yehuda Alkalay

Recently, we read about the passing of a Sephardic leader, the venerable Rabbi Yitzhak Alkalay, in New York. This name, Alkalay, brings to mind another famous Sephardi bearing the same *alcunya* (family name).

I refer to Rabbi Yehuda Alkalay, who was born in 1798 in Sarajevo, Serbia, where his father was the *haham*. The family later moved to Jerusalem, where the young Yehuda received an excellent Hebrew education. He developed such a fierce love and affection for the Holy Land that he began preaching the idea of the establishment of a political state in Palestine.

We've all been taught that Theodore Herzl is called the Father of Zionism. Yet, Rabbi Yehuda Alakalay expressed the idea of *Eretz Yisrael*, as the national Jewish homeland in full details fifty years before Herzl did in his book *The Jewish State*. In hundreds of articles written in all the Hebrew magazines of that period (mid-19th century), Rabbi Yehuda set out to describe plans and specific programs. He was the first to suggest the idea of a Zionist congress, the idea of a Jewish agency, and the idea of a Jewish national fund, in order to buy large tracts of land from the Arabs, to make room for the eventual mass immigration of Jews to *Eretz Yisrael*.

He stated that no historian ever considered Palestine as the homeland for the Arabs, or their country, as such. For all practical purposes, Palestine was at that time a territory which belonged to the Turkish Empire. A deal could be worked with the Sultan to obtain rights of settlement. He wrote and sent scores of letters to Jewish leaders in Europe and other parts of the world, begging them to urge the Jewish population in their areas to come to the Holy Land to rebuild it and restore it once again, from utter ruin into a thriving and productive *Eretz Yisrael*.

Some people considered Yehuda as a "wild dreamer," and as an answer to these scoffers he composed and published a book called *Minhath Yehuda*, in which he presents his carefully prepared future programs, in amazing detail, and in extremely sound logic, about his Zionist and nationalist realization of his ideas. He further stated, in view of the then recent blood-libels in Damascus (1840) and Rhodes (1840), and in view of the inhuman persecution and anti-Semitism suffered by Jews in all parts of the world, that the only solution to these pressing problems is to return to Zion, where all Jews can live as full citizens, with our own flag.

It would take a whole book to describe his prophetic and fantastic plans. I don't know whether Herzl or some other early Zionists ever mentioned Alkalay's schemes and programs. Students of Zionism and eminent scholars who have studied Rabbi Yehuda Alkalay's books and pamphlets agree that "all writers who followed, including Herzl, merely reaffirmed Alkalay's plans, without adding anything to it [sic]."

He even suggested the establishment of a national lottery to raise funds to buy houses for the new *olim* (settlers). He wanted to import from Europe expert farmers and wine-growers and many other types of craftsmen of great ability, to attract business to *Eretz Yisrael*, to build a thriving community, and many, many other wise and clever ideas.

He made a very interesting comment about Jews who would still remain in *galuth* (dispersion). He said, "Let us consider ourselves like a merchant who goes to another city on a buying trip, but whose main thought, ever, is to return to his home."

May 1975   Iyar/Sivan 5735

Ribi Haim Hizkia Medini

In another part of this issue of *La Boz*, you will read about our synagogue board's attempt to help out a family of Georgian Jews, probably Sephardic. The Soviet republic of Georgia is situated right next to Asiatic Turkey on the northern seaboard of the Black Sea.

Beyond this republic of Georgia, in the Caucasus region, there's another Soviet region called Crimea. The Jews living in Crimea and Georgia are believed to be the descendants of the ten lost tribes of Israel.

When King Bulan of the *Kazars* adopted the Jewish faith in the year 732, a large number of Persian Jews settled in that region, thus giving it a Sephardic influence, even until recent times.

For centuries, these Jews of the Caucasus and Crimea, kept a modicum of Judaism, until 1866 when Rabbi Haim Hizkia Medini was invited to be their chief rabbi. Rabbi Medini was born in Jerusalem in 1833 to a very old Sephardic family that had settled in Jerusalem several generations before. Educated in the famous rabbinic *yeshivoth* of the Holy Land, he moved to Constantinople where he filled a position of rabbi, teacher, and *dayan beth din* (judge in the rabbinic court). He was popularly known as the HaHaM (an abreviation of Haim Hizkia Medini).

He stayed in Constantinople thirteen years, when in 1866 he was offered the position of chief rabbi of Crimea, which he accepted. When he came to Karasu-Bazar, he found Ashkenazic Jews (Russian) there, as well as a community of Sephardic-oriented Jews who were called *Kirimastim*. The members of the latter community were for the most part illiterate. So he set up schools, he printed, religious books and other textbooks, together with a *Tatar* translation, that language being the one spoken by the local Jews.

He kept this up for twenty-six years improving the spiritual status of the whole Jewish community. However, after these long years of being away from the Holy Land, he began yearning to return to Jerusalem and to his family. He was torn between his very essential work in Crimea and his love for the Holy City. He had a very difficult decision to make. He finally decided to return to Jerusalem, but not before he convinced a number of *Yehidim* (individual Crimean Jews) to emigrate to Palestine.

On his return, he set out to write his very famous work called *Sede Hemed*, a gigantic, ten-volume rabbinic encyclopedia. We have a set in our *kahal*. They were donated by the late Mr. Isaac Varon. These are mainly reference books. I remember Rabbi Baruch Shapiro, of blessed memory, used to refer constantly to these books whenever he was faced with making a rabbinic decision.

In the introduction to the books, Rabbi Medini says, that he prays to the Almighty, that this work of his, may be considered and accepted as his own personal legacy to the readers, since, as he put it, "*Lo zahiti lebanim zeharim*" (I was not merited with having sons.) probably meaning that the male children he had, *leshos* (May this be kept far from us.), had died during his lifetime. It was as if to say, that these books, his labor of love, should take the place of his heirs, and he is leaving them as an inheritance to posterity. What makes these books so valuable is that Rabbi Medini spent a lot of time gathering a large number of quotations and decisions, and setting them in alphabetical order. Rabbi Medini died in Jerusalem in 1904. *Zihrono livraha.* (May his memory be a blessing.)

April 1975   Nisan/Iyar 5735

Ribi Haim Moshe Bijarano

Rabbi Haim Bijarano became *Haham Bashi* of Turkey in 1920 after Rabbi Haim Nahoum resigned to go to France, and other parts of Europe to pursue his political ambitions.

The following facts are taken from a work by Professor Abraham Galante, who wrote extensively about the recent history of the Jews of Turkey.

Rabbi Bijarano was born in Eski Zagara around the year 1846. This town (Zagara) is situated in Bulgaria, a few miles north of Edirne. At that period Bulgaria was part of the vast Ottoman Empire.

After finishing his rabbinic schooling, he became director of a high school in Roustchouk, Bulgaria, where he also taught *Talmud* for a number of years, where the great Sephardic historian, Solomon Rosanes (see p. 42) attended some classes conducted by Rabbi Bijarano.

From Roustchouk he was called by the community of Bucharest, Roumania, where he occupied the post of rabbi and principal of its high school for thirty years. During all this time, in addition to his duties, he carried on a vast correspondence with great scholars of the times such as Jules Simon, Ernest Renan and other great personalities, as well as writing important articles for serious journals of his day such as *Hamagid, Haivri, Havatzeleth*, and the Ladino newspaper, *El Tiempo*, of Istanbul.

Around the year 1910 he was called to fill the high position of chief rabbi of Edirne, where he spent close to ten years. In 1920, when Rabbi Haim Nahuom left the high position of *Haham Bashi* in Istanbul, Rabbi Bijarano was offered the high post of chief rabbi of Turkey, which he accepted. He guided the religious affairs of the Jews of Turkey with dignity until his death in 1931, at the ripe old age of eighty-five.

Professor Galante tells us of an incident which certainly demonstrates Rabbi Bijarano's ability to deal with difficult and delicate situations. This incident took place during the occupation of a part of European Turkey (Thrace) by the Bulgarian army, in the year 1912. At that time, a large number of Sephardim, including, as I well remember, our family, evacuated, leaving our homes out of fear of terrible rumors of the inhumanity of the Bulgarian soldiers, and settled in Istanbul for nine months. That period of our lives we remember as, *el tiempo del majirlik* (the time of refuge).

At any rate, Rabbi Bijarano, holding at that time the post of chief rabbi of occupied Edirne, was invited to a reception given by General Vazoff, commandant of the Bulgarian Army of occupation. Along with the rabbi, the general invited also the heads of the Armenian, and Greek populations, as well as the Mohamedan mufti. Vazoff asked each of the religious leaders their attitudes toward the new regime, and whether they were happy with the present political situation. All of them, except Rabbi Bijarano answered they were now much happier than in the past. When Rabbi Bijarano's turn came, he answered the following.

"Dear General! Our situation can be compared to a woman who lost her husband whom she loved very dearly. In order to live and avoid an unsure future, she was forced to marry again. Could she forget the undying love she felt for her first husband?" On hearing this, General Vazoff said, "I respect your sincerity, and in my opinion, these sentiments you expressed do you a great deal of honor."

Professor Galante knew Rabbi Bijarano personally, and on many occasions enjoyed visits with him, and his rich library.

March 1980   Adar/Nisan 5740

The Alliance and Nissim Behar

Some few months ago, in one of the articles in *La Boz* (see p. 62, Missionary Schools), I made mention of Nissim Behar and his difficulties in establishing some schools in Jerusalem.

He was also instrumental in convincing the Alliance to open up schools in various communities such as Brusa, Tekirdag, Chanakale, Edirne, as well as in Morocco. In Jerusalem, his plan included not only elementary schools, but also agricultural and professional schools, where youngsters could be trained in some skills to prepare them to earn an honest living, rather than becoming dependent on charity, or go begging in the streets.

At first, the Alliance would select some promising young men from the above-mentioned Sephardic cities. They would be sent to Paris to study at the expense of the Alliance to prepare these students to come back to the Levantine communities as teachers and school directors in the various schools opened up by the Alliance.

Who was this dynamic man, Nissim Behar? He was born in Jerusalem, around the middle of the 1800s, received his education in Jerusalem as well as in various French schools in Paris. The directors of the Alliance in Paris noticed in the person of Nissim Behar, a man not only endowed with a superb intellect, but also a tremendous talent for organization, with a penchant for hard work and a special zeal for achievement.

The archives of the Alliance in Paris contain hundreds of letters written by Nissim Behar from various cities in Turkey and Jerusalem where he was sent to open up their schools. This correspondence is full of details on the conditions prevailing in the different cities at that period. These letters contain so much valuable information, that historians are drawing from this valuable source a tremendous amount of particulars about the Sephardic past, filling many pages of history.

The Alliance Israelite Universelle, an organization founded in 1860 by six Jewish gentlemen in Paris, did so much for us Levantine Jews, that we really owe it a debt of gratitude. [Editor's note: These six men were: J. Carvallo, I. Cahen, A. Astruc, E. Manuel, C. Netter and N. Leven, secretary to Adolphe Cremieux who served as president of the Alliance for almost twenty years.] Its accomplishments in improving the lot of Sephardim in the last 120 years can fill several books.

Mr. Nissim Behar emigrated to New York in the early 1900s where he continued to work in promoting and encouraging young Sephardim to attend English school classes. He was close to seventy years of age, but his advanced age did not stop him from knocking on doors in the slums of New York, where he would talk and convince recently arrived young Sephardic men and women to attend some type of school. His burning desire was to see the Levantine Sephardim receive at least an elementary education, be it in day school or night school.

He was really a remarkable and gentle man. In February of 1928, under the auspices of Mr. Abraham Elkus, the former United States ambassador to Turkey, a banquet was tendered in honor of Nissim Behar. It was attended by many prominent Sephardim as well as a great number of Ashkenazim who were friends of the Alliance as well as personal friends of Mr. Nissim Behar, who was revered for his devotion and dedication to the educational advancement of his coreligionists.

Nissim Behar died in New York, a very lonely man in the early 1930s.

October 1975   Tishri/Heshvan 5736
Ribi Yitzhak Shaki

Recently, my nephew, Benson Jerusalmi, presented me with a book he had bought in Israel. This fascinating book is a bibliography of all the Ladino books and other publications that have ever been printed, and are now in the possession of the Hebrew University of Jerusalem, and the National Library.

Glancing through this book, I came across the name of a book written by the venerable Rabbi Yitzhak Shaki, of blessed memory. The name of this book is *Milleth De Avoth* (a commentary on "Ethics of the Fathers") or "*Trezor Del Judaizmo, Esplicacion De Pirke Avoth, Biografia De Los Savyos De La Mishna, Los Doveres Del Judaizmo*" I remember seeing this book, and, I also remember I had occasion to go visit the rabbinate in Istanbul, with my father. At that time, in 1924, Rabbi Yitzhak was a prominent member of the Istanbul *beth din*, the rabbinic court, where our family obtained their endorsement, a few weeks before we departed for Seattle. My recollection of this great rabbi is that of an outstanding personality. He was one of the last eminent figures on the Turkish Sephardic scene. He left an indelible mark in the literary world, so great that I hope some day, someone will translate his works into other viable languages so that they will not be forgotten.

Who was this eminent rabbi?

The late professor, Mr. Abraham Galante, who wrote the history of the Turkish Sephardim, has the following to say about this noble Sephardi: Rabbi Yitzhak Shaki was a great Talmudist. He succeeded Rabbi Yitzhak Ariel, as the president of the Istanbul rabbinic *beth din*. He died in August, 1940, at the ripe old age of eighty-eight, and he was buried in the Jewish cemetery in Haydar Pasha, the Asiatic section of Istanbul.

He was the author of the very famous work in Judeo-Spanish (Ladino), *La Estorya Universal*, which is a sixteen-volume set of books of the history of the Jews. Next to the *Me'am Lo'ez*, this set of books was a must in every Sephardi house, as our elders will testify.

As we mentioned above, he also wrote the *Milleth De Avoth,* a superb commentary on the "Ethics Of the Fathers." He also wrote other works which unfortunately were left in manuscript.

After Turkey became a republic in 1923, and new rules were enacted relating to the various religious groups, the government authorized only the head of each religious group of having the distinction of wearing ecclesiastical clothes.

However, at this period of Istanbul Sephardic Jewry, we did not have a *Haham Bashi.* Our eminent Rabbi Yitzhak Shaki was chosen and recognized as the "Head Of the Jewish Nation In Turkey," thus granting him the honor and privilege of wearing the rabbinic apparel. The office was also accompanied with a document bearing his photo, certifying his authority so that in the event of any occasion requiring his identification, he could present this photo-bearing certificate. The same honor and privilege were accorded by the Turkish Government to his successor, Rabbi Rafael Saban.

May his memory be blessed.

March 1976   1 Adar/2 Adar 5736

The "Perek" Of Haribi Reuben

Some years ago, an item appeared in the *Seattle Post-Intelligencer* newspaper of the daily feature known as "Believe It Or Not" showing a drawing caricature of a rabbi. The caption under the picture explained that this was Rabbi Reuben Israel of the island of Rhodes, and that the unusual thing about it was, that he was the direct descendant of a line of rabbis that served in the island for the last 250 years.

At the time we read this item, we were wondering where the creators of "Believe It Or Not" obtained this information, and we found that they got this story from a little book written by a Rabbi Marcus, who traced the history of the Israel family at Rhodes up to the time of Rabbi Reuben who died without having children.

I borrowed this little book from Morris N. Israel of Seattle. Morrie's father was a nephew of Rabbi Reuben, who, for a long time was chief rabbi of the Sephardic community of Roumania and later chief rabbi of Rhodes, where he passed away in the 1930s. I remember when the Ezra Bessaroth synagogue in Seattle, whose majority of members hail from Rhodes, held memorial services at the time of Rabbi Israel's death, paying a last tribute to the memory of Rabbi Israel.

Among the many talents of Rabbi Reuben, I think was that he was a gifted writer. I've read many articles of real substance that he wrote for various Ladino newspapers and other periodicals.

Rabbi Israel published a book in 1924, the first part of which consists of a rich translation of *Pirke Avoth* (the Ethics Of the Fathers) using a lucid, modern Judeo-Spanish (Ladino), which gives the reader a much better understanding of the text. We Sephardim call this *mishnaic* work by the name of *perek*, which we chant in Hebrew and Ladino on the six Saturday afternoons from *Pesach* to *Shavuoth*.

The second part of this book by Rabbi Reuben consists of a variety of original articles of his own, which he calls *Pedashos de Moral, Maximas y Poezias* (Selections of Morals, Maxims and Poetry). To give you an idea of his ingenuity in compositions, I've selected the one on page three which he calls *"Drogas Para Flakeza Moral,"* which loosely translated means, a "Prescription For Moral Weakness." Here's the original in Judeo-Spanish, followed by my own translation into English.

Raizes de saviduriya, simyenta de modestia, yervas de fey (emuna), flores de caridad, espigas de consensya, ojas de sobriyedad (contentes de lo poco) lo todo mojado con agua de sinseredad, y mesclado con azeyte de amor y justisyal echo emplasto, y metido en el corason y los rinyones, esto alimpyara la suzyedad del dezeyo, destruyira los microbes del selo, ara despareser el orgoya y otros defectos, y la moral sera perfecsyonada y solida.

Translation:
Roots of knowledge, seeds of humility, greens of faith, blossoms of charity, stalks of conscience, foliage of moderation, all this rinsed with waters of sincerity, and mixed with oils of love and justice, made into a balm plaster and placed in the heart and the kidneys. This will cleanse the filth of lust and desire, it will kill the microbes of envy and jealousy, will help dissolve the ills of conceit and vanity and other defects, thus morality will become perfect and solid.

March 1977   Adar/Nisan 5737

Harav Hagadol Ribi Bension Meir Hai Uziel

Ever since the story named "Roots" was shown on television, I became curious to discover whether any of our Sephardim had ever traced their genealogy. So I read up on this subject, and I came across a very outstanding one in the family history of the late Rabbi Bension Meir Hai Uziel.

It will suffice, for this article, to name just two of Rabbi Bension's forebears who left an indelible impression on Sephardic history through their scholarship, etc.

In an early document we find the name of Rabbi Avraham Uziel. He's called the "glory of his generation." He lived in Castilia, Spain, and after the expulsion of 1492, settled in Fez, North Africa. In this document, it speaks of Rabbi Avraham taking an active role in restoring peace and harmony to the Jewish community in Fez, after a very disturbing episode that shook the population of that city.

One of Rabbi Avraham's sons, Rabbi Yitzhak Uziel, who was born in North Africa, was called to Amsterdam, Holland, where he filled the position of chief rabbi in that important and rich community in the 1600s. Graetz, the great Jewish historian speaks of Rabbi Yitzhak in glowing terms as a great scholar and author. He further mentions the fact that Rabbi Yitzhak became the teacher of the famous Jewish philosopher Baruch Spinoza, and also the teacher of Rabbi Menashe Ben Israel, the very one who was responsible in making it possible for Jews to live in England once again. They had been banned from England for over 400 years.

Later on, the Fez branch of the family moved to *Yerushalayim* (Jerusalem) where it produced great religious leaders, and where Rabbi Bension was born in 1880. In 1900, at the age of twenty, Rabbi Bension was so advanced in his studies, that he was already a professor of Talmud at the *Yeshiva Tifereth Yerushalayim*, later becoming its director in 1904. In 1912, he was thought of so highly that he was elected chief rabbi of Tel Aviv-Yaffo, one of the most important communities at the time.

Before 1948, when it became the state of Israel, the land owned by Jews there, was called the *yishuv* (settlement). This was true also during the Turkish regime, which ended in 1917. Most of the leaders of the new settlements or the *yishuv* were Jews born in Russia. For some reason the Turkish government did not treat these Russian Jews favorably. The Turkish governor of Palestine, at this time was a man called Jemal Pasha, who used to issue cruel and inhuman statements against these leaders of the *yishuv*. A group of these leaders secretly approached Rabbi Bension who was a Turkish subject, to go see Jemal Pasha and try to convince him to change his attitude towards them. Rabbi Bension requested an audience with Jemal Pasha, and after meeting with him, he succeeded in preventing a number of vicious designs that could have proven extremely disastrous to the *yishuv*.

When Rabbi Yaakov Meir passed away in 1939, the rabbinical electors chose Rabbi Bension as his successor to the high position of *Rishon LeZion*, chief rabbi of Israel. He was regarded not only as the spiritual leader of Israel, but all the Sephardic communities of the whole world looked to him as the religious authority. Among many of his writings, we can mention the book *Mishpete Uziel* where he deals with many problems relating to immediate and modern Jewish questions, which are studied and followed by Sephardim and Ashkenazim alike. In almost all of his decisions, rabbis all over agree that Rabbi Bension adopted a very lenient approach, of course always remaining within the province of the *halacha* (Jewish law). He passed away in 1953, having the *zehuth* (merit) to see the creation of the state of Israel in 1948.

May his memory be a blessing.

October 1971   Tishri/Heshvan 5732

Moshe David Gaon

Very few Jews, outside the Sephardic community of Jerusalem, have ever heard of this late prolific writer, who died in Jerusalem only a few short years ago.

For many years his articles, which were of lasting interest, appeared in the Hebrew periodicals and magazines which published literary and historical material written by famous and important writers. Mr. Gaon confined his articles to Sephardic and literary history.

Among numerous other books and pamphlets that appeared under his name, the one that comes to mind at present is, *The History Of*

Sephardic Jews In the Near East and Israel (in Hebrew). He also wrote a pamphlet called *Maskioth Levav*, which is the sole source we possess that reveals biographical facts about the authors of the famous books *Me'Am Lo'Ez*. In this pamphlet, he gives us interesting tidbits about the author of the first two books, Rabbi Jacob Culi.

The gigantic project that occupied Mr. Gaon's time just prior to his death in 1958 was the collection of nearly all the different newspapers that appeared in Ladino in Turkey.

This vast collection, which consisted of more than 290 various publications was donated to the Ben Zvi Institute of the Hebrew University by Mr. Gaon's son, Yoram Gaon (see p. 117). The Institute handed the job to Moshe Katan who is collecting more publications and cataloging what was started by Mr. Gaon.

In one of Mr. Gaon's writings he tells of an incident that struck him as humorous. He says, one day while shopping at a small Sephardic grocery store in Jerusalem, he saw the proprietor wrapping some *halva* in a piece of paper that he tore from a large bookkeeping journal. On further examination, Mr. Gaon discovered that this particular journal book was one that the secretary of the Sephardic community had kept. Somehow, this book and others like it fell into the hands of this storekeeper who for lack of other wrapping material used the pages of this journal to wrap up his wares like *halva* (sesame paste candy), white cheese, *pishcado salado* (salted fish), etc.

Mr. Gaon was able to extract enough information out of this journal to write a whole chapter of the history of the Jerusalem rabbinate and Sephardic community.

It is virtually impossible to enumerate all the works of the late Mr. Gaon in such a small article, which is very unfortunate. It is a pity that he's not more well known and recognized for the value and greatness of his writings on Sephardic literature and history, which, but for his diligence would have been lost to posterity.

November 1972   Heshvan/Kislev 5733

Rabbi Dr. Nissim Ovadia
(A Great Sephardi Leader)

A memorial plaque was dedicated recently in Jerusalem in loving remembrance of Rabbi Dr. Nissim Ovadia of blessed memory (1890-1942). This took place at the central reception hall of the home of the Sephardic chief rabbi in Jerusalem, which also houses a rabbinical academy.

Among the many prominent personalities that attended this ceremony was Dr. Ovadia's widow, Mrs. Mazal Ovadia, who was given the well-deserved honor of unveiling the plaque. She thanked all present for the distinct honor, as well as for their good wishes.

Mr. Eliyahu Elyashar, the president of the Sephardic community of Jerusalem, spoke in glowing tribute of Dr. Ovadia. He told the audience that he knew Rabbi Ovadia personally. He urged the people there to help Mrs. Ovadia in her work for the maintenance of that academy called the *Metivta*.

Also present was Mrs. Rachel Alhasid, originally from Jerusalem, now living in New York. Mrs. Alhasid was the chairman for the day, which included the unveiling as well as donation of funds to establish a special study-room in the academy. She was instrumental in collecting this fund from a ladies group in New York and she declared she'll continue in this worthy endeavor in tribute to the memory of Dr. Ovadia whom she knew and loved.

Dr. Ovadia was born in Edirne, Turkey. As a young man he went to Jerusalem to further his studies, and attended the *Beth Midrash Larabanim Shel Hevrath Ezra*. In the year 1913, at the age of 23, he began his rabbinical career in Vienna, Austria, serving together with Rabbi Michael Papo, who was rabbi of the Sephardim in Vienna. After serving sixteen years in that city, he became rabbi of the Sephardim in Paris in 1929. He was forced to leave Paris when the Nazis occupied this city and for a time he settled in Lisbon, Portugal. From Portugal, he was called to occupy the post of chief rabbi of the Central Sephardi Congregation of New York under one Sephardic union. Unfortunately he was not able to fulfill that dream due to his untimely passing. He was in New York only a very short time, about a year and a half.

Dr. Ovadia has been called by people who knew him as a born organizer. He was instrumental in initiating the first world-wide Sephardic congress which took place in Vienna in 1925. Subsequently another congress was held in London and another in Amsterdam.

He was a dynamic orator and had the very gifted ability of captivating his listeners with his special charm. He was the editor of the prayer book for daily and *Shabbath* worship called *Tefilath Imanuel*. Those of us who have used this prayer book can testify as to the beautiful way Dr. Ovadia gathered together a number of added features from previously published prayer books, and incorporated them in this *tefila* book, a veritable masterpiece which was received and accepted in all the Sephardic congregations.

He also published two other prayer books, one for *Rosh Hashanah* and one for *Yom Kippur* which he called *Tehiloth Avraham*. He wrote many interesting articles in the publication *Le Judaism Sefardi*, which was the leading "spokesman" for world-wide Sephardim, where he manifested an ardent love for Israel.

Even today, people who knew him, have the firm conviction and declare that if Dr. Ovadia had lived his full life, he would've been able to achieve his fervent hopes of laying the foundation to form a strong world Sephardic union.

There is a movement in Israel today, where they're in the process of writing a biography of Dr. Ovadia and republishing all his writings in one book.

May his memory be for a blessing.

September 1982   Elul/Tishri 5743

Rabbi Mizrahi's Library

In one of the Los Angeles Jewish newspapers, there appeared a picture of Mrs. Regina Mizrahi with Dr. Jose Nessim, holding a book. The caption said: Mrs. Mizrahi, widow of the late Rabbi Solomon Mizrahi of Los Angeles, donated his rare collection of books to Dr. Jose Nessim, a Beverly Hills surgeon, founder of the Sephardic Education Center which is located in Jerusalem.

I personally saw this library grow gradually from a modest sized one to one of tremendous size and value. Many times, when I would visit Rabbi Mizrahi in Los Angeles, he would invite me into his library. He was always adding many volumes, and we would discuss Hebrew literature and compare notes on difficult Hebrew words and their meanings in Ladino.

In 1980, my brother Rabbi Maimon and I paid a visit to Mrs. Mizrahi's house. After we tried to persuade her to donate some of those books to our Sephardic Bikur Holim Scharhon Library without success, she let us each have a couple of books, rare and out of print.

When I came back to Seattle, I found, to my amazement, inside one of the books, a very interesting sheet of paper, containing a list of names. On further examination, I discovered that this list consisted of all the chief rabbis of Jerusalem with the instruction saying that the synagogue called *Rabban Yohanan Ben Zakkai*, through the family of Mizrahi, had the solemn obligation of *echar hashcava* (reciting the memorial) for these rabbis, on the night of *Yom Kippur* for generations. This instruction was made official and binding by what was the official seal of the old *Kahal Kadosh* (Holy Congregation) *Rabban Yohanan Ben Zakay*, which was imprinted at the bottom of the sheet.

I considered this a very rare treasure because this seal belonged to this ancient synagogue, which the Arabs reduced to ruins in the 1948 Israel War of Independence, as this synagogue was located in the old section of Jerusalem.

All the rabbis mentioned in the list were authors of important Hebrew books on religion; men who left their imprint in the Sephardic history in Jerusalem.

All those Sephardim who lived around that old neighborhood had to move away in 1948. In 1973 the three synagogues were rebuilt and restored and I wonder if they still *echar hashcava* for all these great men in the new *Rabban Yohanan Ben Zakkai* synagogue. Rabbi Mizrahi himself used to take part in the services in the old synagogue, and his family was the custodian of this seal, which explains the reason why he had it in his possession.

When Rabbi Mizrahi first came to the United States, he occupied the position of *haham* in the Sephardic community of Indianapolis, Indiana. In the early 1930s he was called to fill the post of *haham* of the Sephardic synagogue in Los Angeles, then called *Ohel Avraham* at 55th and Hoover Streets, and now known as the Sephardic Jewish Center. Sometime in the early 1950s Rabbi Mizrahi left the Los Angeles synagogue and began teaching Hebrew and Hebrew literature, for many years, at the Los Angeles University of Judaism. Rabbi Mizrahi died in 1979, leaving a request in his will and testament that his body be transported to the holy city of Jerusalem to be laid to rest with his pious ancestors. Isn't it ironic that, as it turned out, not only was his body taken to Jerusalem, but his great library was returned there also.

As for the library, Mrs. Mizrahi at first held out and would not donate it, expressing the idea that she had a plan whereby she would like to find an individual to buy it from her and the amount, in turn, she would donate either to a hospital or an orphanage or some such charitable institution of her own choice, thus perpetuating her husband's memory.

Obviously, Dr. Nessim, himself born in Jerusalem, has finally convinced her to donate it to his favorite institution in Jerusalem where it could become available to many book lovers and scholars. Dr. Nessim deserves our sincere thanks and gratitude for his generous financial contribution and for his ambition to provide a suitable place where Sephardic youth can obtain that training so dearly needed. This institution is not a school as such nor a *yeshiva* with classes or text books. It is rather a place where our young Sephardim can be developed into leaders who will be trained to defend our Sephardic cause in Israel, protect our share of national interests and instill in others a love for Sephardic culture and history.

Sephardim from many parts of the world are taking advantage of this worthy institution, with good beneficial results. Two of our own Seattle young men have already availed themselves of this treat. They are Morris Varon, son of Jack Varon and now, this year, Sam Mezistrano, son of Dr. and Mrs. Joseph Mezistrano. We would like to see many more do so in the future.

December 1973   Kislev/Teveth 5734

An Interview - Rabbi Abraham Shalem

In one of the recent issues of *Bamaaraha*, the Sephardic magazine published in Jerusalem, I was pleasantly surprised to see an impressive picture of our friend, Rabbi Abraham Shalem, wearing a *jubeh* (a black rabbinic robe) and *memma* (a turban-like headgear worn by Sephardic rabbis in Turkey), with his Van Dyke beard turned almost white. The picture was probably taken on his recent visit to Israel.

This picture of Rabbi Shalem, is accompanied by a two-page article, an interview by a certain Mr. Ben Avraham, a writer for this publication, who asks the rabbi a series of sensible and appropriate questions, and in turn, Rabbi Shalem answers them in his usual inimitable, charming and articulate manner.

Our readers will remember Rabbi Shalem from the time he was here in Seattle as rabbi of our sister Congregation Ezra Bessaroth from 1959 to 1962 when he won the esteem and respect of all Seattle Sephardim. In addition to his erudite scholarship he is endowed with a sweet, melodious, and pleasant *hazanuth* voice.

Rabbi Shalem was born in Jerusalem in 1928, attended the *Yeshiva Shaare Zion*, and was ordained rabbi by his teacher, the late *Rishon LeZion*, Bension M. Uziel. In 1945, he joined the *Haganah*, and later, during the War of Liberation, he saw action in several Israeli military stations. He did post-graduate work in the rabbinical academy called *Mizrahi*, founded by Rabbi Y. Berman, from which he also obtained a rabbi's diploma.

Rabbi Shalem tells us in this interview that upon the suggestion of Rabbi Uziel, he went to Lima, Peru, where he stayed eight years before serving in Seattle. After he left Seattle in 1962, he went to Mexico City, where he had spent some time before, and where he occupies his present position in another congregation.

This interview is a long and a varied one where he covers a lot of subjects, but one question that he answers is a very fascinating one, and I would like, briefly, to relate it in this article, and that is one on the subject of kosher meat. He says, "When I arrived in Mexico City, the *shohetim* slaughtered about forty head of cattle per week, a very small amount considering the large Jewish population here. After much study of the problem and careful planning, we were successful in lowering the price of kosher meat down to the same price level of the non-kosher meat. We got together with managers of several supermarkets, who agreed to handle our kosher meat. Before this, somehow, the quality of kosher meat was inferior to the other meats. We changed this situation so much and we improved the quality to such a degree that non-Jewish customers are also buying our meats because of its superior quality. Now we slaughter 400 head of cattle per week, besides 4,000 chickens."

He also was instrumental in setting up supervised kosher kitchens in three of the big hotels in Mexico City so that those members who wish to celebrate happy occasions such as weddings and *bar mitzvahs* can enjoy their affairs in a real kosher place. Big signs are posted and public announcements are made in the synagogues stating that rabbis reserve the right to refuse to officiate at any wedding held in any hotels which serve non-kosher meats.

There are a few schools and *yeshivoth*, and for these schools, Rabbi Shalem had competent and qualified teachers brought over from Israel and the United States.

He wrote a book called *Eshed Anehalim* in Castilian Spanish. This book, received widely in all Latin American Jewish communities, deals with daily Jewish laws and customs, which proved very valuable in serving as a textbook teaching the Jewish view and rationale to many laws derived from our Talmud and other books of Jewish thought.

"Do you have plans to return to Israel?" The rabbi's answer: "My fondest hope is, someday, G-d willing, to come back home. My son, who came here originally to further his Jewish studies, is at the present time, in the Israeli military service. My daughter also lives here. Naturally, my rabbinic tasks in our community in Mexico City are so vast and so essential that this fond hope has to wait for a while. Added to this, the fact that a large number of my congregants are very firm in their demand that I stay in Mexico City, and will not grant me the luxury of returning to Israel as yet. But my hope is still unchanged and alive." [Editor's note: Rabbi Shalem has since moved to and currently resides in Israel.]

March 1974   Adar 5734

A Sephardic Movie Star

The following is taken from an interview that was reported in a recent issue of *Bamaaraha*, the Sephardic monthly publication from Jerusalem. The author of this fascinating article, Mr. Reuben Kashani, tells us all about his subject, who is none other than the very famous Israeli singer Yeoram Gaon, (or Yoram in modern Israeli pronunciation).

Yoram was born in Jerusalem in the year 1939. Not many people know that he is the son of that excellent Sephardic author and historian, Moshe David Gaon (see p. 110). The late Mr. Gaon, because of his numerous books and articles on Sephardic subjects, is considered by many as one of the four eminent writers and Sephardic historians of the last few decades. The other three are: Shelomo

Rosanes, Abraham Galante, and Abraham Almaleh, all of blessed memory.

Yoram, in this interview, discloses some glimpses of his early youth and tells of his reverent admiration of his father's vast knowledge and mastery of Sephardic history. He remembers his father spending many days and nights gathering all the available copies of old Ladino newspapers that ever appeared in various communities. His father compiled a full catalogue of these *gazetas* and *journales*, which amounted to more than 300, noting when and where they were published, etc.

Mr. Gaon did not live to see all this printed, but Yoram's family donated all this material to the *Mahon Ben Zvi* (Ben Zvi Institute) in Jerusalem. Let us hope that the *Mahon* will find a qualified man to compile this work all together and have it published.

Yoram also tells us that he remembers going with his father to the synagogue, taking part in the services, and many times helping the *hazan* on *Rosh Hashanah* and *Yom Kippur*, etc. He also tells us of the times when his family used to gather around the festive table, for example on Friday nights, singing together the *pizmonim* recorded in his memories and popular albums.

Yoram played the lead character in the Israeli movie called "*Cazablan*," which has been making a hit in all Israeli theatres as well as here in America. Our friends Leo and Liza Azose saw it on their recent visit to Los Angeles. They liked it very much. This movie contains a very charming song called "*Roza, Roza.*" Yoram was recently brought all the way from Israel to Hollywood on the occasion of the annual presentation of the Globe awards, specifically to sing "*Roza, Roza.*" We were fortunate to see this program on television a couple of weeks ago. It was a delight to see and hear Yoram singing this song. Let us hope that this movie "*Cazablan*" will be brought to Seattle so we can all enjoy seeing it.

Yoram tells us also that his father's hopeful ambition was that either Yoram or any of the other children will continue that type of work in history or Ladino research, and when he was asked if this was included in his plans for the future, his reply was, "Right now I'm busy, but I'm thinking about it."

Yoram is making personal appearances in a few United States cities at the present time, and when he will be able to appear in Seattle we will look forward to hearing him with much pleasant anticipation and say to him "*Baruh haba*, Yoram!!" (Welcome, Yoram!)

Chapter Six

Sephardic Literature and Folklore

August 1974   Av/Elul 5734

Me'Am Lo'Ez - A Sephardic Treasure House

The *Me'Am Lo'Ez* is a multi-volume set of books written originally
in Ladino. This gigantic work was initially started by Rabbi Yaakov
Culi who was born in Jerusalem in the year 1690 and later moved to
Constantinople.

In his lengthy introduction to the first book of Genesis, he tells us
what his motives were for composing this tremendous work. It seems
that Rabbi Yaakov realized that the average Sephardi of his time was
terribly lacking in the knowledge of his past history and that only a
small portion of the Sephardim understood Hebrew and therefore our
Torah, our customs and traditions. So, because of his love for the
Jewish people, he set out to compose this work which would fill this
deplorable need. Rabbi Yaakov published his first volume in 1730 in
Istanbul. The initial 1,000 copies were sold very quickly. What
makes this work so popular?

Our author understood the psychology of his people. He knew
exactly what the people enjoyed and, in his charming way, he made
his books extremely attractive. How? He wrote in Ladino which they
all understood, and used a simple and everyday language. His
principal aim was to explain and elaborate on the Bible. He would
take a given subject in a *perashah*, explain it with quotes from our
Talmud, *Midrash*, Rashi and other Bible commentators. Like magic,
he fit all this skillfully together, weaving the whole story into a
beautiful tapestry, all this many times embellished with parables,
stories, etc., to illustrate and prove a point he wished to make.
Moreover, what makes *Me'Am Lo'Ez* most uniquely beautiful reading

is that the author quotes passages out of books that are no longer in print. He had access to a very rich library which belonged to his good friend and colleague Rabbi Yehuda Rosanes, a very famous dean of the rabbinical academy in Istanbul at the time.

When Rabbi Yaakov came to explain a certain *perashah* and reached a certain portion that contained a Biblical commandment, he would leave and set aside the explaining chores and switch over to write down the specific rules and regulations involved with that particular religious practice. At this point he was quoting other relevant sources, like Rambam, Rabbi Yoseph Caro's *Shulhan Aruch*, and many other famous *poskim* (accepted legal authorities).

For example, where the *perashah* made mention of a funeral, he would stop the explanation of that *perashah*, and go over into setting down the rules of burial, *keriya* (tearing of the garment), funeral practices and all the details about the laws concerning *aveluth* (mourning).

Sad to relate, our author died at the very early age of forty-two, so he was only able to finish up to and including the *perashah* of *Mishpatim*, (roughly half-way through *Shemoth*, the book of Exodus).

This work was continued by another *haham* in Istanbul by the name of Rabbi Yitzhak Magriso who tried very hard to imitate both the style and format of his predecessor and he did an excellent job. He is the one who explained the *Pirke Avoth* (which he inserted in total as part of the commentary on the *perashah* of *Emor* in the book of Leviticus because that corresponds to the time when we Sephardim read it, between *Pesach* and *Shavuoth*). Again, after Rabbi Magriso finished the book of *Bamidbar*, he died, and this work was continued by Rabbi Yitzhak Arugete who completed the book of Deuteronomy. [Editor's note: Beyond the five books of the *Torah*, only a few of the remaining books of the Bible had *Me'Am Lo'Ez*-style commentaries written in Ladino. These include the book of Joshua (Rabbi Yitzhak Arugete), book of Esther (Rabbi Rafael Pontremoli) and the book *Shir Hashirim* (Song of Songs, Rabbi Haim Yitzhak Shaki).]

Almost all of our fathers and grandfathers owned a set of *Me'Am Lo'Ez* and used to read it regularly, either at home by themselves or in *pareyas* (family gatherings) where everyone understood Ladino.

Unfortunately, not very many people speak Ladino nowadays so we owe a very big "thank you" to a modern scholar by the name of Shemuel Yerushalmi who translated this whole work into Hebrew. He started in 1968 when he published the first two books on Genesis and, now, they number fourteen books already. [Editor's note: Since 1974 the Hebrew version has been completed, as well as an English translation of it which is published by Maznaim Publishing Corporation under the title *The Torah Anthology, Me'Am Lo'Ez,* in a multi-volume set.]

We, the Ladino-speaking and reading Sephardim always knew the tremendous worth of *Me'am Lo'Ez* and, now, with these Hebrew [and English] translations, the Hebrew-reading [and English-reading] public is also realizing the remarkable Sephardic treasure house that the Me'Am Lo'Ez is.

November 1980   Heshvan/Kislev 5741

Rambam's Letter To the Jews Of Yemen
(Rambam's Iggereth Teman)

Of the many extraordinary works that Rambam (Rabenu Moshe Ben Maimon, also called Maimonides) wrote, few of us are aware of his three famous *iggeroth* (letters) that he wrote to various communities. We will deal with one of these letters in today's *La Boz* article, *Iggereth Teman.*

Teman is the Hebrew name for the country of Yemen. One day, while in Egypt, Rambam received a letter from the chief rabbi of Yemen, Rabbi Yaakov Ben Nethanel Alfayumis, who described in great detail the terrible condition of the Jews there. On top of all the persecutions, Rabbi Alfayumis writes, there's a man by the name of Shemuel Ibn Abas who converted to Islam in the year 1163, and now, some few years later, initiated an intense campaign to have many of his former coreligionists abandon the faith of their fathers and convert to Islam.

This Abas renegade was quoting many Biblical verses, as evidence of the veracity of Mohammed's being a true prophet. For instance, in the verse Gen. 17:20 in which G-d talks to Abraham about his son Ishmael who's the ancestor of all Arabs, there's a phrase in Hebrew *"bimod meod."* This, Abas claims, is an allusion to Mohammed because the numerical value of the letters of these two Hebrew words is the same as the numerical value of Mohammed.

Another verse he quotes is found in Deuteronomy 33:2, *"hofiya mehar paran."* "He shined forth from mount Paran." This also, he claims, has allusion to Ishmael, because Paran was the traditional dwelling place of all *Ishmaelim*, and therefore of Mohammed.

Another verse is in Deuteronomy 18:15 when G-d tells Moses to accept "prophets only from among your brethren," Mohammed is included because Ishmael was the son of Abraham, and therefore a brother. He used many similar verses, trying to prove Mohammed's authenticity.

Rabbi Alfayumis requested from Rambam, as a respected and venerable sage, advice how to deal with this instigator, who had recently declared himself as a *mashiah* (savior).

When Rambam received this letter, it caused him a great deal of distress. He dedicated a large part of his answer to offer his concern and instill and restore confidence in the Jews of Yemen, telling them to hold fast to their ancestral faith; not to despair, G-d will rescue them.

Rambam first sets out in this scholarly letter to explain, in a long thesis, the cause for the universal hatred the rest of the nations have for the Jewish people. Briefly, he maintains, this hatred is a direct result of their envious feelings for our spiritual and cultural superiority. This intense envy drives them to crush our life-giving *Torah* and its enlightened teachings, to the degree that they want to see Israel wiped out from the face of the earth.

Then, the Rambam tackles this renegade's arguments, which were used to prove that Mohammed should be accepted by all Jews. He takes these arguments, and one by one, he disproves them in a remarkable and skillful manner, demolishing every one of these arguments beyond recognition. It's a delight to read such an orderly handling of all the proffered verses. Rambam then says, if anyone takes a good look at history books, he will discover that all these so-called proofs had already been used many times before. They have been effectively explained away by various authorities, thus dismissing them from having any validity. Rambam says further, that even the Islamic scholars who have studied these contentions have rightfully labeled them as ridiculous, absurd and devoid of logic.

Throughout this beautiful letter, one can observe Rambam's strong love for our *Torah*, plus an abiding devotion to Israel, encouraging the people of Yemen not to give in so easily. Because, as he perceives it, this phony wretch of a man is showing signs of having a deranged mind. He should be in a mental institution, in view of the fact that he set a definite date and a time limit as to when he, himself, will be declared the *Mashiah*. Rambam assures the Yemenite Jews that when this definite date arrives and nothing happens, this stupid turncoat will be exposed as a fake, even by the local authorities.

According to many historians, Rambam's *Iggereth Teman* had a very beneficial and profound effect on the stability of the Jews of Yemen; bringing peace and tranquility for some time. As a matter of appreciation, the Jews of Yemen, for a long time, included Rambam's name to the list of saintly sages, on reciting the *kaddish*.

The story goes that when this Abas was confronted by the king, to either substantiate his words that he was *Mashiah*, by valid proofs, or be executed, he answered, "Your majesty, chop my head off and you will see that I will rise and live again." The king, then sensing a pretext, or a dodging scheme or device, said, "That's the best proof I could ever ask for." Immediately the king ordered the executioner to bring the sword and chop the imposter's head off. That was the end of this *povereto's* (poor wretch) misadventure. May we soon see the downfall of all the enemies of the Jews, like the wild Yassir Arafat and his like. Amen.

July/August 1977   Tamuz/Av 5737

Hebrew Letters and Printing Types

On the page following this article, the reader will see samples of five types of Hebrew letters.

The first, of course, is what we call *letras de Meruba* (letters for writing). These square Hebrew letters are the ones used to write *Torah* scrolls as well as all prayer books and many other important Hebrew works. These Hebrew square letters are also known as *ketav Ashuri* (Assyrian script) and as capital letters to distinguish these from the Rashi characters which are known as printing letters. (See style 3.)

The second is the old Sephardic script. These characters or alphabet letters were originally devised for two reasons. One, we find in one of Rambam's *responsa* that the Jewish writers should not use the *Meruba* or square Hebrew letters to write non-religious material, but rather use this script type, and reserve the *Meruba* to write holy books. The other reason is that this type of writing can be achieved much faster than the *Meruba*. Because this old Sephardic script was used mostly by Hebrew scholars to write their compositions, it became known as *escritura de hahamim* (writing of the rabbis), as we've seen thousands of manuscripts, all written in this form. However, this *hahamim* script was later replaced by our Ladino cursive. (See style 4.)

The third printing character is called Rashi type or Rashi characters, although it really is an old style of Sephardic alphabet. Rashi, of course, stands for Rabbi Shelomo Itzhaki, the very famous 11th century French rabbinic scholar who is recognized as the best explainer of both the *Torah* and the *Talmud*. Rashi himself had never used this type at all. His handwriting was a different type of alphabetic letters. The manner in which this so-called "Rashi script" got its name is the following.

After the art of printing was established in the 1400s, the very first Hebrew book ever printed was Rashi's commentary on the *Torah*. This first Hebrew book was printed by a Rabbi Avraham Garton (Gerson) in Italy in 1475. This Rabbi Avraham did not use the *Meruba* letters, but rather designed and cut the Sephardic type because this first book was to be sold in Spain for Sephardim. Everyone in Spain was familiar with this kind of Hebrew alphabet, and from then on this type of printing became known as Rashi characters. All Ladino works, like the famous *Me'Am Lo'Ez* and other books were printed using these Rashi characters. This continued until the 1930s by which time all Ladino was being written in Latin characters because most of the people did not know how to read the Hebrew. Even here in Seattle, we changed the printing of some compositions which we still chant in Ladino like the *Ketuba De La Ley* on *Shavuoth*. Now they're printed in Latin characters.

The fourth is called the modern Sephardic cursive or *Soletreo*. Up to the 1930s all Levantine Sephardim in Turkey, Greece and the Balkans wrote everything in this cursive. We learned it in school, we used it in our business, and other types of correspondence, etc. But now it's hardly used any longer for the following reason.

Professor Abraham S. Yehuda tells us that when a group of scholars met in Palestine (around the 1930s) to discuss the adoption of the Hebrew language as the national language for Israel, some of the delegates suggested that they adopt the Sephardic pronunciation of Hebrew for the sake of uniformity. Some of the Ashkenazim there proposed a compromise and they said, we will accept the Sephardic pronunciation of the Hebrew language provided that the whole convention will agree to have all Jews to accept the Ashkenazic cursive, which was voted unanimously. This of course put an end to our Sephardic cursive or *Soletreo*, and all of which brings us to:

The fifth, formerly purely Ashkenazic cursive was also devised as a faster-writing cursive than the one the Ashkenazim had before, and is the one used now universally by all Jews. Teachers in Sephardic schools, as well as all students, abandoned their Sephardic cursive and changed over to this fifth cursive. Only our generation can still write in *Soletreo*. All others write Hebrew in the fifth style. There's at least this to be said about this changeover. Every Jewish schoolboy or girl, whether in Israel or the United States or anywhere else can read or write each other's Hebrew writing.

1   **Capital Letters**   1

לָמַדְתִּי שֵׁם תּוֹרָה.
מַה כָּתוּב בַּתּוֹרָה?

2   **Old Sephardic Script**   2

3   **Rashi Characters**   3

און אֵמֵנבֵּרי סוֹאֵידִי סֵיכִד מִיל קוֹטסְקִידוֹס סֵין לוֹן
בֵּיזְדֵמֵדִירוֹ אֵמִינוּ. מִיל קֵי סֵייכִי לוֹן קוֹלוֹ אֵמֵינוּ דֵיזִי
קוֹנטֵימֵירסֵי דֵיזֵּחוּ.

4   **Soletreo**   4

5   **Ashkenazic Cursive**   5

אַחַת וְאַחַת־שְׁתַּיִם . שְׁתַּיִם וְאַחַת־שָׁלֹשׁ .

December 1978   Kislev 5739

Hebrew Printing in Turkey

The art of printing, invented in the middle 1400s in Germany by Guttenberg, did not reach Turkey until 1503 when the family of David Nahmias set up a printing establishment in Constantinople. A few years later, in 1530, the famous Soncino family set up a second printing press in Constantinople and later in Salonika. These early publishers were instrumental in printing an enormous amount of valuable books. Historians tells us that if it were not for these early printers in Constantinople and Salonika, many of these books dealing with a wide variety of subjects would have been lost to us forever.

The famous Israeli writer, the late Avraham Yaari, spent thirty years of his literary life compiling an enormous amount of information about the early history of Hebrew books published in Turkey. Among the dozens of books he wrote on the subject of bibliography, he wrote a most interesting book called *Hadefus Haivri Bekoshta* (*Hebrew Printing in Constantinople*), where he traces the beginnings of the printing industry in the Turkish empire. He also wrote the history of Hebrew printing in such places as Baghdad, India, Israel and Izmir. He listed and catalogued about 758 different books published in Constantinople, giving the name of the book, the author and a small paragraph describing the contents and the year of publication for each one.

Mr. Yaari worked mainly in libraries and museums where the books are found at the present time, such as the Hebrew University Library in Jerusalem, the Jewish Theological Seminary in New York and the *Mahon Ben Zvi* in Jerusalem. Some books he lists and says that this particular book is the only one existing today in the whole world. Some are being reprinted in Israel now.

For a long while, printers would publish these books and they would sell them easily to the waiting public. However, after 200 years or more, due to the gradually worsening economic situation among the Sephardim in Turkey, even those customers that loved to read found it very difficult to spend a goodly amount to buy new books. And so, book publishers began feeling the result of the lack of sales, so they slowed down on printing new books.

There came a time when even the formerly prosperous printers simply could not afford to invest the large amount of funds necessary to print books. They didn't have the funds to pay for the paper, the ink, the laborers and other expenses. So they devised a convenient plan, whereby they would print, every week, a few *pligos* (pages) of a certain popular book, take these *pligos* and distribute them every *Shabbath* in various synagogues, where the majority of worshippers would come to *tefilah* (prayer). Those customers who availed themselves of these *pligos*, in turn, would in the course of a few weeks, gather all the pages together and subsequently have them bound into a whole book. Thousands of books, Hebrew as well as Ladino, were published thanks to this convenient plan.

Of course, there were some rabbis who objected to this method, claiming that it looks like doing business on the *Shabbath*, but Mr. Yaari writes that one rabbi by the name of Rabbi Shemuel Ben Hakim defended the system by saying that the public is thus acquiring books, which they would otherwise never be able to read.

These clients were put on their personal honor to pay the printers on a day other than *Shabbath*. The cost of each *pligo* was one Turkish *para*.

Interesting, but sad, it is to read the *hakdama* (introduction) to the *Me'Am Lo'Ez Sefer Bamidbar*, where Rabbi Yitzhak Magriso (see p. 120) the author, is forced to complain about some customers. He says in Ladino, "*La siba' es la pederita de munchos aspros . . . los tomadores de los pligos, ke los tomaron sanos. Kualos los retornaron ratonados . . . y kualos se arepintieron . . .*" (The reason for the delay in printing the fourth book of the Bible commentary was the tremendous loss of money we suffered. Some clients who received the previous *pligos* in good condition, returned them to us even when they were rat eaten . . . and some of them changed their minds . . .)

Printing in Turkish printing characters did not reach Turkey until the year 1728.

January 1976   Teveth/Shevat 5736

The Ladino Kanun Name'

A couple of months ago my brother Rabbi Maimon handed me a super-bound, pamphlet-like book he had received in the mail from a Rabbi Yerushalmi of Cincinnati, Ohio, and said to me, "Here, enjoy yourself." So, I took it home and I found out what this book is all about. I surely enjoyed it.

Rabbi Maimon knows I'm interested in anything that has a Ladino content to it. This one indeed fills the bill perfectly.

This beautiful work turned out to be a Ladino translation of the Turkish penal code, consisting of 264 articles or paragraphs describing the different degrees of crimes and their punishments to be followed by the Turkish courts.

This work is called *Kanun Name'* (Penal Code) and it was translated from the original Turkish into Ladino by Mr. Yehezkel Gabay, the famous owner and publisher of the Sephardic newspaper *El Telegrafo* of Istanbul, over 100 years ago. It was probably printed just the one time and then forgotten.

Rabbi Yitzhak Yerushalmi found a copy of this Ladino *Kanun Name'* in the library of the Sephardic Beth Shalom synagogue of Cincinnati, of which he is the rabbi. He's also a professor in the Hebrew Union College of Cincinnati, Ohio.

The original *Kanun Name'* in Ladino was, of course, printed in Hebrew characters. What Rabbi Yerushalmi did is have each of the 264 paragraphs mimeographed first in Hebrew characters, followed by the transliteration of the same articles in Ladino but in Latin characters, for those that are not familiar with the Hebrew alphabet. In addition to all this, he included an excellent ten-page dictionary explaining the difficult Turkish legal terminology. It's obvious that Rabbi Yerushalmi is very conversant with the Turkish and Ladino languages from the skillful manner in which he records the etymology of all those words of purely legal phraseology.

In his preface to this wonderful work, Rabbi Yerushalmi tells us that there's one copy of this same Ladino *Kanun Name'* in the Jewish Theological Seminary in New York. However, in the New York copy both the first page and date of publication are missing so that the rare copy he found is much more valuable.

He also tells us that this work was translated into both French and English, a copy of which he obtained from the archives of the Library of Congress in Washington, D.C.

I'm reluctant to quote here a "sample" of one of the 264 articles for fear that one might misjudge it, but here's an example of one from page 44, article 161.

Medico o Djerah ke, por hatir, o por la ridja de alguno da eduth por alguno komo es hazimyento, para escaparlo de los servisyos del reynado, sin tener dinguna hazinura, se apena kon aprezarlo de uno anyo asta 3. Y si esta falsiya la izo por

tomar paras, o algun prezente, se djuzgan todos los 2 en la
ley del shohad, tanto de tomador, komo dador.

Translation (my own): A doctor, or a surgeon, that either as
favor to a friend, or on another person's request, gives
testimony to pretend that this person is suffering from a
certain illness, all this for the purpose of making that person
exempt from government service, without, in reality, that
person being ill. This is punishable by a prison term of from
one to 3 years. And if this false report was given to obtain
profit, either of cash or to attain a valuable gift from this
person, both parties are liable and charged with the laws of
bribery, both the taking bribery and the giving of bribery.

We who appreciate the idea of preservation of Ladino owe Rabbi
Yerushalmi a big "thank you" for his efforts in this regard.

September/October 1973   Elul 5733/Tishri 5734

"El Cortijo"

When we speak of the probable future of Ladino, the general
consensus of opinion among the majority of Spanish-speaking
Sephardim is that of a pessimistic nature. They say there's no chance
of it being revitalized.

However, when we see the tremendous amount of literature that's
being produced in this field, one has to realize that there's definitely a
surge and a sort of renaissance which is aimed to recapture at least
some of the Ladino culture of bygone days.

Just this past week, our friend David Balint brought to my
attention a review of a book written by two professors Samuel
Armistead (University of Pennsylvania) and Joseph Silverman
(University of California at Santa Cruz). (The book is *The Judeo-
Spanish Ballad Chapbooks of Yacob Abraham Yona*, University of
California Press.) This 640-page book deals with the history of Ladino
songs and ballads. We shall return, at some future time, to explain
this in an article in *La Boz*. [Editor's note: Unfortunately, the author
never completed his article on this book.]

Today, however, I would like to write about the two stage plays, in Ladino, that have been produced in Israel. The first one, of course, is the famous "*Bustan Sephardi*" ("A Sephardic Field"), written by the very able Yitzhak Navon. [Editor's note: Mr. Navon later served as president of the state of Israel and is currently a member of the Israeli parliament called the *Knesset*.] Briefly, this play, which has played to capacity audiences in Israel for over a year, depicts, in a panoramic dramatization, the life of the Sephardic Jew in the old country.

Mr. Navon has very cleverly blended into the play a large number of favorite and popular Ladino songs which the Spanish-speaking Sephardim recognize with a smile and nostalgia.

When Rabbi Maimon visited Israel with a Seattle group earlier this year, they planned and managed to see this stage play and they all came back raving. They said how delightful it was to hear all those great favorite songs that Mr. Navon shrewdly worked into the play, all of them very appropriately fitting an occasion such as *paridas, birkat mila, espozorios, bodas* (births, circumcisions, engagements, weddings), etc. Mr. Navon produced an album of most of these songs. Those of us that availed ourselves of this recording, always listen to it with great gusto.

Another very talented Sephardic playwright, by the name of Shaul Angel of Jerusalem, has written a very similar play in Ladino called "*El Cortijo*" ("The Courtyard").

While "*Bustan*" tells the story of various social and festival occasions, Mr. Angel's play, "*El Cortijo*," deals with life in the backyard neighborhood as it used to exist in the Old City section of Jerusalem. His characters are composed of *mujeres* (women) gathered in the old *cortijo* (courtyard) gossiping and discussing all the problems of their friends and acquaintances.

In an interview in the Jerusalem magazine *Bamaaraha*, Mr. Angel tells us that he employed a vast amount of materials such as *refranes* (sayings), *consejas* (tales), songs and *romansas* (ballads) that he authored himself in a previous book that he had written.

Mr. Angel also very cleverly worked into the play humorous anecdotes and *estoryicas* (stories) woven into the story that he evolves into the play. All of this goes to make it a very fine Sephardic comedy. I wonder if Mr. Angel will produce an album of "*El Cortijo*"? In case he has made a recording, it certainly would be a treat to listen to "*El Cortijo*."

February 1979 Shevat/Adar 5739

About Sephardic Folklore

Hopefully, one of these days, some enterprising writer will put together a comprehensive work on Sephardic history, devoting several chapters on customs and folklore. Of course, this writer will, as source material, draw from the works of Franco, Danon, Rosanes, Galante and many, many others.

One writer we cannot overlook, for the simple reason that he contributed immensely to Sephardic folklore. I refer to the late Michael Molho, a prolific writer, whose books, articles and other writings contain a veritable source of invaluable material, particularly regarding our Levantine history and our peculiar lifestyle.

Who was Michael Molho and what has he written? A few pertinent remarks will surely help us understand and appreciate his immense contribution to our theme.

Michael Molho was born in Salonika in 1891. His father Rabbi Shelomo Molho, who was head of the *beth din* (religious tribunal), was a descendant of an illustrious family of scholars and rabbis of Salonika. Besides his rabbinic studies, Rev. Molho became very proficient in several European languages. At one time, his great goal in life was to help develop and establish an advanced rabbinical seminary where young scholars could obtain a formal and a superior education. But the tragic fire that devastated Salonika in 1917 smothered that noble project.

From an early age, Rev. Molho devoted untold hours in study and research. He assumed the job of editor of a daily Zionist newspaper to which he contributed many articles of lasting interest. Due to his love for Israel, he helped many of his friends emigrate to Israel in the 1930s. When the Germans invaded Salonika, Rev. Molho was already a marked man because of his anti-Nazi writings. In fact, the Gestapo was looking for him in order to arrest him. However, with the help of some of his friends among the Greek underground partisans, he was able to escape, in the dead of night, with his family. He was able to take with him all his manuscripts which were extremely dear to him. The Greek friends later hid him from the Nazis for the duration of the war.

On his return, he became spiritual leader to those Salonika Jews who chose to return and resettle in their native town. In 1944 he wrote a book *In Memorium*, the story of the Holocaust of the Jews of Salonika.

In addition to his rabbinic duties he began an ambitious project of copying and listing the names on thousands of old tombstones in the Salonika Jewish cemetery where great scholars and rabbis were buried. He recorded their names, dates and other pertinent information which shed considerable light on the history of the Salonika spiritual leaders and *dayanim*.

In 1949 he was called by the Sephardic community of Buenos Aires to fill the position of rabbi and *hazan*, but, for personal reasons he left after only two years.

There exists in Madrid, Spain, a society named *Arias Montano* which publishes a magazine called *Sefarad*, and which encourages writers who do research on Sephardim. Rev. Molho, through the sponsorship of this society, published two important works on Sephardic life. In one of these books, called *Usos y Costumbres* (see p. 200, Sephardic Symposium), Molho writes about Sephardic customs in regards to all our holidays. His book is chock-full of interesting items about *paridas*, *espozorios*, *bodas*, *novyas*, *berith mila* (births, engagements, weddings, bridal events, circumcisions), all written in charming style. He also explains, in great detail, how old ladies used to prepare home remedies for all ailments, real or imagined. He writes about *percantes*, *endulcos* (exorcisms, magical potions), even giving us the old recipes the old ladies used to prepare for love potions. In another book he has a whole chapter on the meaning, history and contents of that famous work, our *Me'Am Lo'Ez*.

Rev. Molho had a fond hope to collect all his scattered articles in various papers and magazines, and other really valuable material, and have them published into one large volume. Unfortunately, he passed away in 1965 at the age of seventy-four, before he could realize his ambition. *Zihrono livraha.* (May his memory be for a blessing.)

May 1979   Iyar/Sivan 5739

More Sephardic Folklore

In addition to the works of the late Michael Molho (see p. 131), we also find an enormous amount of Sephardic folklore in the writings of the late Moshe Atias, the renowned Salonikian, who preserved for posterity hundreds of Ladino *romansas* (ballads) which were sung by our mothers and grandmothers. Among other nostalgic items, Mr. Atias describes, in great detail, the preparations that the *novya's* (bride's) family had to work out in great anticipation of the happy day of the *boda* (wedding).

Here are a few sample bits from Mr. Atias' articles. When the wedding date was getting close, the bride's family would make a trip to the *charihi* (shopping center) where they would purchase a large quantity of sheep's wool and bring it home where a crew of friends and relatives would wash it thoroughly. This was called *lavar y blankear la lana para las colchas* (wash and bleach the wool for the comforters). Then another crew, who were waiting in the backyard, would spread the washed wool to dry in the fresh air and sunshine. This, of course, was followed by a *caveh de mujeres* (coffee for women) accompanied with dancing and singing.

Mr. Atias mentions a singular custom which he calls *almusama* (eve of the festivities, see below). This event was celebrated mostly on the Saturday night before the week of the wedding. A group of female relatives and close friends would assemble at the bride's home to *alegrar a la novya* (entertain the bride). She would be seated in an ornately decorated chair, in the center of the room. All the excited guests would begin dancing around her, singing *romansas de boda* (wedding songs), accompanied by the ever present *pandericas* (cookies) followed by a visit to the table filled with specially prepared delicious food.

In a footnote explaining the origin of the word *almusama*, Mr. Atias says that a great many people figured it to be made up of two Hebrew words *alamoth shama*, meaning "all the young ladies are there." But, he adds, it is more likely that it's a word derived from an Arabic expression meaning "the eve before the festivities."

Sephardim who come from other parts of Turkey had a similar custom, but called it *noche de alhenya*, loosely translated as "the night when the bride's girlfriends used the henna sent by the bridegroom to make her look more beautiful."

Mr. Atias describes the custom *aparap el ashugar* (to exhibit the trousseau). This practice, as some of us remember, consisted of designating a special room in the bride's home, which was filled to capacity with the entire trousseau. Decked out in a fascinating display were all her gorgeous dresses, elegant coats and many other types of wearing apparel, and sometimes, some of her beautiful jewelry. In the course of the evening, a *haham* who was selected by the city's *beth din* (rabbinic tribunal) would arrive in order to appraise the value of every displayed item, the total amount of which was recorded in the *ketuba*. These rabbis were called *preciadores* (expert evaluators of all merchandise). On the following day, all this trousseau would be loaded onto fancy wagons, then delivered to the house where the young couple would make their future home.

The *novyo* (groom) had the pleasant duty of sending certain gifts to the *novya*, like a fancy comb made from the whitest ivory, *el tass de banyo* (the laver of the bath house), *confiete de boda* (wedding bonbons).

Mr. Atias also describes the marriage ceremony, after which the bride and groom would go to a room, all by themselves, have something to eat and come out to be greeted by all the invited guests. For the following eight days, the married couple would sit in a special *talamo* (bridal canopy) situated in the best room in the house (the *hupa*).

Then, Mr. Atias mentions the ceremony called *pasar el pishcado* (to step over the fish). After eight days of the *hupa*, the bridegroom would go to the fish market to buy a whole fresh fish. He would bring it home and place this fish in a large bronze bowl in the center of the room, then the bride would hop over it, back and forth three times. After each time, the parents and guests would shower the bride with appropriate blessings, wishing her long life with children as symbolized by fish, who multiply in the seas. In other communities, this fish ceremony would take place during the wedding festivities.

February 1977   Shevat/Adar 5737

Sephardic Music

Our people often wonder whether our Sephardic tunes, liturgical melodies, etc., can be traced way back to Spain. We can't say for sure which of the songs we sing are of purely Sephardic origin. But we're allowed an educated guess and say that those melodies which all Sephardim throughout the world sing alike, despite some small variations, are most likely to be traditional Sephardic melodies. The tunes I'm referring to, for example, are the *El Nora Alila* of *Yom Kippur*, and melodies like *Ashem Bekol Shofar* of *Rosh Hashanah*. Every Sephardi in the world sings the above named tunes in a similar way.

One more interesting fact is, if you listen carefully to Spanish Flamenco music, you can notice a striking similarity and a close affinity to a lot of our tunes. What about the rest of the types of melodies we sing? Could we say they can be traced back to Spain? For an answer to this question, I read a very interesting article which provides us with an expert opinion.

According to a man named Yitzhak Navon, (born in Edirne, died in Tel Aviv and not to be confused with man of same name who is a current Israeli politician, see p. 130) who was himself a music lover, and who made a very profound study of the history of Sephardic melodies, most of our tunes are derived from Turkish and Arabic Oriental music. Sultan Selim II, who was one of the most benevolent and progressive monarchs (early 1600s) in the history of the entire Ottoman Empire, sent a delegation of musicologists to Persia and other countries. Their purpose was to gather various melodies and so arrange and adopt some of the *makams* that the Sultan had heard and liked on his many travels. [Editor's note: *Makam* means mode of music or leitmotif.]

Among this delegation that went to Persia for this mission, was a Sephardic gentleman from Istanbul. His name was Yitzhak Fresco. This Mr. Fresco, a great musical talent, brought back with him a great number of melodies, which some authorities say, we still sing to this day. The *makam Ajem* is said to be imported during this period.

The word *Ajem* is the Turkish word for Persia, which today is known as Iran. Other *makams* also bear the name of the countries from which they were brought, like *Hejaz, Isphahan* and *Nehavent*, etc. One favorite *makam* in our synagogue is *sabah*, which in Turkish means "morning." That's one of the tunes the *muezzin* (Turkish cantor) sings in the *mishkita* (mosque) for the morning services.

Our *Shabbath* morning *Ashem Meleh* is usually sung in *makam sabah*, as well as the popular *Nishmath* and *Kedusha*. I would guess the reason we picked *sabah* over all the other *makams* is because the name of our synagogue contains the same three letters, sabah. [Editor's note: Sephardic Bikur Holim]

There were *hazanim* who were also famous composers. The most prolific of these was Rabbi Yisrael Najara, who lived in Safed in the early 17th century. (See p. 96.) He wrote three books of *pizmonim* (liturgical songs), *bakashoth* (supplications) and other beautiful Hebrew poems. One of these is the well-known *Ya Ribon Olam*, which can be found in all Jewish prayer books, Ashkenazic as well as Sephardic. A great number of these compositions by Rabbi Yisrael, are sung today in Israel, when groups of Sephardic *hazanim* and talented singers get together around four o'clock on *Shabbath* mornings to sing. I understand these "concerts" attract quite a crowd, despite the inconvenience of the early hour, which, of course brings to mind our own *maftirim* (Turkish Jewish singing groups).

The *maftirim* was a group of talented singers who sang various *pizmonim* and other songs on *Shabbath* in different synagogues in Istanbul and other Jewish communities in Turkey. Our own Rev. Benaroya belonged to one of these groups during his early years first in Edirne and later in Istanbul. Even in our days in Istanbul [Editor's note: early 1920s], some of our Sephardic music lovers used to visit the *mevlehane* (Turkish concert hall) to hear the *dervishes* (Turkish monks) render their religious dirges and other songs. Some of these *dervishes* had marvelous voices.

Another musical influence can also be heard today. A few of our melodies from the old Spanish *romansas* have been adapted to popular Hebrew songs. An example is the *Tsur Mishelo Ahalnu* a *Shabbath* table song which was adapted to the tune of the well-known Sephardic Spanish song, *Los Bilbilicos Cantan*, a very catchy and pleasant melody.

May 1981   Nisan/Iyar 5741

The 1935 Recordings

This story begins way back in 1935 when a Professor Mel Jacobs of the department of anthropology of the University of Washington invited a group of our Seattle Sephardic ladies to the University for the purpose of having a recording session of Sephardic songs, Turkish songs and Spanish *romansas*. It even included one Ladino *estoryica*.

How did Professor Jacobs know all these Sephardic ladies? It all came about because, at that particular time, Emma Adatto (then a member of the Seattle Sephardic community and now with the married name Schlesinger) was writing her college thesis to obtain her degree from the University. In addition to her written theme, she thought it would supply an extra aspect to her work by having an audio section to it. So, she had this group of ladies taken to the University recording department to sing and record some very old, almost forgotten Spanish *canticas*, *romansas* and various other types of familiar songs.

All this took place back in 1935 when the recording facilities available at that time was the old-style large metal cylinders which are very difficult to reproduce. Emma's thesis can still be obtained at the University.

Forty-six years passed. All these recordings were long forgotten. The reason for their reappearance now is that our friend and neighbor Dr. Eric Offenbacher, who is connected with the music department at the University, has discovered the very box containing these old-style recordings. When he saw the word "Ladino" he asked my son-in-law, Eugene Normand, who would know about all these recordings. Eugene mentioned my name to Dr. Offenbacher, and so this was the reason I came to know about them.

First, Dr. Offenbacher had to convince the music department to obtain some equipment that could be used to transfer and reproduce the recordings from the old type, to the modern type cassette recorders. This done, we started listening to the tapes. I could identify some of the voices and some of the songs, and helped Dr. Offenbacher classify them in their respective ethnic groupings.

Although some of the original recordings came out very poorly, we were able to recognize some songs. A little later on, Dr. Offenbacher found some typewritten pages in which Professor Jacobs had written down the names of these ladies as well as the names of the songs and *romansas*. The list included the names of the following: Madam Regina Varon, Mrs. S. Adatto, Mrs. Estreya Barlia, Louise Adatto, two Mrs. Halfons and a Mrs. Eskenazi. At times, one sings a solo, but there is one recording which is sung by a group, which we recognized as *La Cantica de la Parida* (Song of the Mother Who Has Just Given Birth), which starts *Oh ke mueve mezes* (Oh, What Nine Months), etc.

Besides the above-named singers, Mrs. Victoria Viesse is listed as a narrator of *La Estorya Del Pishcador* (Story of the Fisherman). She tells it in such a delightful way that any person who knew her well can close his eyes and visualize the charming way she used to accent her words. One can imagine her dramatic gestures and emotional flare. She had a knack of captivating her audience, which she used in this long but fascinating *estoryica*.

Then, there is a separate cassette recorded by Mrs. Louise Adatto. She introduces it by addressing her beginning remarks to her parents, both of whom lived in Istanbul at the time. She starts: *Keridos genitores-agora vos canto en esta placa de akeyas sharkis de vos plaziya tanto. Kuando vos da escarinyo ke las sientas, ke vos akodresh de me.* (Translation: My dear parents, I shall sing for you now some of the songs you used to like so much. When you get lonesome, you can listen to this recording, so you can remember me.)

Among other songs she sang in this recording was the well known Turkish *sharki* (Turkish ballad) *Soyletma Beni* (Don't Tell Me). She sings also the Spanish song entitled *Manyana Manyana y Tan Demanyana, Kuando Salir Keriya La Estreya Diana* (Morning, Morning, So Early In the Morning, When the Star Named Diana Wanted To Come Out). She had an exceptionally good voice, very suitable to the above type of Turkish and Ladino songs.

Mrs. Becky Souriano tells me that she actually remembers the very day this Professor Jacobs came and took all these ladies to the University to record these *canticas y romansas*. Besides the above ladies, the list included the names of Mrs. Rosa Berro and Mrs. Leah Sadis. I told Dr. Offenbacher that he can go to the Kline Galland Home and meet Mrs. Berro and Mrs. Sadis personally and ask them some questions on those *romansas* from Rhodes that they recorded.

I understand that Dr. Offenbacher did go and interview Mrs. Berro and Mrs. Sadis and I am sure he obtained from them recollections of the whole project. In the event I discover more details about this recording group, I will try to write about them in a future article in *La Boz*. And, if anyone has more information regarding this project, please do not hesitate to call me so we can have a more complete view of this report.

Chapter Seven

Ladino Language and Sayings

November 1974   Heshvan/Kislev 5735

Ladino Language - I
(Ladino)

At the beginning, the word "Ladino" was used to signify the
translation of any Hebrew word into our Judeo-Spanish idiom. This
we can say from our own personal experience. During our school days
in Turkey, anytime we wanted to translate a Hebrew word to our own
idiom, we used to say, *este byervo se Ladina este modo* (this word is
translated in this manner), or *el Ladino de este byervo es esto y esto*
(the translation of this word is such and such). Again, only to indicate
to give the meaning of that certain word.

Incidentally, we used to run across a lot of words that we didn't
understand, because the Bible translators, and our instructors after
them, continued to render some words in the same archaic Judeo-
Spanish. Our generation had already adopted a substitute word for it,
be it of Turkish, Hebrew or Greek origin, that was employed by the
Sephardim in daily use.

As we said, the original intent of the word Ladino was meant to be
used as translation, until it changed so much that it would serve us
well to explain the history and the evolution of this term.

Most historians agree that our Sephardic ancestors were brought
to Spain by the Romans as captive and exiles, from the captivity of the
land of Israel.

Of course, these exiled Jews used Hebrew as their everyday
language, which was their native tongue. However, years later, when
Hebrew ceased being their means of communication, our rabbis, by
necessity, had our Bible translated into Latin. Then, when the whole

Spanish population, Jew and non-Jew alike, switched from Latin into the Spanish language, our rabbis again, had to retranslate the Bible and some prayers into Spanish. This latter translation was called *Barbaro Latino*, or as some pronounced it, to sound like Lathino. Eventually this translation came to be known as the Ladino translation.

In the *Hallel* prayer, which we recite also the night of *Pesach* in the *Hagada*, we say: *Bezeth Yisrael mimisrayim, Beth Yaacov me'am lo'ez* and when we read the *Hagada* in Ladino, this verse we translate: *en salir Yisrael de ayifto, caza de Yaacov de puevlo ladinador.* In short, we transiate the Hebrew word *lo'ez* to mean, as the Radak (Rabbi David Kimchi) has it in his Bible commentary to "any alien language other than Hebrew." And so the Sephardim continued to refer to Ladino as a "foreign language," which to them meant Judeo-Spanish.

Another term was also used to mean Judeo-Spanish, and that was Judesmo. But this latter was used mostly to mean the spoken rather than the written one.

Did our Sephardic ancestors use Ladino before the expulsion in 1492? I would say yes, because of a statement we find in the writings of the famous Sephardic *haham*, Rabbi Yitzhak Bar Shesheth. Rabbi Yitzhak was the rabbi of Barcelona in the late 1300s, who later was forced to run away from Spain and settle in North Africa. This, mind you was 100 years before the Expulsion of 1492.

Anyhow, being that Rabbi Yitzhak was recognized as a great scholar and a respected authority, he used to receive a tremendous amount of inquiries, from Spain, on questions of marriage, divorce and the like. In answer to one of his rabbinical colleagues, he records the fact, that one of these inquiries came to him from Spain asking him to resolve a certain question, and that this particular letter was written in the Judeo-Spanish or in Ladino.

There are two famous Bible translations into Ladino; one dating back to 1547, printed in Constantinople, and the other in 1553 in the city of Ferrara, Italy. The first one used Hebrew characters and the Ferrara Bible used Latin characters.

A Sephardic professor in the University of Paris, who teaches Ladino there, is now in the process of comparing different versions of the Bible translations, and in a scientific manner, analyzing almost every word to explain the variations in the Ladino, as it was then known, and as it evolved now. His name is Vitali Sephiha.

Our own David Romey is presently engaged in almost the same type of work, and what is interesting is that Professor Sephiha mentions David Romey's work and credits David with some ideas that Sephiha obtained from his published works.

December 1974   Kislev/Teveth 5735

Ladino Language - II
(Ladino - Continued)

Ladino, as we Sephardim use it today, underwent many changes from its original Castilian Spanish. On many Spanish words we added a letter, like *mucho* became *muncho*. With many other Spanish words we shed a letter, like *hermano* became *ermano*. In the course of time our Levantine Sephardim sneaked in many non-Spanish words, like Hebrew, Turkish, etc. This time I would like to examine two purely Ladino words, that no one but a Sephardi would recognize, because it cannot be found in a Spanish dictionary.

Alhad. We Sephardim use Spanish words to indicate the days of the week except the one they use for Sunday. Instead of the Spanish word *Domingo* we use *Alhad*, an Arabic word meaning "first" or "one," therefore "the first day of the week." The reason for this substitution is that the word Domingo stands for the day of their Christian deity. As is well understood, our ancestors would never use such a word.

Hadras. This word is also pure Ladino, and cannot be found in any Spanish dictionary. The word itself is derived from the Hebrew, and it has a rather interesting story. We read in 2 Kings - 4, that when Elisha the prophet had occasion to visit the city of Shunem, a man and his wife went to all kinds of trouble to furnish him with a place to stay, and managed to have it there permanently for when he visited that town. So Elisha asked them why they were going to so much pain and trouble for him. The word Elisha uses to ask why they were bothering so much is *harada*, so our Ladino writers turned it into *hadras*. In time this word took the meaning of "Why all the hullabaloo?" Later they added another word and made it into a phrase, "*hadras y baranas*," meaning a person is making a lot of show-off noises. We also refer to a man that's putting a lot of empty airs as *hadrozo*.

When we mention *romansas*, I'm asked many times, to insert in *La Boz* the words to some *romansa* to which people know the tune. This one is called *En La Mar Ay Una Torre* (In the Sea There is a Tower).

En la mar ay y una torre, en la torre ay una ventana.,
En la ventana ay una palomba
Ke los marineros aman.

Da me la mano palomba,
Para suvir a tu nido,
Maldicha ke durmes sola. vengo a durmir kon tigo.

No me mates kon kuchiyo. ni menos kon revolver,
Matame kon tus amores.,
En tus brasos murere.

Translation:
In the sea there's a tower;
In the tower there's a window;
On the window there's a dove
That the seamen love.

Give me your hand dove
To climb to your nest.
Cursed be you that you sleep alone;
I come to sleep with you.

Do not kill me with a knife
Nor with a gun.
Kill me with your love;
On your arms I shall die.

April 1976   Nisan 5736

Ladino Language - III
(Clarification of Ladino)

In a letter printed in the February issue of the *Sephardic Home News* of New York, the sender, who chose to remain anonymous, is astonished to discover that the word "Ladino" found in all Spanish dictionaries is defined as "cunning," "crafty," "treacherous" and other such meanings. And so he asks, through this letter, some expert to "delve into the truth of this dilemma."

All this was pointed out to him when he introduced himself to some Spanish American citizens as a Sephardi-Ladino.

First of all, to say that a person is a Sephardi-Ladino is incorrect. He can say he's a Sephardi who speaks Ladino. We Sephardim use the word Ladino to indicate the language we use, but not to indicate our ethnic group.

How did this term Ladino begin to be employed in the manner that we read and write it? We expressed this before in former articles of *La Boz*. (See p. 139.) However, in order to clarify this dilemma, it's necessary to repeat, in brief, some of the essential points.

Our forefathers were taken to Spain by the Romans. The local language then was Latin. During that period, these early Sephardim, besides Hebrew, spoke Latin also. Our *hahamim* translated our Bible and some of our prayers into Latin. Later on in history a good chunk of southern Spain was conquered by the Moors, whose language was Arabic. All our illustrious Sephardic sages who lived in this region, like Rabbi Yehuda Halevi, Rambam who was born in Cordova and many others, spoke and wrote most of their works in Arabic.

Later on in history, when the Spaniards reconquered this part of Spain from the Moors, the language of the whole country became Spanish. It was at this period that our *hahamim* in Spain saw the necessity again to retranslate these works from Hebrew into the Spanish language to accommodate and help out that segment of Sephardim who were not conversant with Hebrew.

So the original intent of the word Ladino, was to indicate this translation of these Hebrew works from Hebrew into our peculiar and distinct Spanish idiom which they called at first Latino and then evolved into Lathino, with the pronunciation of the letters "th" as in "they" or "them."

As to this letter writer's surprise, he couldn't be more shocked than some of us were when we first heard the term "Jew you down" to mean haggle, to dicker or to drive a bargain. You would expect in an enlightened country like the United States this wouldn't happen, but it did.

I will leave it to expert Spanish language scholars to go back in history and trace back the derivation and etymology of the word "Ladino" and how come the dictionary defines it the way it does. But I suspect the same way that some bigots here in our country defined the word "Jew" in a derogatory manner, the same way Ladino was defined by some Spanish Jew-haters with insulting connotation.

Then again, we have in the English language certain words that are now defined by a different meaning than the original meaning. For instance, take the word "doctor." Certainly an honorable and respectable profession, and yet we find people use "to doctor" defined as to "tamper and to change" as we have seen recently in the Watergate tape scandal.

Then there's the harmless little word "book." When used as a verb "to book" means "to charge a person with a crime," especially at a police station. There are countless such words, that started out harmless enough, but popularly evolved into ominous definitions.

November 1971   Heshvan/Kislev 5732

Ladino Sayings - I
(Ladino: Language and Customs)

It was a delightful sight to see the youth conduct all the religious services in our synagogue on *Simhath Torah*. The president of the day stressed the need of our youth to learn and perpetuate our Ladino language and our heritage. A very good idea!

In line with this trend, it would be apropos to try to understand and trace back some of the Ladino expressions we employed in our daily conversations.

At this time let's take the Ladino saying, *letras de vatodienu.* This saying is meant to indicate the following, "I have explained the matter to you in unmistakable terms." Or, like we say in modern slang, "loud and clear."

The origin of this expression can be better understood by explaining that the Hebrew word *vatodienu* is the first word of a special prayer that we recite on any Jewish festival that occurs on Saturday night. This prayer is printed in our old style festival books in large letters, the reason being that before the discovery of electricity, when synagogues were lit by candle light, the people were not able to read the small print in the book until the *shamash* had a chance to light up those scores of candles.

In connection with this we may mention the custom in our synagogue that the *hazan* reads aloud the middle portion of the *Amida* of the evening services on *Shabbath* or festivals.

According to traditional ruling, the audience is supposed to say the entire *Amida* in silent devotion. Our rabbis, however, eased this ruling, by having the *hazan* read aloud the portion which is read after the first three benedictions have been read by the congregants silently. The *hazan* stops before the last three benedictions. It seems logical to assume that this custom evolved from the time that all the members did not have prayer books.

There is one exception to this rule, and that is on the eve of *Yom Kippur*, the reason being that the synagogue was lighted up from early evening and it was pretty certain that all the congregants had their own private prayer books.

December 1971   Kislev/Teveth 5732

Ladino Sayings - II
(Ladino Sayings)

Continuing with Ladino expressions, we will present two more with their explanations.

First, *al shefoh se sienten las bozes*. Loosely translated it means "We'll see what happens at the end." During the heat of a given argument, one person argues, another shouts, and another one rants and rambles on and on. A detached bystander can philosophize and say, "We'll see what happens at the end of this argument." The Hebrew word *shefoh* is the first word or the beginning of that portion of the *Pesach Hagadah* that we recite after the meal, when quite a few are already either sleepy or feeling the effects of two or three cups of wine, or a little hoarse from shouting the first portion of the *Hagadah* with the initial enthusiasm, so only those that can survive the lively ceremony can really be heard. So this saying evolved in our Sephardic vocabulary to mean: Wait and see what happens at the end.

Second, *ke darshe mi ijo ke seya en Tisha B'Av.* This saying, literally translated means: "I hope my son will make a speech even if it's on the fast of the ninth day of Av." Loosely translated, it's used mostly to mean: Let my son improve his ways even if it takes a little more time than usual.

There is a rather cute story to illustrate this point. Once there was a lady whose son was studying at the academy. He was a brilliant student, except for one thing. When it came to deliver a sermon, he became extremely shy. The mother, anxious to hear her son make a speech went to the teacher, asking him to find a way to cure her son from his terrible shyness. The teacher said, "There is one way." On the night of *Tisha B'Av* when it is customary to put out the lights in the synagogue, I'll have your son deliver a sermon, thus he can overcome his stage fright." The mother replied, "It's okay; *ke darshe mi ijo ke seya en Tisha Beav."*

July 1973   Tamuz/Av 5733

Ladino Sayings - III
(Refran Sephardi)

In the book of the same name, Don Quixote tells his servant Sancho: *"Pareseme, Sancho, que no ay refran, que no seya verdadero."* According to experts in this particular field of Spanish literature, the word *refran*, meaning proverb or popular saying, is found in early books only after the middle of the 15th century. These experts advance the idea that, originally, this word *refran*, was used to indicate the repetition of the last few lines of some popular poem or a popular song, very much the same as we, today, use the English word "refrain." Later on, the Spanish word *refran*, was applied specifically to mean a popular saying.

We, Turkish Sephardim know and employ *refranes* in three languages: Hebrew, Ladino and Turkish. Hebrew because there are countless *refranes* in the Bible, like *Mishle* and *Koheleth* (Proverbs and Ecclesiastes), added to the thousands that are found in our *Talmud* and *Midrash.* Spanish or Ladino, those that our forefathers brought with them from Spain, and are still used by us. Turkish ones, as a natural result, as our people lived in Turkey for many centuries.

It's really amazing to read, how many books, articles and other types of publications have been written up on the subject of *refran Sepharadi* alone. Besides Rosanes, Galante, Kayserling, Danon and many others who have compiled hundreds of these *refranes*, there are a number of Sepharadim living in Israel now, who are collecting all these *refranes*, so that this unique branch of our Sepharadic culture will be preserved and so that they will not be lost to our future generations. Many times, a *refran* is used to illustrate a point, or to clarify an otherwise obscure subject. Following are a few Sephardic *refranes*, with English translations.

Ken al Dio ama no se enganya. Whoever loves G-d, never feels cheated.

Mil mueren de ayin ara; y uno de su muerte. Of all the thousands of people that die, one thousand die from the Evil Eye, and one only dies from natural causes.

El Dio kriyo, y no se kanso. G-d formed many human beings, and He never got tired. (To indicate the difference that exists in each human being, as to character, personality, etc.)

El Dio mos dara buelta y alegria. G-d will make us change our ways, and give us happiness. (Indicates a prayer to G-d that our opponents will act logically and sensibly and so will deserve the blessings of G-d.)

Esta en sus treje. He's standing on his thirteen. (The source of this saying goes back to the days of the Spanish Inquisition, when the priests tried to have some Jews change their religion, and they failed in their efforts. Then these priests would utter this saying, *Esta en sus treje*, meaning these Jews insisted and wouldn't budge from their belief in the Thirteen Fundamental Principles of Judaism.)

July 1975   Tamuz/Av 5735

Ladino Sayings - IV
(Ladino Refranes - Continued)

I've had quite a few requests from a lot of our young readers to write a few more Ladino *refranes*. I'm quite aware that some of our members know these *refranes* already, perhaps better than I, but these are strictly for our interested youngsters, who want to know the origin and some stories that are connected with them.

Izo las malas echas de Zimri, y demanda la paga buena de Pinhas. He committed shameful acts like Zimri, and he asks to be rewarded favorably like Pinhas. The origin of this saying is found in our Bible, Numbers, Chapter 25. Zimri, the villain, despite all warnings, had intimate relations with a girl from one of the idolatrous nations. Someone had to stop this shameful action, but many were either afraid, or didn't wish to get involved. Finally, Pinhas, the grandson of Aaron the high priest, realizing the harm this was causing, stopped Zimri (by killing both Zimri and the woman). *Hashem*, not only agreed with this action but rewarded Pinhas with eternal peace. So, there are some persons that act wrongly (like Zimri) and have the crust to ask people to judge them in a benevolent way (like Pinhas).

Ken va atar al gato? Who will be bold enough to tie the bell on the cat's tail? The story goes that a group of mice had a meeting one day. The purpose of this meeting was to find a way to warn all the mice whenever the cat was chasing them. One of the "smart alecks" in this group suggested: Let's tie a small bell on the cat's tail - this way we hear the bell and we scram." Right then, a realistic mouse happened to come in, and he asked "*Ken va atar al gato?*" Which one of us will have the audacity to tie the little bell on the cat's tail? This *refran* is used to apply to a situation like: It's very easy to say "Let's do this thing," but it's very hard to implement it.

Kedo kon la tinya y la Turkedad. He got stuck with the scalp disease, and his conversion to the Turkish religion.There was once a poor Jew who contracted a scalp disease called in Ladino as *tinya*. After trying everything under the sun to cure this *tinya*, and not being successful, he was advised to go to a Turkish *hoja* (priest), recognized as an expert in curing *tinya*. So this poor Jew, out of desperation, came to the *hoja's* house, who told him. "If you want to get cured, you have to become a Turk, and convert from Judaism to being a Mohammedan." This *prove Judio* (poor Jew) agreed. Unfortunately, after many treatments, the *tinya* was still as thick as ever. Hence the saying "*kedo con la tinya y la turkedad*" Not only did it not help his ailment, on the top of that he got stuck with the *Turkedad*, his unwanted conversion to the Turkish religion.

Cuando ay un metalik solo en la cumbara, aze mucho ruido y barana. When there's only one dime inside the piggy bank, it sure makes a hell of a lot of noise.

I'll let the readers use their imagination, and write their own commentary on this last *refran*.

August 1975   Av/Elul 5735

Ladino Sayings - V
(Ladino Refranes)

Most probably, in another page of this month's *La Boz*, our readers will be made aware of the visit to our community of Rabbi Nissim Behar, formerly of Istanbul, and presently living in Bat Yam, Israel (not to be confused with earlier Nissim Behar, p. 104).

It was a delight to hear his talk, in Ladino. Some of our young members understood quite a bit, and some very little. I could see there was a keen interest shown on the part of a number of our younger members in grasping some of the Ladino. And so, that's the reason for these *refranes*.

Azno batal provecho para el kazal. The neighbors in a village derive a lot of benefit from anyone that's not gainfully employed, even from an idle donkey.

Azno cayado, por savyo es contado. Even if a fellow is not intelligent, if he keeps quiet, and doesn't blurt out all his nonsense, he is considered a wise man.

Lo vites al azno, ni preto ni blanco. On a matter that doesn't really concern you, you will do well not to get involved by meddling, or volunteering information.

Ninguno save lo ke ay en la oya, salvo la cuchara ke la meneya. No one knows what's inside the soup bowl, except for the spoon that stirs it. In other words, you can't realize what's going on, until you really understand all the problems involved.

Ken tiene buen vizino, embeza buen dotrino. If your neighbor possesses good qualities, you can't help but learn to be prudent.

La sedaka balda la gezera. Giving charity has the tremendous power to annul even a severe decree that's been decided against this person who gives the charity.

Inche cuvos echa a la mar. This applies to a person who talks a lot, but what he says contains no rhyme or reason.

El ke bate la puerta, oye su repuesta. There are some circumstances where a person is better off in keeping silent, because if you press the matter too much, you might provoke an unkind and hurtful comment.

Se izo del Mordecai, or *azete del Mordecai.* Mordecai is the Biblical character in the story of Esther who ignored the decree of Haman that everyone bow down to Haman. In other words, a person may know very well what you're asking, but pretends he doesn't by ignoring the issue.

June 1979   Sivan/Tamuz 5739

Ladino Sayings - VI
(Ladino - Let's Keep It Alive!)

We, at Sephardic Bikur Holim Congregation, still chant some compositions in Ladino. For example, *Perek,* which we sing on the six *Shabbat* afternoons between *Pesach* and *Shavuoth.* I think we should encourage our youngsters to learn these and many others, in our Ladino dialect. It seems like a crushing blow to see it gradually fade away.

Recently, a number of young readers of *La Boz* expressed a warm desire to read a few more Ladino expressions. So, following are some that were quite popular. The definitions and explanations are my own.

Lamed holem lo! The Hebrew letter *lamed* joined with the Hebrew vowel *holem,* spelled *lo,* meaning "no!" It was applied in the following manner. For example: David is about to purchase a valuable item from a non-Jewish merchant. A friend, Haim, who is with him at the shop, understands the quality and value better than David, and Haim wants to indicate to David not to pay the price, but doesn't want the shopkeeper to sense that he's trying to spoil the deal. So, Haim starts singing, "*Lamed holem lo!*" as a subtle hint to David - "No! Don't buy it!" - therefore saving David a bundle.

Este es nasido de viernes. He's born on Friday. There was a popular belief that a person who happened to be born on Friday was mysteriously gifted with an extraordinary talent to outsmart any of his friends, having the faculty of a sharp and an intelligent human being. So, you have to be careful in dealing with such a smarty.

Este aroz areyeva muncha agua. This rice will require a lot of water to cook properly. As if to say: in a situation which at first appeared so simple to resolve, it gradually develops that it gets more complicated than it was anticipated. Therefore, it will take more time to wind it up. It may need the intervention of other individuals and the employment of additional funds in order to bring it to a satisfactory solution.

Trokar kazal, trokar mazal. Move to another town, your luck may improve. As if to say: in case you fail to accomplish a certain venture, or you're not able to make ends meet by the usual methods, change your tactics (or location) and you may hit it lucky and accomplish your goal.

Bar minan. Aramaic: Let it be far from us! When someone mentions an accident, an injury, or a mishap, or any other tragic event that happened to someone, we say: *Bar minan!* "I hope it never happens to us or to any of our family and friends." It's a sort of prayer to G-d to keep us safe and away from similar mishaps.

Bivas! May you live long. There's an old tradition that says there was a time in old antiquity, that when a person sneezed, that one sneeze caused his death immediately. Finally, one of the partriarchs pleaded with G-d to abolish this type of death caused by a sneeze. Since then, the custom of saying *bivas* to a person who sneezed started meaning, "Rather than death through this sneeze, we wish you long life." It may be, that our custom of saying to a baby that sneezes, we say *bivas* - if the baby continues to sneeze, on the second one we say *crescas*: on the third we say *te engrandescass*, on the fourth we say *para bien*, on the fifth we say *amen*. If the baby continues to sneeze, you make up your own blessings.

October 1980   Heshvan 5743

Ladino Sayings - VII
(Reflections On Ladino Sayings)

Every language or dialect has its favorite sayings, and so do we Ladino-speaking Sephardim. I will quote here a few of them, and add some maxims based on one single word.

Tu ijo-asta la edad de 5 anyos - es tu amo
a la edad de dies anyos - es tu esclavo,
a la edad de dies y sesh anyos - es tu consejero
de dies y sesh y endelantre - es tu amigo, o tu inimigo.

Translation:
Your son, until he is 5 years old, he is your boss,
When he reaches the age of ten, he is your slave,
When he gets to be sixteen, he is your advisor,
From sixteen on, he is either your friend or your enemy.

Es dezonor al ombre, ser mujer de su mujer: It's a disgrace for a man to be a wife to his wife.

El primer ombre no tomo mujer, asta despues ke el Dio lo adurmesyo: The first man did not take a wife, until G-d put him to sleep.

In Ladino, we refer to a baby or child as *criatura.* If we split this word in two, we get *cria tura.* That is to say, when a mother takes good care of this baby (*cria*), it has a much better chance to grow up and lasts (*tura*) and overcomes the various indispositions that all children go through, much easier.

The word *avramila* means a green, sour plum. Some say that our patriarch Abraham had himself circumcised under one of these plum trees. Thus, they derive the word *avramila,* to say: our patriarch Avram had his *mila* (circumcision) under this plum tree.

Keres matar a un savyo, metele un bovo al lado. If you want to humiliate (or kill) a scholar, have a slow-witted person sit right next to him.

En lugar de Rahel, le dieron a Leah. Instead of Rachel, they gave him Leah. This has reference to the Biblical story, where Jacob wanted to marry Rachel, with whom he fell in love. However, Laban, his father-in-law, fooled Jacob. The night of the wedding, Laban substituted and gave Jacob Rachel's older sister, Leah.

Following are a few sayings, all using the word *cavesa* (meaning, head). *Cavesa de arnaoot:* obstinate, like the head of an obstinate Moslem. *Save alevantar cavesa:* to become prosperous. *Meldar de cavese:* to read by heart. *Sino tiene cavesa, ke tenga pies:* if he has no brains, let him use his feet. *El pishcado fyede de la cavesa:* the fish starts stinking from the head first; to say when things go wrong - it always starts from the leaders. *Conta cavesas, mete bonetas:* count the person's head and buy caps accordingly. *Cavesa de apyo:* a head of Turkish celery. *Le incho la cavesa:* he filled his head with trifles.

September 1981   Elul/Tishri 5742

Ladino Sayings - VIII
(More Ladino Expressions)

Recently I met some of our younger members who are still interested in Ladino sayings or proverbs. A goodly number of these have asked me to write in *La Boz* a few more proverbs. This proves to me that this heritage of our Levantine Sephardim is not really "dead," as some would have us believe.

We know there are several publications and pamphlets that contain a variety of lists of these proverbs, but they only give the proverb with only the literal translations, which sometimes makes little or no sense. What I will try to do is, in addition to their literal translation, supply the way we apply them in their various references, citing some examples.

To that segment of our readers that are familiar with these and many others, I will say this is only for the younger generation.

Golor de kemado, la barva de tu kunyado. Something smells burning, it's your brother-in-law's beard. An example as to when we use this expression is as follows: In a room full of people, one person starts sniffing and says something is burning. As the rest of those present in the room do not smell anything burning, automatically they address this one person with a humorous or sarcastic remark saying to him, "You know what you are smelling that is burning? It is your brother-in-law's beard." This indicates that it is all in this person's imagination.

Azno batal provecho para el kazal. An idle donkey proves an advantage for the village. We use this expression to indicate a situation in which the citizens of a small community see someone that is not occupied, so they ask him to do a few little favors for them. When these villagers see him going around doing nothing, they take advantage of him, and ask him to do some free chores, or fix something in the house that needs to be taken care of. Everyone derives some benefit from him. He's a godsend for their many needs.

Mijor pan seco con amor y non gayina con dolor. Rather eat dry, old bread with love than eat chicken, accompanied with pain. This expression is used when a person would rather do away with all the luxuries in the world, preferring a simple, harmonious life, even though he sees others have all things that money can buy. These affluent people are constantly arguing, depriving themselves of the affection that goes to make a happy and enjoyable life.

Inche cuvos, echa a la mar. Fill up buckets of water and empty them right back to the sea. This expression can be explained and illustrated with a person who is trying very hard to convey an idea or a project to another or to a crowd, but this person uses arguments that are neither logical nor reasonable. His efforts are wasted on the listeners because he repeats his unconvincing approach without adding any new reasons. So because his efforts are falling on deaf ears, he is likened to a person who fills up his buckets with water, but turns around and spills all the water in the bucket right back to the ocean, because, despite all his efforts, the problem is far from being resolved.

January 1982   Teveth/Shevat 5742

Ladino Greetings - I
(Ladino Greetings and Replies)

Some of our members have indicated to me that they're very much interested to learn the proper Ladino greetings for different occasions, as well as the proper reply. So, once again, I have to say to those of our readers who are familiar with these greetings, these greetings are directed only for the benefit of our younger readers who are interested in the preservation of our Ladino culture, so it can continue to live a little longer. When you see a "G," it means a greeting. An "R" means a reply or a response. I will translate only when I think it necessary.

G: *Buenos dias.* (Good day.) R: *Buenas tengas salud y vida.* (Have goodness, health and long life.)

G: *Ke haber?* (What do you say?) R: *Todo bueno.* (All's well.)

G: *Ke ay de muevo?* (What's new?) R: *Salud buena para todos.*

On meeting a friend or a person on Saturday -- G: *Shabbath shalom.* R: *Shabbath shalom mevorah.*

On Saturday night -- G: *Buenas semanas.* R: *Salud y vida.* Some say in Hebrew -- G: *Shavua tov.* R: *Shavua tov mevorah.* Some say -- G: *Semandas buenas y claras.* R: *Amen y tengas.* Or, some say in Hebrew -- G: *Shavua tov mevorah.* R: *Alenu vealah.*

On meeting afternoons or evenings -- G: *Buenas tadres.* R: *Buenas tadres.*

On meeting or visiting at night -- G: *Buenas noches.* R: *Buenas noches.* (Good night.)

On leaving from a visit at night -- G: *Con bien amanescas.* R: *Y amanescas sano y rezyo.*

On *Hanukah* -- G: *Hanukah alegre.* R: *Hanukah alegre.*

On *Purim* -- G: *Purim alegre.* R: *Purim alegre.* (Happy *Purim.*) Some say on *Purim* -- G: *Buen Purim buenos anyos.*

In Israel, in Hebrew, for *Hanukah* -- G: *Hag Hanukah sameah.* R: *Hag Hanukah sameah.* (Happy *Hanukah.*)

For *Purim*, in Israel -- G: *Hag Purim sameah.* R: *Hag Purim sameah.* (Happy *Purim.*)

On the three Jewish holidays, that is, *Pesach* (Passover), *Shavuoth* and *Succoth* -- G: *Moadim lesimha* (Happy holiday.) R: *Hagim uzmanim lesasson.* (Holidays and seasons of joy.) For *Pesach*, some say -- G: *Pesach alegre.* R: Same. Or, some say -- G: *Buen moed.* R: Same. Or, some say -- G: *Moed alegre.* R: Same. In Israel, in Hebrew -- G: *Hag sameah.*

On *Rosh Hashanah* (New Year) and *Yom Kippur* -- G: *Tizku leshanim raboth.* R: *Tizke vetihye vetaarih yamin.* (Wish you many, many years. May you have the fortune to have a long and good life.) For *Rosh Hashanah*, some say in Ladino -- G: *Anyada alegre.* R: *Amen, y tengas.* Others have another -- G: *Escritos en livros de vidas* (May you be inscribed in the book of life.) R: *Amen, este anyo y munchas mas.* (Amen, this year and many more.)

On the end of each holiday -- G: *Buenos anyos.* R: *Buenos anyos.* (Have good years.)

After the eighth day of *Pesach* (Passover) each head of the household tries to bring home a few stalks of green grass and recites the *prasinagua levadura.* (We published this already in a previous article in *La Boz.* See p. 170) The green grass is supposed to represent a good omen that the coming summer will be a lucky and a plentiful one. And when they finish this little poem they greet each other with *enveranada alegre.* (Let's have a pleasant and felicitous summer full of economic prosperity.) Accompanied with, *con salud buena y pas y amor en el mundo entero.* (May we enjoy good health, and may we see peace and harmony in the whole world.) And everyone says *amen.*

We have a few more greetings, but we'll record them in the next issue of *La Boz. Si kere el Dio.*

Ladino Greetings - II
(More Ladino Greetings)

We continue with Ladino greetings and responses. As everyone knows, our Ladino language contains, besides Spanish, a great number of Hebrew words. In our long stay in Turkey, it was inevitable that we adopt some greetings in Turkish, of which I will include just a few in today's *La Boz*.

When a guest drops in, and finds the family at a dinner table, the host invites the guest with the following. Greeting: *Buyurun* (Join us.) The guest declines the invitation. Response: *Afiyet olsoon.* (Enjoy it.) Or, *Salud y beraha* (Health and blessing).

When friends want to welcome back a traveler. Greeting: *Hosh yeldin* (Welcome) Response: *Hosh buldum* (Nice to see you.) The equivalent in Hebrew -- Greeting: *Baruch haba.* Response: *Baruch hanimtza.* In Ladino, *Vengas en buen'ora.*

After a haircut or a Turkish bath -- Greeting: *Saatlar olson.* (It should be in good health.) Response: *Evalla.* (Thank you.)

On seeing a growing baby, etc. Greeting: *Mashalla.* (May G-d preserve him.) Response: *Nazar ke no le toke.* (May the evil eye never affect him.)

On the return of a son, etc., friends greet the father, etc. Greeting: *Yozoon aydi.* (You show a joy in your eyes.) Response: *Gracias* and a smile.

Now we continue in Ladino.

On meeting a friend who is celebrating a birthday or a wedding anniversary. Greeting: *Munchos y buenos.* (Many good ones.) Response: *Y agas.* (You, too.) Some add, *con salud buena.* (With good health.)

On seeing a friend who bought a new car or a new house or a new suit. Greeting: *Con salud.* Some add, *ke la gozesh* (you shall enjoy it), on a house or a car, etc. Response: *Amen, y vozosh ke tengash todo bueno.* (Amen, and you shall have everything good.)

On receiving a donation, the collector or the beneficiary tells the donor, *Para tanyedores* (Wish you many happy events when you employ musicians to celebrate.)

On the recipient -- Greeting: *Tizku lemitzvoth.* (You should merit good deeds.) The donor -- Response: *Tizku laasoth.* (You should merit doing them.)

When offering condolences to a person or family who lost a dear one. Greeting: *Vozosh ke bivash.* (You who are left shall live.) Some add, *mos embaraso' muy muncho.* (We were very sorry.) Response: Just a nod with head bowed. On the last day of mourning -- Greeting: *El ke tenga repozo bueno-y mas por dingunos no.* (He shall have a good rest and this shall never happen to anyone else.) Response: A nod of the head.

Some greet the remaining mourners, *Los ke vos kedaron ke vos bivan.* (The ones that are left shall live.)

It used to be a very beautiful custom among Sephardim, when a friend drops in for a visit, the hostess would offer the guest a cup of Turkish coffee on a beautiful *tavla* (tray) filled with various types of *dulce* (sweets). Sometimes it was *dulce de conja* (a jelly made from rose petals) or *dulce de cayissi* (apricot compote) or *dulce de bimbriyo* (quince) or *naranja* (orange marmalade or other citrus fruits) all personally prepared by the housewife. Before the guest would eat this delicious treat or drink the coffee, he would offer his good wishes -- Greeting: *Dulces alegres* (sweets). Some would add the Turkish word *dovletlis* (wish you all the best). Response: *Dulces siempre.* (May it always be sweet.)

On inquiring about a friend's health -- Greeting: *Ke tal estas* (How are you?) or *Ke mos kontas* (What's new?). If everything is okay -- Response: *Bendicho el Dio* or *Gracias a Dio.* (Thank G-d.) If things are not all that well -- Response: *Diremos bueno, ke mos se aga todo bueno.* (Let's say well so everything will be well.) *Arogar al Dio salud buena.* (Ask G-d for good health.)

When friends wish to offer congratulations to the parents of a *bar mitzvah* boy -- Greeting: *Novyo ke lo veamos* (We hope to see him grow to be a bridegroom.) Some add, *Con padre y madre y todos justos.* (With father and mother and none missing.) Response: *Y lo veremos todos con salud buena.* (And we shall see them with good health.) On talking about a friend who is doing well -- Greeting: *De tura ke le vayga.* (I hope his success continues.)

On greeting a friend or relative going on a trip -- Greeting: *Caminos buenos* (good roads) or *Caminos de leche y miel* (roads of milk and honey).

In Hebrew -- Greeting: *Nesiya tova* (a good departure) or in Ladino *Ke vayash y vengash con salud buena.* (You shall go and come back in good health.)

On meeting a person who just did a favor, *Para bueno ke te topes.* (We shall find you for good things.) Sometimes the above greeting is used to express a regret for what he did, in a sarcastic way.

On seeing a member of a family that is expecting a blessed event, *Escapamiento bueno.* (You should have a good ending.)

On offering wishes to a person who is embarked on a project, *Kolay y livyano.* (Easy and light.) This is a greeting exchanged by ladies who are beginning to clean house for *Pesach* or beginning preparation and baking for a wedding, *bar mitzvah* and such.

On seeing a healthy increase in members of a family or some other additions, *Pujados y no amenguados.* (You shall multiply and not subtract.)

On wishing a friend success in a project -- Greeting: *Reushita buena.* (Good success.) Response: *Y tengas.* (And you, too.)

There are many, many more.

This will suffice for now.

Shalom, beraha vetova! (Peace, blessing and good!)

February 1976   Shevat/Adar 1 5736

La Ija De Yiftah

We have a saying, partly in Ladino and partly in Hebrew, that goes: *"Ben kach uven kach bulo la ija de Yiftah."* Very loosely translated it means "Between the one and the other, Yiftah's daughter perished." This saying is actually based on an episode we find in our Bible, in the Book of Judges, where the story of Yiftah is related.

As is well known, after Moses died, Joshua was appointed the nation's leader, under whom the Jewish people conquered and settled in the Holy Land. After Joshua died, there began a period in our history known as the era of *Shofetim* (Judges). This period lasted for quite a few years, after which the prophet Samuel, the last of the judges appointed Saul as the first king of Israel.

One of these judges was called Yiftah, who ruled over Israel for six years. Being the tenth in line Yiftah was selected as *shofet* because the Jewish nation needed an experienced warrior to fight the enemy and recapture some of the land they had lost in previous battles.

After he was selected for this mission, he took a very solemn oath and he made a formal *neder* (a vow) and said: If *Hashem* will help him win the war, and be victorious against the national enemy, the first thing he will see come out of his house, on his return, he will offer it as a sacrifice.

According to our sages, this declaration, in the form of a solemn promise, was extremely irresponsible on the part of Yiftah. They say, supposing, on his return home, he would've seen an unclean animal, which was unfit for sacrifice, how would he ever have accomplished the *neder*?

As it happened, unfortunately, his daughter was the first one that came out of the house to greet her heroic father. Now Yiftah found himself in a quandary. He, naturally, loved his daughter very much, yet he had to keep his solemn oath. Torn between his affection for his daughter, and his obligation to fulfill his vow, he finally chose to keep his promise, thinking that his word of honor came first, and therefore he thought he was duty bound to offer his daughter as sacrifice.

What Yiftah didn't do was ask the advice of Pinhas, the high priest. Had he asked, Pinhas would've found a way out of his *neder* by the process of annulment, thus absolving Yiftah from any binding vow, and thus Yiftah's daughter would've been spared.

Yiftah thought it beneath his dignity to seek advice from Pinhas, and Pinhas, in turn, figured and said to himself, "a person who has a toothache, it's up to him to go to the dentist." The result was "*ben kach uven kach bolo la ija de Yiftah.*" Meaning that two leaders of the nation, for lack of communication, caused this tragedy. Between Yiftah's arrogance and Pinhas' complacency, Yiftah's daughter perished.

Some biblical commentators explain that Yiftah's daughter ran away to the mountains, and there lived until her death, all alone, like a hermit.

April 1978   2 Adar/Nisan 5738

Ladino Endevines (Riddles)

Before the advent of radio and television, Sephardic families used to get together in the evenings; sometimes they held interesting conversations about timely topics, and at other times they resorted to other ways *para pasar el tiempo y para devirtir* (to pass the time; to entertain). Especially around *Purim*, if the family circle was blessed with a clever individual, he would introduce a variety of Ladino riddles, which we called *endevines* or *bilmejekes* in Turkish. This person would challenge the listeners, saying to them: "See if you can figure out the answer to this riddle?" I came across a few of these *endevines*, and I insert them here. After all, these *endevines* form part and parcel of our Sephardic lore.

For the benefit of our non-Ladino speaking readers, I've translated each one from Ladino into English. A good, fun way, would be to read the riddle and try to guess the answer before the reader takes a look at the answer, which I listed by number at the bottom of the page.

1

Yo so una criatura blanca
(I'm a white creature.)
Mi madre me izo en lo ke estava cantando
(My mother made me while she was singing.)
Ni cola tengo, ni cavesa
(I have neither a tail nor a head.)
Yo no so ni ombre ni animal.
(I am neither a man nor an animal.)

2

Mas muncho se alarga, mas muncho se akurta.
(The longer it gets, the shorter it gets.)

3

Mas muncho kitan, mas grande seaze.
(The more they take out, the bigger it gets.)

4

La boz se siente, la cara no se ve.
(You can hear it, but you can't see it.)

5

Mi ermano viene a vijitar,
(My brother comes to visit me,)
Yo se la do a chupar
(I put it in his mouth to lick it.)

6

Corona tiene, rey no es.
(He has a crown, but he's not a king.)

Ora no tiene, y save ke ora es.
(He has no watch, yet he knows what time it is.)

7

La manyana camina con cuatro pies
(In the morning he walks on four legs)
La mediodia con dos
(At noon he walks on two)
La tarde con tres
(In the evening, he walks on three legs.)

Answers:
1. *El guevo* (the egg)
2. *La vida* (life)
3. *La foya* (the grave)
4. *El trueno* (thunder)
5. *La cuchara de dulce* (a spoonful of candy) This one needs a little explanation. It used to be a Sephardic custom, that when a relative or a friend came over to someone's house to visit, the first thing the hostess would do was to offer the visitor a *tavla* (tray) with *dulce* (a sort of home made marmalade or a preserve made from rose petals or grapefruit peels, etc.); this followed by Turkish coffee. It was a beautiful custom.
6. *El gayo* (the rooster)
7. *El ombre: ninyo, mansevo, y cuando se aze viejo, camina con baston* (man: baby, grownup, and when he gets old, with a walking stick).

October 1974   Tishri 5735

Consejas

What did we ever do before radio and television? To pass the time, that is. For one thing, the art of conversation is being lost, and what a pity. Between stories, programs, news and sports, our children's eyes are glued to the "tube."

As a matter of comparison, I would like to tell our young readers how we passed the time at home when we were young. No doubt, every family had a favorite *tiyo* or *tiya* or some other relative that was an expert story teller. These stories were known as *consejas*. In our case, we had a *Tiyo* David, my Dad's younger brother, who was a fantastic *contador de consejas* (storyteller). He had an uncanny ability to dramatize the events to such a degree that he had all of us curious with suspense to hear the outcome of the story.

On long, cold winter nights, we would gather around him, heat radiating from the *ogar* (a charcoal burner) in the middle of the room, and when we could afford it, some of us would have a bag of *pipitas* (dried pumpkin seeds), or *bilibizes* (roasted chickpeas), or *garvansos* (salted chickpeas), listening intently to those enchanting tales of a princess romatically involved with the young hero of the story.

Children's stories in English usually begin with "Once upon a time" and in our Ladino version they always started with "*Aviya de ser un rey.*" (There once was a king.) One explanation why most of these stories had to do with kings and princesses, I think, is a holdover from the time our ancestors lived in Spain where these *consejas* probably originated. In fact, some of the stories had to do with *la ija del rey de Castilia con el ijo del rey de Aragon* (the daughter of the King of Castilia with the son of the King of Aragon), so that it could very well be an extension of our Spanish origins. Many of these *consejas* are being collected in Israel now from various sources and are being translated into Hebrew and being published in different publications in order to preserve every type of literature related to Ladino.

I would like to give you a sample of one of these *consejas* that they discovered recently from a very old source. Some of our readers perhaps have come across a similar story in the literature of other people's folklore, or in another version, but for our simple purpose we will not be critics, but just plainly enjoy a *conseja*. [Editor's note: Examples of *consejas* in English can be found in *Folktales of Israel*, Dov Noy, editor, University of Chicago Press.]

It seems that the king of Aragon had a very beautiful daughter who had a sweetheart whom she loved since childhood. Their love developed to such a degree that they decided to get married. Of course, they needed to have the consent of her father. But the king had other plans and ideas, namely, that some day his daughter would marry a wealthy *sinyor* and thus the king would have a rich son-in-law.

As it happened, this young man was not well to do, so the king refused to give his consent, and prevented the marriage. But the king agreed to a plan that the young couple came up with. That is, the young man would go away, seek a fortune and come back a rich man. The king heard this plan but he agreed on one very strict condition.

The king would give this young lover three years' time, and if he did not show up by that time, the princess would be married to someone else.

So the young man went away, won a fortune, and returned to Aragon a few hours after his grace expired and only a very short time after his sweetheart got married to another man, whereupon the young man collapses and dies, and at his funeral, the princess passes out and dies from a broken heart.

What a sad ending!! Oh well, never mind! It's only a *conseja*.

Chapter Eight

Sephardic Customs

July 1976   Tamuz/Av 5736

Sephardic Customs - I

Not long ago, a young Seattle Sephardi asked me where he could find either a book, or some other type of written material in which he could, research Sephardic customs, and those customs that are different from the ones used by our brethren, the Ashkenazim.

I told him there's an excellent book, in English, on this subject written by a Rabbi Dr. Zimmels from London, England. The name of this book is *Sephardim and Ashkenazim*. There's another book on this subject, written in Hebrew only, this latter book deals with different liturgical prayers. The name of this book is *Keter Shem Tov*, written by Rabbi Shem Tov Gaguin, from London, England, also.

When I explained to this young man the contents of these books, being of a highly *halachic* nature (relating to Jewish law), I could tell by his facial expressions that this was not what he had in mind. What he really wanted to read about was the nontechnical customs and differences, like how come on the *Pesach seder* night the Ashkenazim eat horseradish, while the Sephardim use romaine lettuce instead, and similar types of custom differences.

So I decided to write for *La Boz* a series of three or four articles, enumerating Sephardic customs, and also mentioning some differences that exist between the two groups concerning *minhagim* (customs).

First, though, we have to make it very clear that both Ashkenazim and Sephardim are first and foremost Jews. We believe in the same Creator, our *Torah*, our *Mishnah, Talmud, Shulchan Aruch* are one. In other words, our basic laws are exactly the same. The only differences that do exist arose only after many years of living in exile in different countries and climates. Like the Sephardim, who use Ladino or Arabic as their second language after Hebrew, the Ashkenazim use Yiddish as their second language after Hebrew. Lately, though, to pinpoint how to distinguish between the two groups, some authorities came out with a new definition of Sephardim and that is: A Sephardi is any Jew that is not an Ashkenazi.

Now it's only logical to start off with those customs that pertain to when a Jewish child is born, or even before he's born. Soon after the future mother notifies the family she's expecting, both families get together and designate a day when they will invite all the female friends and relatives to a gathering called: *cortar fashadura*, that is, to cut, measure, and sew the baby clothes that will make up the layette. Naturally, this calls for a celebration. That's when they have *caveh de mujeres* (coffee klatch). It starts out as simply "coffee and" and it ends being the most sumptuous *jonbush* (party), with a large variety of goodies. Those ladies that know, would sing *canticas de parida* (songs for the expectant mother) in Ladino.

Then comes the *paridura* (birth). In the olden days the *haham* would write out *shadayim* (two papers) and send them to the house, one for the baby, and one for the *parida*, as blessings and protection from all accidents (see p. 190). This custom is not in vogue any more.

If it's a boy, naturally they notify the *mohel* (the ritual circumciser) and make preparations for the eighth day, when they will have the *berith mila* (circumcision) or *birkath mila*, or as the Ashkenazim call it the *bris*. Another old custom, which is not very popular now, was on the night before the *berith*, the *parido* (father) would invite to his home a few men who would recite some psalms and some special appropriate prayers. This night's ritual is called *shemira*. The Ashkenazim have a very similar custom. They call it *sholom zahor*, only they get together on the Friday night before the *bris*. On the eighth day, the *parido* and the *parida*, designate someone to act as *kitado*, and his wife to act as *kitada*. Another name for these two, the godfather and the godmother is *sandak* and *sandaka*. On the first male child, this honor is given to the paternal grandfather and grandmother. For the succeeding male child born, this honor of *kitado* and *kitada* is given to the maternal grandfather and grandmother. On this auspicious day, the *kitado* sits on a special chair, decorated with *chevres* (ornamental, embroidered cloth). This chair is called *la siya de Eliyahu Hanavi* (Elijah's chair), because we have a traditional belief, that this saintly prophet attends all the *beriths* and brings blessings and good tidings from our Creator.

August 1976   Av/Elul 5736

Sephardic Customs - II

In last month's *La Boz,* I mentioned *canticas de parida* (songs for the mother). Here is a small sample of one of the more popular ones. *Ya vino el parido, con los combidados se trusho en la mano, menta y buen pishcado y la otra mano yena de ducados ya es buen siman, esta alegria,* etc. (The father of the baby came, with all those who were invited, he had in his hand mint and good fish, and the other hand filled with gold coins, and this is a good omen, this happiness.) Also in last month's article, I stated that the *kitado* (godfather) sits <u>on</u> the special chair of *Eliyahu Hanavi.* Rather, it should be corrected to say the *kitado* sits <u>next</u> to that chair. Then, those men present start chanting appropriate *pizmonim* (Hebrew songs), then the *kitada* (godmother), who is with the baby, waits for a signal from the rabbi, and she marches down the aisle carrying the baby, wrapped up in fancy clothes, sometimes with a tiny *taleth,* and wearing a cute little *kipa* (skull cap).

The circumcision takes place, after which the father recites two blessings. The Ashkenazi father recites only one blessing, the one that says "Enter the newborn in the Covenant of Abraham" omitting the *sheeheyanu beraha.* They claim that this last *beraha* is omitted wherever any *sekana* (danger due to the operation) exists. The Ashkenazim also have the custom of *sandak* (the one who holds the baby during the circumcision), however they do it differently. They call him *kvater,* and those who are so honored hold the baby for a minute, and then transfer it to the other relatives that are also picked for this honor.

Then comes the naming of the baby. We Sephardim have the practice of naming the child after a living relative, like a grandparent, while the Ashkenazim never do. The reason for this, they maintain, is that they don't hold it as a good omen so they pick a name of a dear departed relative. *Kiddush* is said on wine. In addition, we have the custom of saying a blessing on either a lemon, a sprig of romero, or *murta* (rosemary, or fresh myrtle). The reason for this, some *hahamim* say, is we bless the Almighty for our sense of smell, which is the symbol of *neshama* (soul), in that He is the one that gives us the breath of life.

Incidentally, here is a good spot to mention the word *mumya* (foreskin). After the rabbi cuts the foreskin, in times past, he used to hand over this piece to an elderly lady, who in turn used to take it, dry it and then use it whenever necessary, as a mysterious cure of some illness. I don't think this practice is prevalent any more, because there are no persons left that know how to do it, or what to do with it.

Let us not forget to include the fact that if the baby happened to be a girl, there's a special celebration for her also. The friends and relatives get together, and have what they call *fijola*, where the parents hold the baby girl, usually dressed in fancy little clothes. Everyone present takes a look at the baby, and all congratulate the father, the mother, and relatives on how beautiful the baby is, and wish her *novya ke la veamos* (that we should see her as a bride), etc. After this they finally bestow upon her the name they selected. Usually the first born girl is named after the paternal grandmother, and the succeeding girl is named after the maternal grandmother. (The Ashkenazim, as we explained concerning naming the boy, also do not name the girls after living relatives, and so they pick a name from a former generation.)

Sometimes, the naming of a girl is done at the synagògue, when the father is called to *sefer*. The rabbi then conducts a *misheberah*, accompanied by selected, and appropriate portions from *Shir Hashirim*, extolling the virtues of the gorgeous newborn girl. At the end of this ceremony, the rabbi asks the father the name he and *parida* have selected for their daughter. The rabbi then announces her name with a hearty *mazal tov*, and blesses the whole family. We Sephardim greet a *parido* and a *parida* or the grandparents with: for a boy - *Besiman tov* and if it is a girl, the greeting is *Bemazal tov*.

September 1976   Elul/Tishri 5736

Sephardic Customs - III

The Sephardic name for *bar mitzvah* is *cumplir minyan* (completing the quorum of ten males). Our practice is to have the young man come to *kahal* on that *Shabbath*, read the *perashah* or *Torah* portion of the week, and call him to *sefer* as *samuh* (next to the last). The Ashkenazi *bar mitzvah* chants the *haftarah* (weekly portion from the Prophets). That's the only main difference. Here's a good spot to mention the fact that the Ashkenazi young man reads the

haftarah not only on his *Shabbath* of *bar mitzvah*, but when he is a
bridegroom, he chants the *haftarah* on the Saturday before the
wedding. The only time the Sephardim ever read the *haftarah* is when
one has to commemorate a dear departed (as on the week of the
meldado, see p. 178) or when one is *betoh shana* (during the year of
mourning). Both customs are based on traditional reasons. The
Sephardic boys wear the *taleth* (prayer shawl), even starting during
their very young years, while the Ashkenazi young man, once he wears
it on the day of his *bar mitzvah*, does not wear it again until after he's
married or when he goes up to *sefer*.

The Ashkenazim call the *Shabbath* before the wedding as
Shabbos Auf Ruf, literally meaning "Being called up [to *sefer*]." The
groom, his relatives and friends come to *shul* (synagogue) where the
hatan chants the *haftarah* followed by a *kiddush*, accompanied with
special songs and festivities. The Sephardim call this Saturday
Shabbath de novyo (*Shabbath* of the groom), but the Sephardic *novyo*
does not read the *haftarah*. Lately we've been seeing that the
womenfolk start throwing down *confites de boda* (candy) when the
novyo is finished reading the *beraha* for the *sefer*. This custom is
prevalent among the Jews of Israel. The Ashkenazi *hatans* fast on the
day of the wedding. They maintain it's their day of atonement when
all their sins are forgiven. Most of the Sephardim did not adopt this
custom.

All Jews have the *hupa* (bridal canopy). The Sephardim have the
added custom of *echar taleth* (spreading of the *taleth*). The bride's
parents on one side, and the groom's parents on the other, hold on to
the fringes while the *taleth* is placed on the head of the *novyo* and the
novya. The real significance of this very old custom is explained to
mean that the groom is saying to the bride "from now on you're under
my shelter and my protection," and so they become as one unit,
bearing in mind also the symbolism of the *taleth*, which is considered
a very solemn article of clothing. Incidentally, a Sephardic father and
mother of a growing young man, considered this action of *echar taleth*
so important, that they used to say, as a solemn oath, "*Asi ke mos
ayegue el Dio echar taleth a mi ijo*." (Let G-d . . . help us be able to
spread the *taleth* over my son.)

The Saturday after the wedding is called *Shabbat de Avraham Siv*.
On this Saturday, the *novyo*, the *novya*, all relatives and friends come
to *kahal*, and in addition to the regular weekly *sefer*, a special *Sefer
Torah* is taken out for the *novyo*. The rabbi reads the appropriate
portion (Genesis 24, 1), and those men in the congregation who know
chant the Aramaic translation starting with the two words *veavraham*

siv (and Abraham became old). This custom, which is very old, and is purely Sephardic, is not very prevalent nowadays.

The custom of breaking a glass at the end of the wedding ceremony is based on a story found in the *Talmud*. Mar, the son of Ravina, was giving a party on the day of his son's wedding. He took a look around, and he saw all the scholars clowning immoderately and carrying on too long. So, in order to attract their attention, and to put a stop to all this joshing, he took a very expensive crystal glass and shattered it to pieces. Our *hahamim* offer the explanation that, from this incident related in the *Talmud*, we should derive the lesson, that even in our times of joy and happiness we should remember the destruction of our sacred city of Jerusalem and the sanctuary, which was the symbol of our national existence. The Ashkenazim, some of them at least, have the custom that just before the wedding ceremony starts, the bride goes around the groom seven times, sometimes accompanied by both mothers, and sometimes with candles. The Sephardim never adopted this custom. From the above story of the *Talmud* we see that the groom's family sponsors and makes all the expenditures for the wedding. Sephardim nowadays, usually share the wedding expenses, by both families.

November 1976   Heshvan/Kislev 5737

Sephardic Customs - IV

In this, the fourth of the series, we will mention a few customs about Jewish holidays. In order to accomplish the *mitzvah* of eating *maror* (bitter herbs) on *Pesach*, the *Mishnah*, which is part of the traditional oral law, prescribes several kinds of greens, but they recommend, at the top of the list, *hazereth* (romaine lettuce), wherever available. Since the Sephardim lived in moderate climates around the Mediterranean regions, romaine lettuce was available around *Pesach* time. So we kept that custom. However, for the Ashkenazim, living in the northern European regions, where the snow was still on the ground around April, no lettuce was available. So they used horseradish, which, by its very nature grows in cold climates. In Turkish, the lettuce is called *maror*. There might be a connection there, somehow, linguistically. I remember when we used to cut into a fresh romaine lettuce in Turkey, the first taste had a small bitter flavor to it. That, possibly accounts for its being called *maror* (bitter).

There is another difference in customs on *Pesach*. We Sephardim do eat string beans and fresh peas on *Pesach*, while the Ashkenazim don't. Their *hahamim* put a ban on dried peas over fifty years ago, because there may be some housewives who would take these dried peas, grind them into a fine flour and make a breadlike dough and bake it. To avoid any misunderstanding, and to make sure that some people wouldn't be driven to believe that these housewives are baking bread on *Pesach*, as a safeguard measure they banned the eating of dried peas on *Pesach*. The same applies to any leguminous dried vegetable, and they went even further and they applied this ban also to fresh peas, string beans, and other legumes.

The night after the last day of *Pesach*, we Sephardim have a custom, on the way home from *kahal*. We cut a bunch of green grass from a field or lawn, bring it home, and recite a humorous little poem that starts this way. *Prasinagua levadura, con su buena paparuna. kishca de gayo, cola de cavayo, aki mos vinimos, un ijico mos trushimos*, etc. (Precious dough with its good tulips, wattle of a rooster, a horse's tail, we came here, we brought a boy.) This grass is a symbol of abundance. We wish each other *buenos anyos* (good years), a prosperous summer with a healthy wheat crop and plenty of produce, fruits and vegetables.

On *Rosh Hashanah* (Jewish New Year), the Sephardim eat certain foods and we say special prayers at home, called *yehi ratsones* (literally, may it be Thy will). This also is a symbol. Each one of these food items is mentioned in the *Talmud* and accompanied by its reason why we eat them. As an example, they say we should eat apple dipped in honey, so that we should have a sweet and happy year, etc.

On the fifteenth of the Jewish month of *Shevat* (*Tu B'Shvat*), called by the Sephardim *Frutas, Fruticas,* or *beraha de las frutas,* we have the custom of eating certain kinds of fruits like figs, dates, pomegranates, *ahrovas* (carobs), grapes and we drink wine. The women bake *coluras, panizicos* (type of roll) and other goodies to say the *beraha of mezonoth*. Some housewives make *prehito*, a pudding made from bulgur, but some call this *mustrahana*. The word *prehito* is of a very obscure origin, but some maintain that it's two Hebrew words: *peri hita* meaning "the fruit of the wheat." Sometimes they serve that delicious candy-paste made from dried apricots called *pitagra*, or they make *halva de bimbriyo* (candied quince). Some even preserve a honeydew melon to have the night of *Frutas*, which is *mahpul* (a rare and welcome commodity).

Somehow, the Ashkenazim do not go to any elaborate steps as we do on *Rosh Hashanah* and *Tu B'Shvat*. It seems, at a quick glance, that the Sephardic *hahamim* (sages) have introduced into the holiday family gatherings a little bit of extra celebration. Possibly because, in feeling the public pulse, they saw that there's a great social and psychological benefit in all these added tidbits, in all these rituals, and that it tends to generate that beautiful feeling of family solidarity.

On *Tisha B'Av* (ninth of Av), we in Seattle say the *haftarah* in Ladino, alternately chanting one Hebrew verse followed by its Ladino translation. I've heard that not many communities preserved this old Sephardic custom, which some authorities say is 500 years old.

To go to another type of Sephardic custom, it's interesting to mention the practice of children standing up in *kahal* (synagogue) whenever one of their older relatives gets called up to *sefer*. This, of course, is done as a sign of respect and deference to your elders. This custom is applied also to younger brothers. They stand up for an older brother, uncle or some other relative. Nowadays, we see even girls in the *azara* (women's section) stand up whenever a big brother, an uncle, a cousin and needless to say whenever their father gets called up to *sefer*. This is a carry-over from the younger males.

August 1972   Av 5732

Marriage Customs - I
(Reflections of Bygone Days)

One doesn't have to be too old to remember some customs that have almost disappeared from the Seattle Sephardic scene. Nowadays, as soon as the wedding ceremony is over, the rabbi takes the *ketuba* (the religious marriage contract) and hands it over to the bride's mother. In bygone days, it was one of the chores of our *shamash*, Mr. Avram Barlia to deliver the *ketuba* to the mother the next day. If one saw him leave that house in his usual fashion, that meant he received the normal payment, which was *un dolar y un raki* [one dollar and one shot of raki (raisin brandy)]. But, if he was seen coming out smiling and happy, that meant he got *dos dolares y dos rakis* (two dollars and two shots of raki).

In the early days of our community, printed invitations were mailed only for weddings. But if a certain family wanted to invite to a party to celebrate *espozorios, birkath mila*, etc., the head of the family used to hand Mr. Barlia a list of names for him to go and *conbidar* (invite) the *parientes, vizinos y amigos* (relatives, neighbors and friends). There was no problem, because everyone used to live in the vicinity and Mr. Barlia knew all of them.

There was one particular occasion that we don't see anymore, and that was *aparar el ashugar* (display the trousseau). The mother of the bride appropriated a special room in the house, where she used to hang and display every stitch of clothing and other assorted accoutrements that the bride was to take with her. This also contained family heirlooms, *lavraduras* (needlework) and *chevres* (embroidered cloth), etc. This occasion was celebrated on the Saturday before the wedding, so naturally Mr. Barlia was given the list of *nombres para conbidar* (names to invite). Sometimes, also the father of the bride used to call over from Friday, the *haham* and the *cosfuegro* (in-laws) for the purpose of *apresiar el ashugar* (to appraise the value of the trousseau) and that amount agreed on by both parties, was duly inserted in the *ketuba* (wedding contract).

Speaking of *ketubas*, last year I had occasion to visit a Jewish museum in Berkely, California, with my son-in-law, Eugene Normand and among many old Jewish books and other articles of interest we saw a room full of *ketuboth*. Some of them are written in our old Sephardic script. One of them caught Eugene's eye in that it contained a little extra than the usual writing in a *ketuba*. This *ketuba* was written in Alexandria, Egypt. In the *ketuba*, the city is called No Amon, which is the rabbinic and historical name for Alexandria, Egypt.

The *ketuba* is written on the upper part of the document. On the lower part, they wrote what they call the *tenayim*, a Hebrew word meaning conditions of agreements. The father-in-law agreed and accepted upon himself to fulfill the amount of the dowry he promised the *novyo*. On this particular *ketuba*, in addition, the father-in-law agreed to give the *novyo* the privilege of *meza franca* for the whole year. I remembered this term was used in the old country to indicate the right of the bridegroom to stay with his bride -- live, eat, drink, etc. -- in her father's house free for a specified time. Often times, the *esfuegro* gave the *novyo* spending money also. These terms were legally binding, as the rabbinate had the authority from the government to enforce the laws.

Nowadays, because we're not used to this custom, we could classify the *novyo* as a freeloader. But even today, in the old country, the custom of giving a dowry to the *novyo* is in full force and many times, the father of a bride gets himself in debt considerably in order to have the daughter married.

March 1981   1 Adar/2 Adar 5741

Marriage Customs - *II*
(A La Boda y Al Biscocho)

There are an enormous amount of customs connected with the procedures leading to and including the wedding day (*la boda*). Each city in Turkey, North Africa and the Balkans had its own Sephardic practices and traditions, either original or borrowed from among the people with whom we lived.

In this article we will deal mostly with some customs prevailing in some homes interested in preserving the beautiful, time-hallowed, Sephardic traditions. We will start with the engagement, a special night set aside to celebrate this happy occasion at the bride's home, *nochada d'espozoryo* (evening of the engagement). First, they have the *haham* or rabbi read the *tenayim* (marital agreements) and then the haham would make it authentic by the *kinyan* (a form of acquisition) with a white handkerchief, held by both sides of each family, to indicate that the groom promises to bind himself to his chosen, and no other. This was followed by cheerful greetings like *mazal tov*, *besiman tov, ala ora buena, con salud y alegriya* (good luck, with a good omen, to the good hour, with health and happiness, etc.), etc., plus the *confites de boda* (wedding candies).

In years past, the bride then would do the honor of going over to kiss the hand of her future father-in-law, who had ready the *aniyo despozoryo*, a beautiful gold ring, the size and value of which depended on the economic status of the groom's family. Wealthy families in Turkey used to send their gold to expert jewelers in Paris, or Venezia (Venice) to have an exquisite design or creation for the *novya's* (bride's) pleasure. The groom would then go over and kiss the hand of his future *esfuegro* (father-in-law) who would hand over an appropriate gift or something else they would call *besa mano* (kissing the hand). Then someone in the family would announce the date of the forthcoming wedding, and other important details.

The bride's family would rush the preparation of the *ashugar* (bride's dowery wardrobe), which consisted of every item of apparel the bride would need during her early years of marriage, like dresses, jackets, coats, lingerie. As a matter of fact, each mother would start accumulating the *ashugar* even when the daughter was only three years old, which included items knit or embroidered or crocheted, even *chevres* (embroidered cloth). So by the time of the engagement she already had *el baul yeno de cozas lavradas* (a trunk filled with items of fine needlework), etc., *para la ora buena* (for the happy occasion). I venture to say, even today there are some of our ladies that can boast and display some rare pieces and say, *"Esto es del ashugar miyo."* (This is part of my dowery.)

All this, of course, would tend to lighten the financial burden of the father of the bride, who otherwise would have to spend all this in one lump sum. As it was, there was a popular saying, *"Ija de cazar, fierro mashcar"* (a father who had a daugher to marry, had the rough ordeal of chewing hard items, like iron). There was another saying, *"Bath, banoth, bavonoth."* (One daughter was *bath* (Hebrew), more than one was *banoth*, and more than two was *bavonoth*, an expression meaning, a multitude of sins, a lot of expenses of course.) This does not apply today because all girls can get good jobs now and help with the *gastes* (expenses), while in years past girls never had the opportunity to earn money.

There are so many more customs to mention, but these will suffice for now. However, I would like to make mention of the fact that right after the *espozoryo*, some families would begin rehearsing *canticas de novya, y canticas de boda* (songs of the bride and of the wedding). There are a number of these which we, in Seattle still sing. We will mention some in next month's article. But one comes to mind now, which is generally sung by some ladies from Rhodes, which is called *Dize La Muestra Novya* (My Bride Says). This is a nice song, with a catchy tune, that contains many stanzas. The main theme of the song is to extol the excellent parts of the body of the *novya*, like praising her face, her eyes, her lips, her teeth, the neck and other parts. It's too long to insert here, but I'll give a sampling.

Dize la muestra novya, como se yaman las caras. Esto no se yaman caras, sino ricos masapanes. A mis ricos masapanes a mi pendola descrivibriva la novya con el novyo. Dize la muestra novya. Como se yaman los dientes, esto no se yaman dientes. Sino perlas denfilar . . . amis limones del limonar, ami tavla de contar, ami redoma de plata, ami pala denfornar, amis perlas denfilar. Amis ricos merjanes, a mis ricos masapanes, ami pendola descrivir, a mis ricos

*ezmeraldares, ami arcol de tirar, a mi espada reluziente, a
mis brieles de lavrar, ami toronja de tornjal, a mi campo
espasiozo, biva la novya con el novyo.*

Our bride says - How do you call the cheeks? These are not
called cheeks, only rich marzipan cake. To my rich
marzipans, to my pen that writes, long live the bride and the
groom. Says our bride - How do you call the teeth? These
are not called teeth but pearls to string. To my lemons of the
lemonade jar, to my plate which deserves to be counted, to my
silver jug, to my spade in the oven, to my pearls to string, to
my rich (merchants?), to my rich marzipans, to me a pen to
write, to my rich jewelry, to my pulling rainbow, to my
resplendent sword, to my brilliant things to knit, to my
grapefruit of the grapefruit tree, to my spacious field. Long
live the bride with the groom.

April 1981   2 Adar/Nisan 5741

Marriage Customs - III
(A La Boda y Al Biscocho - II)

Last month we described some of the customs that were practiced
by the Sephardim, in connection with the preparations for
engagements. We continue now, to mention the wedding and its
various ceremonies.

Noche de alhenya The night before the wedding, the bride would
invite some of her close friends over to her house where these friends
would attend to her. One of these friends would be an expert in
applying the *alhenya* (henna) as a rouge, or finger nail polish. All this
was followed by singing, dancing, eating and having a good time with
the bride.

Caveh de banyo A day or two before the wedding, the mother of
the *novya* would take her to a big marble building known as the
Turkish bath, for the ritual bathing before the wedding. In Seattle, it's
known as the *mikveh.* After the bath, family and friends gather in the
mother's home to enjoy what they call *caveh de banyo* (coffee of the
bath), where the guests would *alegrar a la novya* (entertain the bride),

with special *romansas* (songs) and appropriate songs with *panderos* (musical instruments).

El talamo   Meanwhile, over at the *novyo's* house, a group of ladies would get busy preparing one part of the house, installing a *talamo* (canopy) decorated tapestries, with elegant *almadas, chevres, brilles, kirlantas* (pillows, embroidered cloth, sequins and beaded bride's crown). These throne-like fancy quarters is the spot where the *novyo* and *novya* would spend most of the eight days of *hupa* following the ceremony.   The groom was never allowed to leave, because it was believed that if he did leave, the *mazikim* (evil spirits) would cause him some harm.

Conbidador   In the old country, as well as the early days in Seattle, wedding invitations had not come in vogue as yet. So, in order to invite some relatives and friends to the wedding, there was a person known as *conbidador* (inviter).   In Seattle, many of us remember Avram Barlia, as the official *conbidador*. The father of the groom would hand him a list of names to be invited. In those days almost every Sephardi used to live within the confines of *maleh Judiya* (Jewish quarter) and Barlia used to know exactly where everyone lived without the benefit of home addresses. Later on, when the members started to spread out, this idea of *conbidador* was abandoned.

Echar taleth   This is strictly a Sephardic custom (see p. 168). The groom would buy a new *taleth* to be used first for this wedding ceremony. Both sets of parents would stand next to the bride and groom, each one getting hold of the fringes respectively, while the *haham* was reciting the *sheva berahoth*. This practice of *echar taleth* (put on a *taleth*) was so solemn and of such importance, that when a parent wanted to express a hope for his family, he would say: *Asi el Dio me ayegue a echar taleth a mi ijo*. This was followed by the smashing of the glass, as a remembrance to our state of exile due to our national suffering by the destruction of our glorious Holy Temple. After the ceremony, people would shower the newly married couple with rice, as a symbol of plenty, and *confites de boda* (Jordan almond candy) as a symbol of a sweet and harmonious life together. The reception would follow, first *pranso de boda* (wedding dinner), accompanied by *panderos kieman, tamboura, romansas, poeziyas y baylar chiftetelli* (tambourines, violin, drum, romantic songs, poems and dance Turkish-style).

Limousine ride   This practice was only used in Seattle and it went out of style long ago. During the early days, even during the early 1930s, a couple that just got married in *kahal* would hire a fleet of black fancy limousines to have the bridal party taken for a nice leisurely ride around Lake Washington Boulevard. I remember hiring four limousines from Benny Cohen, who usually dressed up in a blue uniform like a fancy chauffeur, and directed the parade. In those days this was considered a treat, because not everyone had an automobile to go for a ride.

El peshcado (The fish) I remember, we did it in our *boda*. A person would buy a large, fresh (live) fish, bring it to the home where the bride and groom are staying. Someone would bring a sort of large tray or such, place the fish on it, and the guests, one by one, would take the bride, and skip over the fish's back a few times. Some would *apegar* (take dollar bills and stick it on the *novya's* forehead). This was done as an omen for good luck, as well as to ward off the evil eye. In some communities the *peshcado* ceremony was done on the eighth day of the *hupa*, when the groom himself would buy the large fish and bring it home, along with a nice present for his new wife.

Avraham Siv This is still practiced in Seattle (see p. 168). This ceremony takes place the *Shabbath* after the wedding. This custom is very old, as we find it mentioned in old books. The *novyo* is given the honor to go up to *sefer*, a special one is taken out in his honor, and the reader chants from a portion where it recounts the story of our patriarch Abraham selecting a wife for his son Isaac. Each Hebrew verse is followed by someone in the congregation chanting the same verse in *targum* (Aramaic) with a beautiful cantillation. This is followed by a special *kiddush*, where friends enjoy the "three Ds": drinks with delicious delicacies.

For lack of space, we will forego other details and we will limit ourselves by mentioning only one of the many popular *canticas de boda*. Here is one.

Escalericas l'ize d'oro y de marfil (2)
Para ke suva el novyo (la novya) - para ke suva a dar kidushin
No pasesh por mi varandado (2)
Ke tengo ijo onrado y pasare
Pasariya y tornariya y le dire
Ke la novya era miya y no del rey (2)

Translation:
Stars of gold and ivory he made
So the (bride/groom) would climb to give kidushin.
Do not pass by my patio
Because I have an honored son and I shall pass

I shall pass and I shall return and I shall tell him
That the bride is mine and not the king's.

Besiman tov!

February 1972   Shevat/Adar 5732

Meldados

Our religion teaches us that a people that cherishes the memory of
its loved ones, is a people worthy of being called "a wise and
understanding nation."

And so our rabbis have devised a variety of ways of
commemorating our loved ones. There are some communities that
conduct memorial services by sitting around the graveside, reading
from the immortal Psalms or rabbinic literature, and many other
methods are used by the different groups of Jews around the globe.

One can see a distinct underlying theme in all these types of
services and that is they all stress the importance of "prayers for the
dead and charity for the living."

Now, in the following we will try to explain briefly what we do in
the *meldados* (memorial services) we conduct in the Sephardic Bikur
Holim Congregation and which is typical of most Turkish Sephardim.
First, there's the candle that is lit by the relative. This is a reference to
a verse in the bible "the light of G-d is the soul of man." So in
lighting this candle we indicate symbolically, that the memory of this
loved one is engraved in the hearts and minds of the living.

The books which are then distributed to those present are called
Mishna (or *Mishnayoth* for plural), a Hebrew term meaning books of
the Oral Law. The reason we read from these books is that the Hebrew
term for soul is *neshama*, which, with the letters changed around,
make up *Mishna*. An ingenious way to indicate that we're reading
Mishna for the *neshama* of our loved one in praying to our Maker that
the soul of our loved one is elevated to that ineffable and spiritual bliss
which G-d has laid up in Heaven.

The name we're commemorating is achieved by the selection of
the first letter of a chapter in the *Mishna* to correspond to the name of
the departed. For example if that name was David, we find the
Mishna chapters starting with the Hebrew letters *daleth*, *vav* and

daleth to make the Hebrew spelling of the name. Then we add those letters which make up the name of that person's mother. In addition to these we read from the three *Mishnayoth* of *Avoth*, *Midoth* and *Tamid*, which make up the Hebrew word *emeth* (truth) to indicate our belief in the one only true G-d.

The *hazan* then reads the *Idara*, part of the mystic book of *Zohar* where it narrates the events that took place on the day that the author of that work, Rabbi Shimon Ben Yohai, died.

Kaddish, the age old recitation of "the prayer for the dead" (see p. 70) is said. The mourner or the person that's making the *meldado* joins the *hazan* in saying this *kaddish*. If they say the evening service, the *Arvith*, they join the *hazan* in saying the *kaddish* that occurs in the *Arvith* service.

Hashcava is recited and the *hazan* has those present stand up. This is a memorial prayer in which the name of the deceased is mentioned along with appropriate phrases like "May his soul rest in peace," etc. What we serve after this service is a leftover from the old custom of offering charity to the poor. Whenever a man had a *meldado* for one of his parents or relatives, this man used to invite to his house a *minyan* (required quorum of ten men) of poor men who conducted a reading session. At the end this man used to serve these poor individuals a full course meal, thus achieving the double duty of prayer and charity.

In passing, I would like to mention the beauty and the spiritual benefits that used to prevail in the *meldados*, when we used to make them at home. First the *hazan* used to say a few *divre Torah* (words of wisdom of our *Torah*) words that are sorely lacking in many Jewish homes. Then the *Arvith* service which they recite the night of the *meldado*, bringing a little bit of "religion" into this house, which is valuable since G-d only knows whether such prayers are ever uttered in most Jewish homes the rest of the year. At the end, when the relatives leave, the custom with Bikur Holim members is to say *para munchos anyos* (for many more years) and other appropriate greetings. The members of Ezra Bessaroth synagogue have a custom of saying *bivos y sanos siempre* (alive and always healthy).

The members of Ezra Bessaroth have another custom, and that is the *Shabbath* before the *meldado*, the son, or the person in whose house the *meldado* takes place, lights one of those long candles, and all the relatives make it their duty to go visit that house on that particular *Shabbath*. They call this Shabbath *El Shabbath De La Candela* (*Sabbath* of the Candle). The visit on this Saturday is called *Acompanyar La Candela* (Accompanying the Candle). They're all good customs that evolved in the different communities. If we but try to understand them, we'll find that they all make good sense.

April 1972   Nissan/Iyar 5732

The Behor (First Born Son)

There is an endless string of laws and regulations connected with the *behor* (first born male) in our religion. First, there is the rule whereby the *behor* is entitled to a double share of his father's inheritance. For a time, the office of priesthood belonged to the *behoroth* (all first born males, collectively). Later, this office was transferred to the tribe of Levy.

As we read in the *Hagadah*, G-d punished the Egyptians by inflicting them with ten plagues, this tenth plague, being the killing of their first born. At the same time G-d saved the *behoroth* that belonged to the children of Israel. G-d's attitude was: As long as I saved them, they belong to Me. Therefore, they were consecrated to G-d. When a baby *behor* reaches the age of one month, his father can buy him back from G-d by handing five *shekels* (silver coins) to a *kohen* (priest), who acts as an agent of G-d for this purpose. This ceremony is called *pidion haben* (redemption of the son). After this trade, the parents celebrate the occasion by inviting friends and relatives to a festive party.

To show our gratitude to G-d for his great miracle that he had saved the first born, the rabbis instituted a fast day for *behoroth* on the day preceeding the festival of *Pesach*. They also ruled, that as long as the *behor* in the family is too young to fast, his father must fast for him.

The rabbis, however, gave the *behoroth* a convenient way out of this fast by attending, on *erev Pesach* (day before Passover), a *siyum* (completion) of a section of the *Talmud*, by a rabbi. The rabbi then invites the *behoroth* to join him in a small *seuda* (meal). This *seudath mitzvah*, absolves the *behoroth* from fasting the rest of the day.

In Sephardic lore, the *behor* is called a *bovo* (fool), meaning, they were considered naive or not too bright. Some say the origin of this insinuation is found in the story of Joseph and his brothers. This story can be found in Genesis 42.

On their first visit to Egypt, Joseph accused his brothers of being spies. He told them to bring their younger brother, Benjamin, the next time, so they could prove they were not spies.

When their supply of wheat was exhausted, the brothers told their father, Jacob, but he refused to let Benjamin go with them. Then, Reuben, who was the *behor*, pleaded with his father by telling him "You can kill my two sons if I don't bring Benjamin back to you." Jewish lore tells us that's when Jacob called Reuben, "*Behor bovo*."

Jacob told Reuben, "Don't you know that your sons are my grandsons, and that they're just as precious and dear to me as my own sons?" In our Sephardic tradition, we hold the *behor* of the family in high regard. Often times, it is second only in importance and authority to the father. They used to call the male firstborn *basya*, and the female *bulissa*. These terms carried with them an indication of authority, and the respect given to a head of the family.

August 1978   Av 5738

Vender Las Mitzvoth
(Selling the Mitzvoth)

This practice of *vender las mizvoth*, auctioning off the various honors as a preliminary to reading from the *Torah* goes back over 600 years.

Our *hahamim* state, that since all Jews respect and revere our *Torah*, some members love to show their admiration for the *Torah* by offering monetary gifts for these honors that precede the actual reading of the *Torah* on *Shabbath* or holy days. Unlike popular belief, this practice is not purely of Sephardic origin. Rabbi Yaakov Ben Asher, a 14th century codifier, mentions in his famous *Turim* that this was a practice in many Ashkenazic synagogues. Rabbi Yoseph Caro comments on this practice (O.H. 147). It seems that after many centuries, the Ashkenazim discarded this practice, we Sephardim held on to it. In fact, we even retained the Ladino idiom in the bidding procedure.

The purpose is twofold; one is because it's a source of revenue for the *kahal*, and second to avert any possible controversy that might result by showing favoritism in passing the honors.

For those unfamiliar with what goes on, we will explain how the congregation bids for the various honors, which are six in number.

1. First, the *gabay* auctions off the *petiha*, the honor of opening the doors of the *ehal akodesh* (holy ark) where the holy scrolls are deposited.

2. *Yevar y trayer el Sefer Torah*, the honor of carrying the scroll to the *teva* (the readers' desk) and return it.

3. *Rimonim*, the honor of placing the crowns on the scroll which is to be read that day and removing them on their return to *ehal*.

4. *Gelila*, the honor of unclasping the *sefer* belt, and clasp it back at the conclusion of the reading session.

5. *Akama*, the honor of lifting the open scroll before the reading. This is done to show the worshippers the exact place from which we read. The congregation then extend their hands as to kiss the scriptures, and then each one recites a formula we call the "pledge of allegiance" of our religion. [Editor's note: "This is the *Torah . . .*"]"]

6. *Maftir*, the person buying the *haftarah* which can be found in the printed *humash* (pentateuch) at the end of the weekly *perashah* (*Torah* portion). The *maftir* goes up the last of those called and is actually an "extra" reading and the portion read for him from the *sefer* is a small part repeated from the end of the *perashah*. The *hazan* repeats the last three verses of the *perashah*. The *haftarah* usually corresponds with the subject matter of the weekly *Torah* portion. This honor of *maftir* is usually offered to a member who wishes to commemorate a dear departed.

The one called up next to the last is called *samuh*, usually reserved for a younger man. The last one called up to sefer is called *mashlim*, usually reserved for an older gentleman.

In order to avoid the appearance or the sound of a business transaction on *Shabbath* or holidays, our leaders devised a unique method of bidding in numbers rather than dollars. For example, when the *gabay* announces *sien dan*, *sien* (100) is the equivalent of 100 pennies, or one dollar. If he says *kinyentos* (500), it's the equivalent of 500 pennies or five dollars, or if he says *mil dan* (1,000), it's the equivalent of 1,000 pennies or ten dollars. And so, if a person buys the honor of *petiha* he wishes to offer to a friend or relative, for *dies mil*, the *hazan* makes a *misheberah* (blessing) and the bidder knows he bought this particular honor for 100 dollars and so on.

The laws governing this practice fill up scores of pages. We can only mention a few. At times a person buys the *petiha* with the express purpose of offering it to a relative or a good friend whose wife is expecting a blessed event. It's believed this acts as good luck, that the *parida* will have an easy delivery. During the ninth month, the future father has someone else close the doors, as if to say "We do not close the doors on prayers and blessings."

A few recent changes. Our president instituted the practice of offering the *petiha*, without bidding, to a member about to celebrate his fiftieth wedding anniversary. The young man on his day of *bar mitzvah* is honored by the congregation with the honor of carrying the *Sefer Torah*. This practice applies to the *novyo* (bridegroom) on the *Shabbath* before the wedding, as well.

Regarding the bidding for the *haftarah*, our rabbis urge the bidders to use their discretion, and avoid any fierce competitive clash, since the whole purpose is to pray for the peace of the soul or the memory of the departed. The *hahamim* say that this discretion should be used also in bidding for all other honors, since controversy defeats the purpose of synagogue attendance which should be permeated by *shalom* (peace).

July 1982   Tamuz/Av 5742

Saturday Night Live

In order to give our youngsters an idea what the elder generation did in the way of diversion, which we called *pasa tiempo* (pass the time away), there are quite a few of us who still remember the *noches de alhad* (Saturday nights), when some neighbors would get together at a friend's home for a fun night.

The festivities always began with everyone singing the Ladino song called *Al Dio Alto* (The Heavenly G-d). Here are a couple of stanzas as a sample. It is a beautiful Sephardic melody, ushering in the new week.

El Dio alto con su grassia mos mande muncha ganansia no veamos mal ni ansia nos y todo Yisrael

The heavenly G-d with His grace, He should send us a good living, we should not see bad things nor anxiety, neither us or all of Israel.

*Bendicho el abastado ke mos Dio dia onrado kada Shabbath
mijorado a nos y a todo Yisrael*

Blessed be He the plentiful One, that He gave us an honored
day each Shabbath is better to us and all Israel.

This was followed by other Ladino songs.

After some refreshments (which included a large variety of
mezelikes (appetizers) like *pishcado salado, kezo, azitunas,* (pickled
fish, cheese, olives), etc., even some *borekas* (cheese filled pastry)left
over from *Shabbath*), there would always be one person in the group
with a wonderful comical talent who would captivate the listeners with
his antics or his *estoryicas* (stories). Some of the younger generation
would sing some timely Ladino songs. Here are a couple of stanzas of
a song that was very popular and romantic.

La agua pasa, l'arena keda, el amor me kema, en mi corason

The water passes, the sand stays, love burns me in my heart

*Avlar te kero, el anyo entero, contar te kero, con la me
passion*

I wish to talk to you, all year around, I wish to tell you, with
my passion.

By this time everyone was ready to play a fun game called
Finjanes or *Filjanes* (small coffee cups). This game was played as
follows. Suppose there were ten persons in the group. They would
split into two competing teams, often men against women. Each team
would select a captain. For the sake of identifying them, let us call
one team "K Team" and the other the "D Team."

The housewife would provide a good-sized *tavla* (tray) on which
one could fit eleven coffee cups, some small Turkish coffee cups of
different sizes, shapes and colors. These cups would be placed upside
down. Under one of these eleven cups one would place a gold ring.

In order to gain initial possession of the *tavla*, let's say the captain
of the K Team would try to buy it by offering the rival team so many
points, say twenty-five. This would give the K Team the privilege to
take hold of the *tavla* and try to earn some points for the K Team.
This was done as follows.

The captain of the K Team would take the tray to another room, out of sight of the D Team, and arrange the cups, placing the ring under one of the eleven. The D Team would take turns in trying to find the ring either on the first lift or the last. Every time the D Team failed to do this, as many cups that were left on the tray would count as score for the K Team. The captain of the K Team would again hide the ring for more points.

In the event that a member of the D Team was lucky enough to either lift the "ring cup" at the first try or to lift all the cups and leave the ring cup for the last, this person would be hailed as "champion" of his respective team. He not only scores eleven points for his side, but he also takes possession of the *tavla*, giving his captain the privilege of arranging the tray, thus trying to add up to his team's score. The game was won with a score of 101.

Points would be acquired the following way. For example, if a person from the rival D Team lifted the ring cup on the fourth try, then the K Team would be given a score of eight points, that is how many cups were left when the D person lifted the ring cup.

We call the team that possesses the tray as the K Team because they get to control and "keep" the tray either until they accumulate 101 points, or until the rival team gets lucky in the way we described above. The other team, we call the D Team because the persons in the D Team are the ones that take turns to "draw" or lift the cups that were arranged by the K Team. Until either team gets to a score of 101, the game goes on. The losing team would have to buy *uno oka de halva* (a loaf of *halva*, sweet sesame paste candy) or some such prize, to be enjoyed by everyone at their next gathering.

Some players would tease their rivals by making some snappy remarks. When there were only two cups left on the tray, some would burst into the Turkish: *Ya shunda dir ya bunda!* (It's either in this one or that one!)

It is a lot of fun. Try it, you'll like it.

April 1980   Nisan/Iyar 5740

The Molejas

The Bible tells us that a *kohen* (a member of the Hebrew priestly family) was entitled to keep three different parts of every animal offered by an Israelite, by law, as compensation for the services he rendered in the Holy Temple, plus other services. In a broadly similar form, a *shohet* (an ordained ritual slaughterer) in all Sephardic communities in Turkey and Balkans, had the traditional right to keep for himself, from every animal that he declared *kasher* (kosher, ritually acceptable), the *molejas*, as a bonus for the extra services he rendered the Sephardic community.

Molejas are what we call sweetbreads, or a piece of gland found in a young lamb or young calf. The season for good *molejas* was very short, because they were *mahpul* (a rare delicacy) and occurred mostly in the springtime when these animals were still young and tender. My father, *Alav Ashalom* (May he rest in peace.), was the *haham* of the city of Tekirdag (Rodosto) before we came to Seattle in 1924. A *haham* in a Sephardic community in Turkey performed the job of five or more religious employees. He was, at the same time, a rabbi, a *hazan*, a *Torah* reader, a *shohet*, a *mohel* (ritual circumciser) and teacher, a veritable full-time occupation.

Being a *shohet*, my father was the recipient of these *molejas*, bringing them home from the *salana* (city slaughter house) where he had to trek two or three times a week. This was because there was no proper refrigeration. The *salana* was at least five miles from where we lived. For lack of other form of transportation, he had to walk all that distance, sometimes before dawn. So these *molejas* were very well deserved.

Of course, there was no way our family could eat all these *molejas*, so during the height of the season when they were so tasty when fixed properly, a number of prominent members of our city had a standing order with my father to obtain a supply of these *molejas*. I remember when I was a youngster, my father would hand me a few packages of these *molejas*, with the names of the various members written on each package, and I would take them and deliver them to the various homes of these prominent members. Of course, there were no house addresses in Tekirdag. But because almost all Jews in Tekirdag lived in the *Mahle Judia* (Jewish District), we knew where they all lived. Some of the names of these prominent members come to mind, names like Shemuel Bahar, Moise Naon, Shelomachi Altaras, Bohorachi Bensushen, and many others. [Editor's note: Descendants of some of these men still live in Seattle.]

My younger brothers would also deliver some of these packages to the homes. Once in a while, we would receive a small *regalo* (gift) from some generous member, which would make the delivery a little more pleasant. Of course the payment for these *molejas* was made directly to father. We had no knowledge as to how much they cost, or how they paid for them.

People tried *molejas* in Seattle, of course, purchased from the kosher butcher, but they never could compare or come up to the delicious taste as the ones from the old country. Some skeptics claim it's all *enganyo de meoyo*, in other words these doubters say "It's all in the mind," an imagination, or a false impression.

But let us not be too hasty in judging these matters. For example, when I was in Jerusalem, I bought some large black figs, and they tasted out of this world. Is it because the fruit is tree-ripened or vine-ripened? Who knows? *El Dio ke no mo lo trayga a dezear.* (G-d should never make us want.)

September 1980   Elul 5741

Past Practices

There are some customs and practices that our ancestors used which are unknown or forgotten. The customs whose descriptions follow, are those which are not used today. Of course, those of us that came from the old country, remember them all. So, what follows is intended for the edification of the younger element of our readers.

La agua de la tekufa. The Hebrew word *tekufa* means "season of the year," having to do with the seasons and equinoxes. On the exact day when one of these four seasons ended and another started, the custom was that people used to spill all drinking water stored in *cantaros, jarros* (pitchers and jars) because there was a strong belief that anyone who drank any of this stored water during this *tekufa*, would contract some swelling or other mysterious disease. This was closely connected with astrological phenomena. This only applied to drinking water, which we as youngsters used to go and fetch from public fountains because, even if we had a well inside the precincts of our home, this well water was not fit for drinking.

Rain water was collected in large barrels, but this rain water was only good for laundry and the cleaning of laundry mixed with *leshiya*, a sort of home made bleach.

Messalayim. This Aramaic word means "pray." *Leshos leshos* (May it be far from us.), when a person was very close to death, the *haham*, would take a *minyan* (quorum of ten men for prayer) to *kahal* and there read a form of a prayer starting with the word *messalayim*. Essentially, this was for the purpose of changing the patient's name. For example, if the patient's name was Reuben, most of the time they would either add Haim (meaning life) or Refael (meaning G-d heals), petitioning the Almighty to add life to the patient and to accord him a full recovery. They said, this changing of the name would confuse the Angel of Death, who would have difficulty in recognizing Refael from the patient's original name, Reuben. Hopefully this would work, and the patient would be well again.

Mercado or *mercada* (purchased). This practice of "purchase," was followed by a family that was blessed with a newborn baby, but had previously suffered the loss of an infant before the new arrival. In order to ensure the life of the *muevo nasido* (newborn baby), they would go through a formality in which, a relative or friend would "purchase" this baby from the parents, thus transferring ownership. This was done to outsmart the evil spirits, and ward off their fatal hold on this family's offspring that was marked for a fatal accident. So, if it was a boy, he was called *mercado*; or, if a girl, she was called *mercada*.

Shedim, demons. A great number of people would believe in the existence of these evil spirits and their tendency to harm people. We used to call them *los mijores de mozotros* (the ones who are better than us), or *los de abasho* (those from below). Many rabbis preached against this belief, quoting the Biblical verse, Deuteronomy 32-17 *Tamim tiye im amonay*, "You should believe only in the power of the Almighty." I still remember, when my father, Z"L, was asked his views about these *danyadores* (harmful spirits), he answered, "As far as Seattle is concerned, we shouldn't worry, because these *shedim* didn't cross the Atlantic Ocean." Nowadays people rather believe in psychotherapy or relieve their anxieties by tranquilizers, or other types of "little dolls."

Kapara (slaughtering for atonement). Many families would have the *shohet* (ritual slaughterer) come on the day following a tragedy or the day before *Yom Kippur*, or on the day of *Hoshanah Rabbah*, to slaughter a rooster for each male member of the family or a white hen for each female. The *shohet* then would raise this fowl over the heads of each member, and would recite a certain prayer to atone for their sins. The head of the family would then take some of these chickens, add a few dollars and send them to some poor family as a form of charity. This custom has gradually faded away. Rabbi Yoseph Caro in his code of Jewish laws is against this practice, adding that it bordered on heathen practices.

October 1972   Tishri/Heshvan 5733

I Remember - Superstitious Practices

On the way to *kahal* (synagogue) from my house in Tekirdag there was a one block square, enclosed building we used to call the *Tekye*. This was a sort of Turkish monastery, which served as living quarters for Turkish *hojas* (priests) and *dervishes* (Turkish monks).

One very weird item that sticks in my mind about this, and other similar places is, that in one corner of this vast enclosed place there was an old broken down window where there were a number of old knotted pieces of cloth, obviously tied there a long time since the cloth was worn out. They used to tell us that these cloth knots had some mysterious connection with sorcery *ichizos*, or witchcraft.

When the parents of a sick child, after having the child under a physician's care, had not shown any sign of improvement, the child was then taken to this place, the *Tekye*. The child was left there by himself all night, and through some hocus pocus, we used to hear that some children were cured. Or were they? Maybe it was all in the mind. Is this type of "curing method" allowed by our religion? Is this considered a superstitious act which borders on idolatry?

It wasn't too long ago that some women in our own Seattle community performed *endulcos* (superstitious practices using magical potions). A certain woman Tiya Fulana or Ermana Fulana, who was acquainted with the process used to take water from four or seven different places, mix it with rose water and sprinkle it in the patient's room reciting a certain formula or prayer. Some used different methods, some used *mayorana*, a spice or an herb named marjoram in English.

It was regarded as dangerous to perform *indulcos* when a neighbor's wife had given birth to a child. They were careful also about the time of the month, like *Rosh Hodesh* (first day of Hebrew month).

Then there was the practice of *apercantar* or *azer por espanto*. *Apercantar* (exorcism) where the *haham* or some knowledgable, learned and pious man would take some whole cloves in his right hand, and recite a prayer while he passed his hands on the head of the patient. At the end of this ceremony, the cloves would be thrown to the fire, to burn away all the *males* (evil spirits).

Who remembers *mumya* (circumcised foreskin)? Some persons in our community were always on top of the *mohel* to obtain the foreskin of a child after the circumcision ceremony. They believed that eating this foreskin (the *mumya*), obviously after preparation, would cure a woman of sterility or some such similar disorder, thus enabling her to have children.

How about *kemeya* (amulets)? I don't remember any here in Seattle, but in the old country there were some men who were expert in writing these amulets, which were supposed to have a secret or mysterious power of curing certain diseases or disorders. I remember here in Seattle, whenever there was a male child born in certain families, the *haham* would write a certain formula on parchment. He would take two of these to the *parida* (mother). She used to pin up the one on herself and the other one on the newborn baby. This was effective in keeping away any bad accidents from the baby and the *parida*. These are just a few. There are many others, but this will suffice for now.

Chapter Nine

Jewish and Sephardic Institutions

September 1977   Elul 5737

The Haham Bashi - I

The first capital of the Ottoman Empire in Turkey was in the city of Brusa. When Sultan Orhan conquered Brusa in 1326, the Jews there received a royal *firman* permitting them to build a synagogue, which still exists, being the first in Turkey. It wasn't until 127 years later when Sultan Mehmet II conquered Constantinople in 1453, that the office of *Haham Bashi* (chief rabbi) was established by a royal *berat*, a Turkish word meaning, "the privilege of franchise, immunity and exemption." [Editor's note: See Appendix I for full list.]

Rabbi Moshe Capsali was given the honor of becoming the first *Haham Bashi* under this royal *berat*, affording him the additional rights and privileges of appointing rabbis and other leaders for the rest of the Jews of the whole Ottoman Empire. He was the recognized central authority of all the Jews in the Empire, until sometime later when some of the powers were taken away, and the subsequent chief rabbis were known as *kaymakam*, meaning a substitute of that office, or one who served in an unofficial capacity.

The chief rabbi who held one of the longest tenures of this high office was Rabbi Moshe Halevy, sometimes known as *kaymakam efendi*. His regime started in 1872 after the death of Rabbi Yakir Geron. Rabbi Moshe Halevi was born in Brusa and received his religious education in the *yeshiva* of Brusa, at that time one of the most prestigious *yeshivoth* in all of Turkey.

To give the reader a small idea of how much power the *Haham Bashi* had in bygone days, I will cite an episode Professor Avraham

Galante tells us in his book on the *History Of the Jews of Istanbul* (in French).

It seems that Mr. David Fresco, the leading journalist of his day, and the editor of the Sephardic newspaper *El Tiempo* of Istanbul, found some discrepancies in the balance sheet of the communal finances. Mr. Fresco published his impressions and his personal criticisms. But Mr. Fresco went a little too far, accusing some members of the rabbinic council with misappropriation of public funds. After the *Haham Bashi* had the whole matter investigated, and he was convinced that Mr. Fresco's charges against the council were absolutely unfounded, he demanded from Mr. Fresco a retraction and an apology. Mr. Fresco declined to do so, and continued his accusations mentioning some very influential members of the Istanbul Sephardic community. Rabbi Moshe tried again, this time warning Mr. Fresco of the embarrassing consequences. When Rabbi Moshe was convinced of Mr. Fresco's stubborn and unyielding attitude, he resorted to a couple of unusually tough punitive measures which were in his power to do. One was, he placed Mr. Fresco under a strict religious ban, which curtailed some of his personal rights. The second measure was, Rabbi Moshe appealed to the government and had Mr. Fresco suspended from his job as editor of the newspaper for a given time.

Obviously, Rabbi Moshe succeeded in doing this because he knew Sultan Hamid personally and had tremendous clout with the Turkish government. This state of affairs continued for a while. Through the personal intervention of Mr. Fresco's father who was an eminent *haham* and a very close friend of the *kaymakam*, Rabbi Fresco succeeded in convincing his son to appear before the rabbinic council, where Mr. Fresco offered his apologies and asked them for their forgiveness, admitting only to the section where he incriminated some innocent rabbis in the scandal. In order to avoid a further scandal, he promised he'd be more sympathetic in forthcoming articles of *El Tiempo*.

Professor Galante, who relates all these events, was able to find all the original documents dealing with this fascinating episode. He had access both to rabbinic archives as well as the Turkish government archives. He shows us the "ban" containing the signatures of the Istanbul *beth din* and signatories to this ban.

When the Young Turks forced Sultan Hamid to accept and sign a new Turkish constitution in 1908 divesting the sultan of a lot of dictatorial powers, there were a great number of high Turkish officials who lost their lofty positions. Among these, the *Haham Bashi*, Rabbi

Moshe Halevi was asked to tender his resignation because of his close connection with the sultan. And so, after thirty-six years, he ended his long regime.

After he resigned, the rabbinic council and the administrative council in charge of electing the next *Haham Bashi*, were faced with a most difficult decision, because it involved Rabbi Haim Nahoum and his father-in-law, Rabbi Avraham Danon, a highly qualified scholar. The councils finally elected Rabbi Haim Nahoum because of his personal relationship with some members of the new Turkish regime, as well as his previous close association with the office of the Istanbul rabbinate.

The period of this new Turkish regime, where they attained a great number of guarantees of freedom and liberty through a new constitution, was known in our time as *el tiempo de el huriyet*.

October 1977   Tishri 5738

The Haham Bashi - II

It was customary for the *Haham Bashi* to pay state visits to Sultan Hamid on special occasions, such as the sultan's birthday, or on some Turkish *bayram* (holiday). In addition to the chief rabbi, the head of the Greek church of Istanbul and the head of the Armenian church of Istanbul also paid their respects to the sultan on such occasions.

Professor Avraham Galante tells us that besides these regular official visits, Sultan Hamid had, on two separate occasions, extended royal invitations to Rabbi Moshe Halevi. The first one was in 1893 and the second in 1902. On the first visit, the sultan expressed to Rabbi Moshe his great satisfaction of the faithful manner in which his Jewish subjects had conducted themselves toward the Ottoman Empire. Without previous notice, the sultan asked Rabbi Moshe a very leading and puzzling question. Hamid asked, "Is the Jewish population of Turkey ready and willing to render a useful service to their beloved country?" Rabbi Moshe was taken by surprise, and he answered, "Your majesty, we have nothing to do but to follow your orders." Then the sultan continued, saying, "I'm aware that the Jewish people are constantly being persecuted in a number of European countries, and quite a few Jews have found refuge in my country. I would be willing to open my doors and let in a considerable number of

Russian Jews or others that would be willing to settle in Turkey. I have a plan to install these newcomers in eastern Anatolia. These new immigrants will join the local Jews in furnishing me an army of 100,000 men which would be attached to our Fourth Army. If any difficulty arises concerning *kasher* or *trefa* for these Jewish soldiers, we can create a *kasher* kitchen for them. What do you say to that, *Haham Bashi efendi?"*

Rabbi Moshe thanked the sultan for the great honor which he conferred on the Jewish community, and as a reply to this leading question, told Hamid, "I will submit this royal plan to the high council on religion," which he did without delay. After much deliberation, the high council composed and signed their reply to Hamid, which, in effect, projected and presented to the sultan their pleasure to follow the sultan's royal orders.

Abdul Hamid referred this petition to the Turkish council of high government ministers, who expressed their satisfaction at the loyal attitude of the Turkish Jews. However, they added, due to a variety of reasons, and especially in view of the attitude of the other non-Turkish minorities of the Empire, they did not deem it plausible at this time to put this plan into execution. And so the matter was postponed indefinitely.

The second invitation came a few days after Rabbi Moshe Halevi had finally obtained an audience for Theodore Herzl with Hamid. Mr. Herzl asked Hamid some pointed questions about the Jews and Palestine, which at that time was under Turkish rule. The sultan was very polite with Herzl, but his answers were very guarded and vague. Mr. Herzl interpreted these answers in a very favorable way for his future plans for the Jewish question.

A few days after Herzl left Constantinople, Abdul Hamid invited Rabbi Moshe Halevi, the *kaymakam*, to come to the royal palace. Rabbi Moshe made every effort to arrive at the palace early in the day. But, after waiting there the whole day, somehow he was not called in to see the sultan, so when evening came Rabbi Moshe returned to his home. The next morning, he made another trip to the palace, and the same thing happened again, so he returned home without seeing Hamid. On the third, when he realized he was being deliberately ignored again, he talked to the king's chamberlain who went in to get instructions as to how to deal with the *Haham Bashi*. Sultan Hamid finally received Rabbi Moshe. The sultan gave him a very sharp lecture as to why Rabbi Moshe intervened on behalf of Herzl, in view of the fact that Rabbi Moshe knew Hamid's attitude against Zionism. Rabbi Moshe, who became very confused and flustered assured the sultan that he did not mean to offend the sultan and that the only reason he intervened was that being Mr. Herzl was a famous journalist, he thought he would ask from his majesty concerning the Jews in general. After Hamid listened to Rabbi Moshe, he replied, "Now, I'm convinced that you're innocent of any intrigue."

As a result of this emotional experience and the terrible nervous ordeal, Rabbi Moshe had to spend a few days sick in bed. When Hamid heard about the *Haham Bashi's* state of health, he sent a special palace officer, carrying a royal purse containing 100 Turkish gold liras as an imperial "*regalo.*"

June 1974   Sivan/Tamuz 5734

The Rishon LeZion

Elsewhere in this issue of *La Boz*, we'll probably read a full account of the visit of Rabbi Ovadya Yoseph to New York and Rabbi Maimon's interesting get-togethers with the present *Rishon LeZion* (chief rabbi of Israel).

Reliable authorities say that the first chief rabbi to be honored with this title *Rishon LeZion* was Rabbi Moshe Galanti who held this office around the year 1665, and after him subsequently by all the other Sephardic chief rabbis of the Holy Land.

The eminent Israeli historian, author, and journalist, Abraham Almaleh, Z"L, in a book that he wrote about the history of this high office, devotes a whole chapter describing the way in which the *Rishon LeZion* was chosen, elected and the ceremony that was celebrated on the day of his inauguration.

Mr. Almaleh deserves a lot of credit, because were it not for his diligent search in old archives, many of these facts would have been lost to us forever. He was able to dig up records of each of the numerous rabbis, as to where each was born, educated and what books they wrote, including which remained in manuscript and which were published, where and when. [Editor's note: See Appendix II for list.]

There was a special committee that was delegated to select the chief rabbi from among many candidates. They were ever to keep in mind that the one they selected was to be a man blessed with many qualities of wisdom, erudition, as well as one endowed with leadership, and one who commanded the affection and respect of his people. After the election, and after the morning service in a large synagogue in Jerusalem, the ceremony of his inauguration was started by the newly elected chief rabbi, delivering a very articulate *derasha* (sermon) suitable to the occasion, with everyone listening attentively. Then, one of the other rabbis who was a dear and intimate friend of the *rashal* (*Rishon LeZion*) would step up to the *teva* and present him with a brand new, pure wool *djube* (elegant caftan) bought with money from the communal funds. At that time the *rashal* would recite the blessing of *sheeheyanu* (recited on using a new item), and all the audience would respond with the word *amen*.

Then the chief *hazan* would chant the blessing for the government, the mayor of Jerusalem, and a special blessing for the new *Rishon LeZion* who was thus the recognized leader of all the Jews in Israel, an authority granted officially by the Sultan in Istanbul.

After this ceremony a large portion of the audience would march out, and accompany the *rashal* to his house where they would be served a light breakfast. Just before the *rashal* reached his house, the chief *shohet* of Jerusalem would be ready at the front door with a lamb, which he would then slaughter, say the *beraha* (blessing), everyone responding *amen*. Then the *rashal* would step over this lamb, and before going in the house, the *shohet* would dip the palms of his hands in the blood, and would imprint a design of a hand with five fingers on the top of the door, this being a good omen that no accident of any evil would befall the newly elected *rashal*. In other words, they were wishing him good luck.

The meat of this lamb was then distributed to the poor, representing *tzedaka* (an act of charity). This ceremony of the lamb has been discontinued in recent years.

Because we now have two chief rabbis in Israel, one Ashkenazic and one Sephardic, even the method of choosing candidates and voting for a *rashal* has been changed.

August 1980   Av/Elul 5740

The Nagid of Egypt

The Talmud tells us that there was a large Jewish community in Alexandria, Egypt, even during the time Jews had and ruled their own country, even building a beautiful synagogue large enough to contain over 5,000 congregants. However, when the Romans swept the whole Middle East, this Alexandrian community was also taken capitve, dispersed and sold into slavery.

Today's article deals with an event that happened to Jews in Egypt who resettled there after many centuries, when a group of Jews established a *kehila*. For a time, they did not have a central religious authority, like Jews of Baghdad had the *resh galutha* or *exilarch*, who were accorded vast and absolute powers by the Moslem *khalif* of Baghdad.

We see a little later in history, the *kehila* in Egypt had, as their central authority, the *nagid* (president). The origin of this high office goes the following way. One of the princesses of the Abassinian *khalifate* in Baghdad married a Fatame Khalif in Egypt. One day, this Moslem queen inquired from her husband how the Jews of his kingdom were governed. When she learned that the Jews of Egypt did not have a recognized head, she told and advised her husband about the Jews of Baghdad with their *resh galutha*, so he appointed a scholar, called him *Rais Al Yahud* and the Jews called him the *nagid*. This exalted office lasted nearly 500 years.

The first appointed *nagid* on record was a scholar by the name of Rabbi Paltiel Hasar. He was accorded full power to appoint judges, presidents, community leaders, *hazanim*, *shohetim*, scribes and tax collectors. He was chief of the Jewish supreme court. Every document had to be approved by the *nagid*.

After Rambam (Rabenu Moshe Ben Maimon) settled in Egypt in the year 1165, the *khalif* was so pleased to have such a renowned philosopher living in his kingdom, that he appointed the Rambam as *nagid*, an office which he held until his death (1205). In addition to being the *nagid* the Rambam later became physician to King Saladin, the conqueror of Jerusalem from the barbaric rule of the Crusaders who had banished all Jews from the Holy City. No Jew lived in Jerusalem for over eighty years.

After Rambam passed away, his son, Rabbi Avraham Maimon was appointed as *nagid*. Rambam's descendants continued to hold this famous office for over six generations.

In 1492, when the exiled Sephardim settled in various communities in Turkey and the Balkans, a large group settled also in Cairo, Alexandria and other cities in Egypt. The office of *nagid* was still the head of the *kehiloth* existing at the time. The name of the *nagid* during that period, was a scholar by the name of Rabbi Yitzhak Hacohen Sholal, who later on emigrated to Jerusalem to fill the office of *Rishon LeZion* there. Solomon Rosanes, the Sephardic historian tells us that Rabbi Sholal had a pleasant relationship with a number of the *hahamim* that came from Spain.

After Rabbi Yitzhak left Egypt a member of his family, Rabbi Yeonathan Sholal, became the *nagid*, but he didn't last too long because when the Ottoman Turks conquered Egypt in 1530, under Sultan Selim, all ethnic authority was taken away from local leaders. The Jewish leader, the *nagid* was removed from office, and in his place, the sultan extended this right to the *Haham Bashi* in Constantinople, for him to appoint someone to be the central authority in Egypt, thus ending an era that existed for nearly 500 years. The first *haham* sent over from Istanbul to replace the *nagid* was a scholar by the name of Haham Tacher, and instead of *nagid* they called him *chelibi*, a Turkish word meaning a nobleman.

When Rabbi Yehuda Halevi, the famous Sephardic philosopher and poet, spent a few days in Egypt on his way to Jerusalem in 1141, the *nagid* in those days was a certain Rabbi Shemuel Ben Hanany or Ibn Mansur, who was also chief physician to the *khalif* Al Hafiz. Commenting on the *nagid* Rabbi Yehuda was quick to add, that though the *nagid* had absolute and despotic authority, and could easily have treated his subjects with an iron rod, the fact was that the *nagid* was a very decent, fair-minded, pleace loving gentleman, and a superior human being.

April 1973   Adar 2/Nisan 5733

Report on New York Sephardic Convention

Mashalla!   Are all these people Sephardim?   It was really heartwarming to see all those new and interesting faces. From New York, Los Angeles, Detroit, Miami Beach, Atlanta, Chicago and many other cities, all assembled to represent their respective communities at the first convention of the American branch of the World Sephardi Federation.   The convention was held on February 25th and 26th at the *Shearith Israel* synagogue in New York.   In short, the purpose of this convention and the Federation is to get together to promote and improve the lot of Sephardim, both here and in Israel.

Seattle was represented by seven delegates sent from the newly formed Seattle Sephardic Federation.   Two were chosen from Congregation Ezra Bessaroth, one from Seattle Sephardic Brotherhood and four from Sephardic Bikur Holim Congregation.   Besides these seven, we had a ready-made Seattle youth delegation that was attending school in New York. These are Linda Capeluto, David Angel, Michael Galante and Frank Varon.

I'm very proud to report that our S.B.H. delegates made a worthwhile impression, not only in numbers, but also in making the other delegates aware of the fact that ours is a vibrant and extremely active congregation, doing our share in promoting and preserving our Sephardic culture and tradition.

Headed by Rabbi Maimon, our S.B.H. delegation included the very able Dr. Rene' Levy, my wife Lucy, and, yours truly. Each of us was equipped with a red kit, containing the program for the two day convention, as well as other literature and brochures, and the articles of confederation for the Federation and other similar papers.

All day Sunday, we were kept busy. After attending the general assembly meeting, each delegate was assigned to a certain room where various workshops and discussion groups took place. I was assigned to the workshop that discussed how to improve and implement Sephardic education. We discussed various problems and made some suggestions which were incorporated in the agenda to be dealt with at some future time.

Dr. Rene' Levy chose to take part with the group that dealt with social and welfare problems, and thanks to his diligent work and efforts, many substantial projects and resolutions were advanced and voted on.

Was it all work and no fun? No, not by any means. Sunday evening we attended a wonderful banquet, which was preceded by a cocktail hour, during which we were introduced to a number of charming people. The main speaker at the banquet was Shelomo Hillel, the Israeli minister of police. After that they cleared the floor to present the entertainment, highlighted by that wonderful Israeli *hazan*, Meir Levy, who sang so sweetly that nobody wanted to go home.

I cannot end this article without mentioning the gracious host and hostess who fed and entertained us all on the Friday night and *Shabbath* that we were there, prior to the convention. I mean none other than Mr. and Mrs. Sam Ashkenazie and family of Brooklyn, New York. They went out of their way to see that we were fed and made comfortable. At one time, on the Sunday morning before leaving for the convention in Manhattan, we actually counted sixteen Seattleites at the breakfast that Mr. and Mrs. Ashkenazie prepared for us. May the Almighty bless them.

All in all, it was a very productive convention.

May 1982

The Sephardic Symposium in Madrid

My son-in-law, Eugene Normand, brought me a book he borrowed from the University of Washington library called *Actas Simposio de Estudios Sefardies*. It contains 781 pages, *Meldo y meldo y no s'escapa*. (Read and read and there's no end.) The book was published under the auspices of the famous *Institute Arias Montano* of Madrid, Spain.

This institute is made up of a group of several professors at Spanish universities. These professors are very much interested in all aspects of Sephardic studies. Because they have access to all the Spanish libraries and to all the ancient Spanish archives, they are discovering a wealth of material about our ancestors while they lived in Spain before the expulsion of 1492. From time to time they come up with some new unknown facts about Sephardim and they publish these in the magazine called *Sefarad*.

In 1964 this same group of Spanish professors invited a vast number of people, all expert in Sephardic history, literature, folklore, etc., to come and present scholarly papers. Experts came to Madrid from all over, from the United States, from Israel, from England and many other countries. The published proceedings of this gathering were called *Actas del Simposio de Estudios Sefardies* (*Proceedings of the Symposium of Sephardic Studies*).

This distinguished array of personalities that accepted the invitation included experts like Henry V. Beso, Professor Mair Benardete, Andre Chouraqui, Baruh Uziel, Professor Samuel Armisted, Ovadia Camhy (founder of World Sephardi Federation), all very talented, and many, many more. They all presented scholarly papers on various aspects of Sephardic life, including history, literature, folklore, etc. On other days, several of these experts participated in discussions about Sephardic topics, sometimes developing into dialogues and debates.

All this vast material was recorded, transcribed and put together by a staff of secretaries. The host scholars appointed one of their own as chief editor, to gather all this vast amount of papers and recordings so it could eventually be published in book form. The name of this editor is Jacob M. Hassan. It took a long time to sort out the hundreds of pages and finally, in 1974, ten years after the symposium was held, the book was published in Madrid, *Actas del Simposio de Estudios Sefardies*. An extremely interesting book.

Besides all the experts and scholars I mentioned above, I particularly liked what two other scholars contributed to this conference. The names of these two are Moshe Attias and Michael Molho.

Moshe Attias was born in Salonika in the year 1891. At the age of fourteen, on the suggestion of his teacher, he emigrated to Israel where he graduated with a degree in education. Although his regular profession was teaching, he somehow developed a special love for Sephardic *romansas* (ballads), so he devoted all his spare time to contacting some elderly Sephardic ladies in Jerusalem, asking them to sing to him some of the old *canticas y romansas* (songs and ballads), that they, in turn, had learned from their grandmothers. He would record and write down all these Sephardic gems. Some of these ladies were from Salonika, some from Istanbul, some from the island of Rhodes and other places.

In time, Moshe Attias collected literally hundreds of these *canticas y romansas* and finally he published two books full of these. One book he call *The Romansero Sefardi*. The other he called, *Cancionero Sefardi*. So, when he was invited to this conference in Madrid in 1964, he presented his story of how he came to collect all these ballads. The book contains a few *romansas*, as a small sample. Moshe Attias died in Jerusalem in 1973.

The other great personality that was invited to this conference of many experts was Michael Molho who was also born in Salonika in 1891. (See p. 131.) Besides his Hebrew and *Talmudic* education he mastered some secular studies and other languages. He was a contributor to many journals.

His most famous literary product, I think, was a book called *Usos y Costumbres de los Sefardies de Salonica*, in which he describes the many, many customs of our people encompassing daily, *Shabbath*, holiday and other occasions. He cites the many laws regulating our way of life in all its ramifications. Many writers refer to this book as source material and as authentic reference. I hope some day someone will translate it into English so our non-Spanish speaking members will derive full benefit from this precious volume.

Another book written by Mr. Molho is *Literatura Sefaradita de Oriente* (*The Literature of the Sephardim of the Orient*) containing many important chapters. In this book, Mr. Molho included a chapter on the *Me'Am Lo'Ez* (see p. 119), giving the authors, dates, of the

contributors. I translated this interesting chapter into English. I hope
some day I will find some means to have it published.

February 1978   Shevat/ 1 Adar 5738

The Kotel

The Seattle *Jewish Transcript* of January 19, 1978, printed an
article to the effect that a large American corporation by the name of
Borg-Warner distributed a 1978 calendar to its clients in a section of
New York, as a token of the holiday season. This beautiful calendar
contains various recipes and each of the twelve months is accompanied
by pictures of scenes from various countries around the world.

The American Jewish Congress called on Borg-Warner
Corporation to withdraw this calendar from circulation because on the
December 1978 page, it contains a view of the Old City of Jerusalem
as seen from Mt. Scopus. It explains that the Old City of Jerusalem is
situated in Jordan and credits Suleiman the Magnificent, Sultan of
Turkey in 1542, with building our *Kotel*, the Western or "Wailing
Wall."

It's a well known fact that this *Kotel*, the "Wailing Wall,"
composed of huge, uneven stone blocks are a remnant of Solomon's
Temple. [Editor's note: In reality the Kotel is from the Second Jewish
Temple and was built by King Herod.] How can this calendar say that
it was first built by Sultan Suleiman?

In connection with the foregoing item, I remember reading a story
in a Hebrew book. The author copied it from a book written by the
famous Palestinian Rabbi known as Moharam Hagiz. Rabbi Hagiz says
that he heard the episode from the mouths of very reliable Moslem
scholars and historians (around the end of the 1600s). Here's the
story: When Sultan Suleiman conquered the city of Jerusalem in 1542,
he rebuilt a large number of ruins left over from the many wars that
the city had suffered throughout the years. He had his people build for
him a mansion and a government house opposite the *Kotel*. One day,
while he was looking out of his window, he happened to see a very old
lady carrying a large basket of what appeared to him as garbage.
When this old lady approached the vicinity of the *Kotel*, she stopped
and dumped the whole basketful of garbage around the *Kotel*. The
Sultan, gripped by curiosity, sent a couple of his officers to bring this

old lady to the government house. Suleiman asked her, "What nationality are you?" She answered: "I'm a descendant from the ancient Greek-Romans." He asked her, "Where do you live now?" She said she lived far away, almost a two-day journey from here.

Upon further inquiry, she admitted she's following her solemn duty which was established long ago by the Greek-Roman patriarchs. Every member of this society is to bring a basketful of garbage and dump it in this place in Jerusalem at least once every thirty days. Their priests explained that it's their moral obligation to destroy the dwelling place of the G-d of the Jews and erase it completely from the face of the earth.

Suleiman ordered her locked up until such time he made sure that she was telling the truth. Meantime, he told his officers to place secret patrols to see if there'll be other members of this society who would do the same. Sure enough, these patrolmen caught a group of the same society carrying baskets full of garbage. After intense inquiries Suleiman found that the old lady was telling the absolute truth - that it was part of their faith to dump this garbage on the *Kotel*. Suleiman had all these people punished.

In order to clear all this debris that accumulated around the *Kotel* for so many years, Suleiman hit upon a brilliant idea. He got a shovel and a pail, and he filled hundreds of money-sacks with silver and gold coins. He announced a royal proclamation, saying: "Anyone that likes the king, come with me!" He took all these coins and he scattered them around the debris which covered almost the whole spot. A great many of the local citizens, most of them very poor people, came and took advantage of this treasure hunt. Suleiman continued this project for a few days until finally the *Kotel* became visible. Suleiman is credited with restoring a great many other historical places around the city of Jerusalem. Whether this story of Suleiman and the *Kotel* is fact or legend, I'll leave it to the readers to draw their own conclusion. Obviously, Rabbi Moshe Hagiz believed it because he heard it from reliable people.

December 1981   Kislev/Tevet 5742

The Dura Europos Synagogue

On Saturday night, November 14, we attended a lecture delivered in our S.B.H. (Sephardic Bikur Holim Congregation) social hall by Dr. Jo Milgrom. We were expecting to hear a lecture from her husband on the Temple scrolls but, for some reason, he was unable to attend that night. So, as it turned out, Dr. Jo, the wife, had to fill in that night. Her specialty is Bible through art, so she brought with her a large number of slides of the ancient synagogue of Dura Europos.

Dura, or as the town is called today A-Salhia, is a city situated on the northeast side of modern Syria, close to the river Euphrates. In the olden days Dura Europos was a prosperous town. Historians say that a number of Jews, on their way back from Babylonia to reach *Eretz Yisrael* to rebuild the Second Temple passed through Dura. Some of these settled there, establishing a Jewish community when they built the synagogue.

When this synagogue was first discovered in 1933, the roof was gone so that the interior was filled with rocks and dirt. This was done on purpose, and also to other buildings adjacent to this synagogue, as a way of preventing the enemy from entering into the town of Dura, because it was located right on the Syrian border.

According to experts, it is estimated that this Dura synagogue was built around the year 245 C.E. After the dirt and rubble were cleared, they found some Aramaic writing, indicating that it was built by a prominent member by the name of Samuel Ben Idi, the Elder, of the Jews. This synagogue did not last too long, only approximately twelve years, when the Persian troops conquered the whole region, reducing the whole town to rubble and ashes.

What made the discovery of this synagogue so extra special is that it electrified the Jewish world for two important reasons. First, it was the oldest synagogue in existence, 1,700 years old. The other reason was that this Jewish place of worship contained art paintings and murals painted on all the walls, all depicting scenes of events taken from the Bible, and all these art drawings in exquisite color.

As is well known, our religion prohibits these types of art paintings inside the place of worship because of what it says in the Ten Commandments (Exodus 20:4) "Thou shalt not make unto thee any graven image, or any likeness of anything . . ." and here we find an ancient synagogue whose walls were painted with all kinds of "likenesses." It really poses a perplexing problem, with people asking the very obvious question of "How come?"

According to Dr. Milgrom that night the answer lies in the fact that the *Torah's* objection and prohibition of not having any likenesses is not on the paintings per se, but the objection lies in what the commandment says in the next verse, that is, "Thou shalt not bow down thyself to them, nor serve them." In other words, the scripture's only concern is that no Jew should worship these "likenesses." This interpretation of scriptures was already advanced some years back by the famous Jewish archeologist Y. Sukenik, who visited this Dura synagogue back in 1933. I am not sure whether this interpretation is accepted by our traditional authorities.

The paintings are undoubtedly of a Jewish motif, such as the holy ark, *menorah, lulav, etrog*, etc. They contain some beautiful scenes, such as the binding of Isaac, the exodus from Egypt, Moses and Aaron and many, many more. There's a special Aramaic sentence in the bottom of a scene which reads *Moshe kad nefak min Mitzrayim, ubaza yama* meaning "Moses, when he left Egypt, split the sea." Other scenes show Samuel the prophet anointing King David, Ahashverosh with Queen Esther, etc.

On the western wall of this Dura synagogue there's a sort of alcove in which can be seen the *ehal akodesh* facing west towards Jerusalem.

As we said, the original art work on the walls of the synagogue has been preserved extremely well, despite the fact that it was covered with dirt for centuries. A few years back, the Syrian government engaged some very skilled experts who were able to cut deeply through all these walls, shaped them into panels, had all these wall panels removed intact, and had these panels carefully transferred to a specially built museum in Damascus, Syria. It is slides of these panels that Dr. Milgrom showed us. The director of this project was the eminent British architect and engineer H. Parsons. Will Jews be fortunate enough to view these paintings of this marvelous discovery ever again? Let's hope so.

December 1979   Kislev/Teveth 5740

Museum Of the Diaspora

This past *Succoth*, we were listening to Lilly DeJaen's spirited conversation telling us how much she enjoyed her visit to the Museum of the Diaspora (*Beth Hatefutzoth*), on her last trip to Israel. She described it and praised it to such a degree, it almost makes you go and see this thrilling place.

Later on, I came across some articles written about this incredible place, with pictures in vivid colors. So, I would like to share this information with our *La Boz* readers who are planning a trip to Israel, to include this historic site on their tours. It is a place where they can also trace their family roots and background, with the help of a minicomputer, which supplies all types of personal information.

This fabulous museum is situated on the campus of the Tel Aviv University.

The idea for this spectacular and impressive project was originated in the 1960s by Dr. Nahum Goldman (head of the World Jewish Congress), along with experts from the United States, Israel, and England, working on the extraordinary exhibits. The museum opened in May, 1978, and already close to a million persons have visited this educational site.

These experts used the most modern technology to produce all the magical life-like effects. Everyone who sees the several exhibits is so enraptured by the unusually vivid exhibits, that each will want to come again and take in what they missed. These groups, which include thousands of school youngsters, are led by a well-informed guide who helps make every tour a delightful educational experience.

These guides are required to read up on all the available information, so they can answer any and all questions a viewer may ever care to ask.

One visitor said, "This certainly is not the popular or usual concept of a museum, with sleepy or musty-looking halls and dead displays. This is a living dynamic, magical presentation of Jewish history, encompassing the entire world, wherever Jews have lived."

It's almost impossible to describe it. Even when you see it, it's difficult to give an account adequately unless you happen to be a gifted novelist.

Visitors are taken through seven well-arranged sections of this museum. Each section is especially and uniquely designed, portraying in a vividly animated style, the various creations, the historic concepts of Jewish historical themes of each era, all this representing the ethnic, cultural and historical events of each country and its Jewish people. Each theme is enhanced by talking models, and magnificent murals illustrating thousands of wonderful scenes.

One of the most outstanding feats of these highly skilled engineers who designed the fabulous museum, is the section containing the model synagogue exhibit.

Sephardim from Turkey will have the unique thrill to discover, in this section the beautiful life-like model synagogue of the town of Sardis.

The town of Sardis was situated in Turkey, in Asia Minor (Anadol), about sixty miles from Izmir. Sardis is mentioned by early historians (about 1,800 years ago), in connection with a Roman emperor's generosity affording the Jewish community of Sardis the freedom of religion, with special privileges. The Jews of Sardis were allowed to import religious articles, kosher meats and other commodities. This magnificent reconstruction of the synagogue of Sardis, is based on archeological excavations. The synagogue was estimated to be the oldest and the most beautiful in the world at that time. They say that it could accomodate over 1,000 worshippers.

It included the minute details in vivid particulars, including the traditional *lampara* (sacramental oil lamp). In the course of subsequent centuries, vandals plundered the town and its various historical places, and Sardis is now in ruins. Sephardim who are interested are also treated to view a fabulous recreation, in true-to-life design, of a fourteenth century *Pesach seder* in Spain which must be a joy to behold.

In brief, you have to see it again and again, to believe it.

June 1982   Sivan/Tamuz 5742

The Adventures of the Oldest Bible

By the time the Rambam (Rabbi Moshe Ben Maimon) decided to write his very own *Sefer Torah*, he had examined many texts, both in Spain and later in North Africa, but he found that they contained a variety of textual errors, especially in the arrangement of every *perashah* (weekly portion).

However, when he arrived in Egypt in the year 1166 (at age thirty-one) he found one that satisfied him completely as being the most authentic and the most reliable text to copy from. Rambam tells us all this in his famous book of laws the *Mishnah Torah* (*Hilhoth Sefer Torah*, Chapter 8:4).

It is believed that this text was written by Ezra in Jerusalem and later annotated by a very prominent Bible expert by the name of Aharon Ben Asher who lived in Tiberius around the year 800. Ben Asher added the vowel points and the *taamim* (musical notes) according our Jewish tradition (*masorah*).

There are two distinct differences between what we know as a *Torah* scroll and this ancient text. First, this Ben Asher Bible contains not only the five books of Moses (*Torah*) but it also contains the rest of the twenty-four books of our holy Bible. Second, this ancient Bible is not in a scroll form but it looks like a modern book with numbered pages.

Where is this Ben Asher Bible now? We will attempt to trace its history very briefly. When the Seljuk Turks destroyed Jerusalem, some dedicated Jews left Jerusalem and they settled in Cairo, taking this Ben Asher Bible with them. This is when Rabbi Moshe Ben Maimon saw it and copied his own *Sefer Torah* from this text.

It is believed that some 250 years later, when one of the Rambam's descendants moved to Aleppo, he transferred all of his ancestor's manuscripts with him, taking along this precious Ben Asher Bible. This descendant, Rabbi David Maimon, deposited this ancient Bible in the great synagogue in Aleppo, Syria. The Jews of Aleppo felt very fortunate to have this valuable text in their midst. Ever since then, this Ben Asher Bible has come to be known as the Aleppo Codex.

However, during the terrible times in 1948, when the fanatic Moslems in Aleppo set fire to all the synagogues in the city of Aleppo, they also destroyed the great synagogue in which this precious Codex was deposited. But, it was saved thanks to a very courageous and dedicated group of Jewish members. They defied the flames, went in and rescued this cherished Bible and secretly hid it in one of their homes, waiting until the safe and opportune time to move it out of the country and possibly take it to Israel.

In the meantime, one Syrian official found out where the Codex was taken for safe-keeping. He was able to steal it, moving it to Lebanon. Somehow, this Syrian government official was persuaded to bring it back, with promises of large amounts of money and other forms of bribery. So, it was once more in the possession of the Syrian Jewish community.

But, there still was that fearful feeling that some other type of accidental disaster might occur in which event they might lose the Codex forever. So, one day, a Jewish resident of Aleppo decided to move to Jerusalem with his family. Those were very dangerous days for all Syrian Jews when the Syrian Arabs treated all Jews in an extremely inhuman and cruel manner. This man, whose name was Murad Faham, decided to leave Aleppo, leaving behind all of his considerable wealth including home, business, valuable properties, etc. But, before he left, he had a plan to take the Aleppo Codex with him. So, he got the consent of the Syrian Jewish community to try and take along with him the Codex.

After many difficulties with the Syrian Arabs' customs authorities and after great financial sacrifices, he was successful in hiding this Codex among his belongings, and finally rescuing it. He brought it with him to Israel. When Mr. Faham arrived in Israel he handed it over to the then president of Israel, Yitzhak Ben Zvi, for safekeeping. President Ben Zvi placed it in the Sephardic Ben Zvi Institute in Jerusalem, in a vault. Some skilled electricians and engineers devised a clever mechanical device whereby if ever there would be a disturbance, this Codex would automatically sink into an underground vault, where it would be safe from any molestation.

We know there are many versions of the holy Bible. There are several old translations in many languages including Greek, Latin, Armenian, Syriac, Aramaic, etc. Experts use all these for references.

For the first time in Jewish history, a team of Biblical scholars at the Hebrew University in Jerusalem got together a few years ago to produce one single authentic version. When they finish their long research and study, then they will publish it, in several volumes, under the name the Hebrew University Bible. This Bible will contain not only the text, but thousands of notes, quotations, commentaries, interpretations, etc. One of the most frequently used books in this study, as basic and authentic, is this very same Ben Asher or Aleppo Codex Bible we described above. The late president Ben Zvi made it available to this team of Bible scholars who have testified to the fact that they find it the most authentic. This Aleppo Codex was never available to scholars before. This Bible project published a facsimile edition a few years ago so as to preserve the original in good condition.

January 1972   Teveth/Shevat 5732

The Ben Zvi Institute

On my first visit to the Ben Zvi Institute, which is located on the third floor of a building in the Hebrew University in Jerusalem, I knew that my curiosity was only partially satisfied. I had read so much about this institute that I decided to go again. As it happened, I was very fortunate in obtaining an interview with the institute's dynamic and busy director, Dr. Meir Benayahu.

He was gracious enough to show me around, even to open up a portion of the place that contains some very valuable old printed books and some very rare manuscripts. These are kept under lock and key. He gave me a few samples of some publications that were issued by the institute.

In order to give you an idea of the history and purpose of the institute, I quote, in part, from one of these samples.

This institute was established in 1949. Four years later, in 1953, under the auspices of the Hebrew University it was named *Mahon Ben Zvi*, after the late president of Israel, Yitzhak Ben Zvi, who was the head of the organization and who contributed considerably to its progress and growth. The principal aim of the institute is to preserve the spiritual heritage of the Oriental Jewish communities. It has collected photographs of the manuscripts of the different Oriental Jewish communities dispersed throughout the great libraries of the world in England, Holland, etc. [Editor's note: By Oriental Jews, the Institute refers to what we call Sephardic, i.e., all those Jews who are not Ashkenazic, those that spoke languages such as Ladino, Arabic, Greek, Judeo-Persian, etc.] Today the institute possesses nearly half a million pages in microfilm containing historical and literary material in all the dialects spoken by the Oriental Jews. In addition, the institute has acquired some 1,700 original manuscripts.

I was amazed at the amount of books that these gentlemen have been successful in collecting in this one place. It would take more than ten or twenty articles of this size to explain and enumerate some of the literary treasures that this place contains.

Dr. Benayahu has already published ten volumes of a publication that appears annually called *Sefunoth*. How wonderful it would be to find one of our members to make a generous donation to buy these

volumes of *Sefunoth* to add to our synagogue library. What better way
to commemorate a dear departed one?

Another phase of this place that had me pleasantly surprised was
when I visited the Ladino room, a whole room full of books that have
been printed over a period of 400 years in Ladino. These consist of
original works in Ladino as well as works that were translated from
Hebrew. I knew we had quite a few books printed in Ladino but I had
no idea that so many existed.

Incidentally, Dr. Benayahu uses a pen name. He is actually the
son of the present Sephardic chief rabbi of Israel, Rabbi Yitzhak
Nessim. I've been told that the reason he doesn't use his family name
is that he doesn't want to capitalize on the fame of his father's name.
He chose a pen name which contains, in brief, his family name.

June 1975   Sivan/Tamuz 5735

Mashalla - Misgav Yerushalayim

A few weeks ago, Mr. Isaac J. Levy, professor of romance
languages at the University of South Carolina, made a visit to our city.
He spent almost all of his time here, gathering precious material in the
way of *romansas, canticas, consejas* (ballads, songs and folklore
stories) and other Sephardic goodies. All these items, mainly from
members of our Sephardic Bikur Holim Congregation - *Mashalla!*

A week later, we had another distinguished visitor. This time it
was Dr. Issachar Ben-Ami, currently senior lecturer in Jewish folklore
at the Hebrew University in Jerusalem. He was introduced to us
through Rabbi Maimon, and he was fascinated by the Sephardic Bikur
Holim Congregation of Seattle.

This proves that we do have *kavdal* (substance). *Mashalla!*
Moreover, it's a very definite proof that we have members who are
loaded with that specific type of information that international
scholars are looking for.

Is all this Sephardic cultural, historical and literary heritage worth
preserving? The answer is: definitely! But: how? As you will see in
the following lines, they're doing something about it in Israel now,
too!

There are thousands of books, an abundance of historical material
of Sephardic interest, but it's all scattered in many and varied places.

All this needs to be gathered and deposited in one appropriate location.

When Dr. Ben-Ami was here in Seattle, he gave us a magnificent folder, explaining fully a brand new institute to be called *Misgav Yerushalayim*, which is designed to house and display all of this Sephardic material. In other words, this building will take the place of a combination library, museum, archives, and research center. In addition to all this, this institute will present seminars in which Sephardic scholars and historians will offer classes in various Sephardic studies.

This institute is being constructed in the same exact location as that of the Sephardic hospital *Misgav Ladah* in Jerusalem. In 1948, the Arabs captured the whole area of the Old City and destroyed the hospital completely. In 1967, of course, the location reverted back to the Sephardic community. Mr. Elie Elyasher, president of the Sephardic council of Jerusalem, who is also chief administrator of Sephardic public properties and foundations, made this site available to a group that decided to build the *Misgav Yerushalayim* Institute. This group is made up of three main organizations: the Sephardic Council of Jerusalem, the World Sephardi Federation, both operating with full cooperation of the Hebrew University of Jerusalem.

At the initiation ceremonies, attended by a number of celebrities at the Hebrew University, half a million dollars was already raised from various individuals, and one of the generous donors was Mr. Nissim David Gaon, who is the president of the World Sephardic Federation. He donated the sum of $100,000. He's an industrialist who lives in Geneva, Switzerland, and is originally from Egypt.

Anyone who wishes to see this excellent folder of the *Misgav Yerushalayim*, please contact me. I'll be glad to lend it to you.

May 1976   Iyar/Sivan 5736

The Sassoon Collection

On my recent trip to Chicago, where we visited our children and grandchildren, I had occasion to go to a Jewish college called, Spertus College, with my son-in-law, Eugene Normand. There's a fantastic library in this college. The amount of books and other literature, especially about Sephardic subjects is incredible. Almost anything you ask for can be found there.

Among the interesting books that I found is a two-volume catalogue of the fabulous collection of rare and priceless manuscripts of the Sassoon Library, located in the garden city of Letchworth, forty-seven miles from London. This catalogue is called *Ohel-David*, and contains 1,112 pages. It was published in England in 1932 by Rabbi David Sassoon. I was curious as to who started this collection. Here is what I found.

The dynasty of the Sassoon family goes back to David Sassoon (1792-1884). Born in Baghdad, he moved to Bombay, India. There he and his family became so rich, the people used to call them the "Indian Rothschilds."

However, the real book lover of the family was David Solomon Sassoon (1880-1942), who spent a veritable fortune in acquiring thousands of rare books and manuscripts. Then the family moved from Bombay to London. After the Nazis began to conquer Europe in 1938, Rabbi David was very much afraid of what might happen to his priceless collection. So he started to divide up his library sending portions to different locations. In his diary on April 11, 1938, he wrote, "I was afraid lest the Nazis bombard London. I felt it my duty to preserve my manuscripts. I took a number of them to the Winchester Safe Deposit, Broad Street, London. I placed them in the strong-room. I embraced them, I kissed them and I reflected whether I should ever set my eyes on them again." Unfortunately, his premonition came true. *Zavali, no los vido mas.* (The unfortunate one never saw them again.) He died in 1942, without ever having the luck of seeing his manuscripts again.

After the war, it was his son, Rabbi Solomon David Sassoon, who was able to reassemble the famous Sassoon Collection. In 1970, he found it necessary to auction off a few of his rare books, which brought him a formidable sum.

Recently, he made up his mind to move and go live in Israel so he had dealers and private collectors bid on some more of his collection. The amount of what he was selling was so unusually large, that it was reported as extraordinary news in the *Wall St. Journal*.

As an example of the contents of this fabulous library, there is the Farhi Bible, with 359 illuminated illustrations, and 1,058 pages. The illustrator was a Sephardic Jew by the name of Elisha Crescas, who worked on it for over seventeen years - a most excellent achievement of the Sephardic Jewry of the Spain of the 1300s. Another very important manuscript is described as Rambam's commentary on the second order of the *Mishnah*, which contains the first draft of this work, along with Rambam's corrections and additions. There is also another Bible, the Shem Tov Bible, written in the 1300s. It includes twenty-four different types of synagogue services for Jews from communities like Yemen, Persia, and Corfu.

December 1972   Kislev/Teveth 5733

The Silver Chandelier

In the November issue of the *Jewish Transcript*, we read an extremely interesting article, written by a former Seattleite, now living in Jerusalem. In this article, Mrs. Jennie Adatto Tarabulus, describes the historic rededication ceremony of the four Sephardic synagogues in the old Jewish section of Jerusalem, which she attended with her husband.

The largest of these four synagogues is called the *Raban Yohanan Ben Zakkai* synagogue, now restored largely with money contributed by the Rothschild family. It was completely demolished by the Arabs in 1948, and until 1967 it was used by the Jordanians as a stable for donkeys and sheep.

There's a very fascinating story that I've read about this synagogue in the history of Jerusalem. In the early 19th century, a very beautiful silver chandelier was donated by a group of European Jews to the Jewish community of Jerusalem. Obviously, the donors did not designate or specify in which one of the many synagogues this chandelier was to be used, nor did they say, whether this chandelier was to be used by a Sephardic or Ashkenazic synagogue.

So the leaders of the various synagogues got together, and came to an agreement. They decided that this chandelier shall be installed and used in the Sephardic synagogue (the *Raban Yohanan Ben Zakkai*) for one year, and at the conclusion of the year it shall be installed in the Ashkenazic synagogue that was named the *Hurva* or *Beth Yaakov*, which was situated in the same district of the old Jewish quarter of Jerusalem.

And so this arrangement continued for many years until 1864, during the time that the *Haham Bashi* of *Eretz Yisrael* was Rabbi Haim David Hazan. All the Sephardic chief rabbis of Israel are also known as the *Rishon LeZion* (see p. 221). This arrangement, of having the chandelier moved from one synagogue to the other at the end of each year, was terminated because the Sephardic community of Jerusalem was having a very difficult time maintaining its charitable institutions. After consulting with other rabbis and leaders, the chief rabbi negotiated a deal with the respective rabbis and leaders of the Ashkenazic community then called the *parushim*. This deal stipulated that from that date on, the Sephardic community shall transfer all rights and privileges related to this silver chandelier to the *Hurva* synagogue, and in exchange the *Hurva* was to pay to the Sephardic community the sum of 2,458 groshes and 30 paras, Turkish money.

This information is contained in an ancient document which was published in Jerusalem in 1928. It also tells us that the reason Chief Rabbi Hazan was compelled to sell his rights to this chandelier was that the Sephardic community of Jerusalem at that time had already borrowed a large sum of money from some creditors who were pressing for payment. The income that used to come in from collections from charities donated by the different Sephardic communities around the world had decreased considerably. This silver chandelier, the document says, weighed 1,405 dramas (about eighty-eight pounds). In addition to Rabbi Hazan's signature, this document was also signed by three other Sephardic rabbis, probably members of the Jerusalem rabbinical council: Rabbi Mordecai Refael Binnun, Rabbi Moshe Yehuda Mizrahi and Rabbi Yedidia Suzen.

It would be very interesting to find out whatever happened to this chandelier. Were they able to save it from the Arabs?

July 1979   Tamuz/Av 5739

La Gabela

Besides the many ways of raising money to support various budgets of each *kehila* (community), there existed in our countries of origin, the famous *gabela*, a tax imposed on the three main commodities that needed special supervision, thus sold in the stores with the certification of the rabbinate. These three commodities were kosher cheese, kosher meat and kosher wine.

The word *gabela*, some say , is derived from the Hebrew word *gaba* (to collect). Some take the word *gabela* and break it down to the first three letters of the word, that is *gimal*, *beth*, and *yod* (with the

Ladino suffix *-la*). They explain, *gimal* stands for *gevina* (cheese), *beth* stands for *basar* (meat) and the *yod* stands for *yayin* (wine).

Cheese

Many families would make their own cheese at home. However, in order to make cheese for export, they had the *mandra* (a Turkish word meaning dairy farm).

I remember many of our Sephardic young men in Tekirdag would be employed during the spring months in some neighborhood *mandras* where they made tons of *kezo blanco* (feta cheese), *cashcaval* and other cheese specially for shipment to Istanbul and other Turkish towns. Some of these young men would work long and hard during the busy season earning enough money to last them the rest of the year in case there were no jobs. After satisfying the proper authorities, with the proper supervision by the rabbinate, these cheeses would bear the seal or a kosher certificate, and then be shipped to Istanbul. There the public would buy them with the firm assurance of its being in conformity with the rules of *kashruth*.

Meat

Every town had its *shohet* (ritual slaughterer). Every animal slaughtered for kosher consumption was of course examined by the *shohet*. The ones that reached the butcher were taxed a certain amount each. This amount would be assigned to the local *gabela*. Even chickens, when slaughtered by the *shohet*, had to be taxed a few cents each. Sometimes the congregation had special coins minted to cover the cost of each chicken when these chickens were brought to the *shohet* by individuals. A kosher butcher in Turkey would very seldom sell chickens. The owners of these chickens would send them to the *shohet* either by a member of the family or a hired person we called *mosicos*.

Wine

Many cities in Turkey had their own local wine makers. However, as concerns making wine for export, it involved having special supervision by a person or persons delegated by the proper rabbinic authority.

I remember, in our town of Tekirdag during the late summer and fall season, wagons full of real delicious ripe wine grapes would arrive at Bohorachi Morhaim's home. (He was Mrs. Donna Baruch's father.) In the basement of this home, there were some unbelievably enormous barrels, so huge they could hold at least 1,000 gallons of wine. As mentioned above, this wine made by the Morhaim family was only for local consumption.

As for making wine for export, the most famous town in the whole of Turkey was on the island of Marmara. The reason, they claim, was that Marmara was blessed with the best and most suitable types of grapevines in the whole region. Added to that was the fact that the island contained master winemakers. They also manufactured *raki* (anise-flavored brandy made from raisins) from these flavorful grapes. After proper supervision, this wine was shipped in big sail boats (*kayikes*), to Istanbul and other parts.

Most of the Marmarali members in our *kahal* were engaged, to some degree, in making and exporting this wine, *raki* and *pishcado salado* (fish salad).

Other sources of revenue for the congregations were assessments, selling the *mitzvoth*, and many wealthy members would make substantial donations for charitable and benevolent societies to fill the city's budgets.

Appendix I

Rabbis Who Held the Office Of *Haham Bashi*
(Chief Rabbi of the Turkish Empire)

Name	Years In Office
* Moshe Capsali	1453-1497
* Eliyahu Mizrahi	1497-1520
Tam Ben Yahya	1520-1542
Elie Benyamin Halevi	1542-c.1550
Menahem Bahar Samuel	c.1550-c.1580
Eliyahu Ben Haim	c.1580-c.1605
Yehiel Bassan	c.1605-1625
Yomtov Ibn Yaish	1639-c.1650
Yomtov Ben Yakar	c.1650-1677
Haim Camhi	1677-1715
Yehuda Ben Rey	c.1715-1727
Samuel Levi	1727-c.1735
Abraham Rosanes	c.1735-1743
Solomon Haim Alfanderi	1743-c.1758
Meir Ishaki	c.1758-1762
Eliyahu Palombo	1762-c.1800
Haim Yaakov Ben Yakar	c.1800-1835
* Abraham Levi	1835-1836
* Samuel Haim	1836-1839
* Moise Fresco	1839-1841
* Yaakov Behar David	1841-1854
* Haim Hacohen	1854-1860
* Yaakov Avigdor	1860-1863
* Yakir Gueron	1863-1872
* Moshe Levi	1872-1908
* Haim Nahoum	1908-1919
* Sabetai Levi	**March-May 1910
	March-July 1912
* Yitzhak Ariel	**1918, 1919
* Haim Moshe Bijarano+	1920-1931

	Haim Yitzhak Shaki+	**1931-1940
*	Raphael David Saban+	1953-1960
*	David Asseo+	1960-present

Taken primarily from A. Galante, *Histoire des Juifs d'Istanboul* and *Encyclopedia Judaica*.

* Officially recognized by the Turkish government as representing the Jewish community. Other Haham Bashis headed the rabbinate in Istanbul and led the entire Jewish community, but received no official recognition from the Ottoman Empire.
** Interim position, e.g., while Rabbi Nahoum was outside Turkey.
+ Served under the Republic of Turkey

Appendix II

Rabbis Who Held the Position Of *Rishon LeZion*

Name	Years In Office
Moshe Ben Yoseph Galante	c.1670
Moshe Ben Shelomo Ben Habib	1689-1696
Avraham Ben David Yitzhaki	1715-1722
Nissim Haim Moshe Mizrahi	1748-1749
Raphael Shemuel Meyuchas	1756-1771
Haim Raphael Avraham Ben Asher	1771-1772
Yom Tov Algazi	1772-1802
Moshe Yoseph Mordechai Meyuhas	1802-1806
Yaakov Moshe Ayash	1806-1817
Yaakov Korah	1817-1818
Raphael Yoseph Hazan	1818-1821
Yom Tov Danon	1822-1823
Shelomo Moshe Suzain	1824-1836
Yonah Moshe Navon	1836-1841
Yehudah Raphael Navon	1841-1842
* Avraham Haim Gagin	1842-1848
* Yitzhak Ben Hizkiya Kovo	1848-1854
* Haim Nissim Abulafia	1854-1861
* Haim David Hazan	1861-1869
* Avraham Ashkenazi	1869-1880
* Raphael Meir Panezel	1880-1892
* Yaakov Shaul Elyashar	1893-1906
* Yaakov Meir	1906-1939
Bension Meir Hai Uziel	1939-1953
Yitzhak Nissim	1955-1972
Ovadia Yoseph	1972-1982
Mordechai Eliahu	1982-1992

* Officially recognized as *Haham Bashi* of *Eretz Yisrael* by the Ottoman government.

Appendix III
Chronological List Of Articles

Appendix IV

Index of Articles by Subject Matter